PENGUIN BOOKS

All Dressed in White

Carol McD. Wallace, author of *The Penguin Classic Baby Name Book*, has been fascinated by social behavior ever since childhood. She was one of the coauthors of *The Official Preppy Handbook,* contributing sections on preppy rituals like weddings and college parties. In *To Marry an English Lord* (with Gail MacColl), she examined the late-nineteenth-century phenomenon of American heiresses marrying into the British aristocracy. She has been collecting material for *All Dressed in White,* her nineteenth book, since the late 1980s. Wallace was married in 1983 wearing ivory linen and pale pink shoes. She lives with her family in New York City.

Praise for *All Dressed in White*

"*All Dressed in White* reads like a drama in three acts, gloriously telling the story of what has become one of the greatest of American theatrical events. . . . This book is a must for brides-to-be and dramatists alike."
—William Ivey Long, Tony Award–winning costume designer

"Carol Wallace's detailed research takes us from the quaint and romantic customs of the proper Victorian world into the whirlwind nuptial extravaganzas of the twenty-first century."
—John R. Burbidge, former Priscilla of Boston senior
  designer and three-time father of the bride

All Dressed in White

THE IRRESISTIBLE RISE OF THE AMERICAN WEDDING

Carol McD. Wallace

PENGUIN BOOKS

PENGUIN BOOKS
Published by the Penguin Group
Penguin Group (USA) Inc., 375 Hudson Street,
New York, New York 10014, U.S.A.
Penguin Books Ltd, 80 Strand,
London WC2R 0RL, England
Penguin Books Australia Ltd, 250 Camberwell Road, Camberwell, Victoria 3124, Australia
Penguin Books Canada Ltd, 10 Alcorn Avenue,
Toronto, Ontario, Canada M4V 3B2
Penguin Books India (P) Ltd, 11 Community Centre, Panchsheel Park, New Delhi – 110
    017, India
Penguin Books (N.Z.) Ltd, Cnr Rosedale and Airborne Roads, Albany, Auckland,
    New Zealand
Penguin Books (South Africa) (Pty) Ltd, 24 Sturdee Avenue, Rosebank, Johannesburg
    2196, South Africa

Penguin Books Ltd, Registered Offices:
80 Strand, London WC2R 0RL, England

First published in Penguin Books 2004

10 9 8 7 6 5 4 3 2 1

Illustration credits appear on page 323.

Photo research: Ellen Horan

LIBRARY OF CONGRESS CATALOGING-IN-PUBLICATION DATA
Wallace, Carol, 1955–
    All dressed in white : the irresistible rise of the American wedding / Carol McD.
Wallace.
        p. cm.
    Includes bibliographical references.
    ISBN 0-14-200216-X
    1. Weddings—United States—Planning. 2. Weddings—United States—History.
3. Weddings—Equipment and supplies—United States. 4. Wedding etiquette—
United States. I. Title.

HQ745.W34 2004
395.2'2'0973—dc22   2003058226

Printed in the United States of America
Set in Simoncini Garamond
Designed by Beth Tondreau

To my sisters Eve and Josephine,
with whom I went to my first wedding

Contents

Contents

Contents

All Dressed in White

"Ritual Is Dynamic and Creative"

Sandy Bass and Junius Oliver Chambers V had a beautiful wedding. The weather didn't exactly cooperate (heavy clouds threatened rain throughout the ceremony), but the flowers were gorgeous and Sandy was a truly ravishing bride. Pretty enough to stop traffic—literally. For Sandy and JJ were married in Times Square on May 17, 2002, on the television show *Good Morning America.*

It may not have been exactly the wedding the bride and groom had dreamed of. For one thing, 8 A.M. is a terrible time to try to look your best. And then the traffic island where ABC set up the ceremony could only accommodate a handful of guests in addition to the cameramen, security men, wedding coordinators, electricians, and anchors Diane Sawyer and Charlie Gibson. It was impossible to get a camera angle that didn't include a car or a stoplight, and at one point Sandy and JJ were caught in front of the army recruiting station as they waited to cross the street.

And though the event wasn't blatantly commercial, it came pretty close. Luther Vandross sang for the bride and groom—he was promoting a new album. The wedding ceremony itself had to be squeezed between commercial breaks, and the first people to kiss the bride and groom were . . . Diane and Charlie. They weren't actually part of the family, though ABC wanted you to think so. The reception would be held at a restaurant called Le Cirque, so viewers were treated to several moments of promotional video showing celebrities like Robert De Niro posing with the owner.

Nevertheless, it was a real wedding, touching and emotionally genuine. JJ welled up when Sandy came down the aisle, and the bridesmaids flicked tears from their cheeks with French-manicured nails. Sandy's dad looked ready to burst with pride. The smiles on the new couple outshone all the Times Square signs, many of which had been programmed to say "Best Wishes Sandy and Junius!" And the producers added a brilliant touch. Once the ceremony itself was over (as well as the next round of ads), a coanchor led the newlyweds on a tour of Times Square. They dashed across Broadway, with Sandy's tulle veil floating behind, into a sea of red-jumpsuited street cleaners, who threw confetti all over them. They shook hands, they hugged strangers, they collected wedding presents in festive shopping bags. After English country weddings of the eighteenth century, the bride and groom would parade up the village street, greeting all their neighbors. Broadway and Forty-second Street was a village that morning, and Sandy and JJ were surrounded by beaming faces.

The whole thing was oddly moving and a nearly surreal mix of the public and the private—like most weddings, actually. Getting married, though it involves issues of profound emotional intimacy for the couple, is also an important civil transaction. It is not enough for a couple—in any kind of society, anywhere—to pledge permanent fidelity and commitment to each other in seclusion: they must do so in front of witnesses. Every community has a stake in marriages, because marriage represents both the formation of a new family unit and the promise of continuity in a new generation. Government also gets involved, keeping track of who is married to whom (mind-boggling when you think about the scale of the enterprise). In addition to creating social entities, marriage also ensures the orderly passage of property from one generation to another. Religion has gotten in on the act as well. In medieval Europe, beginning in the thirteenth century, civil unions for Christians could be blessed by the church. In the fourteenth century Jewish weddings began to require the intervention of a rabbi, and in 1563, at the Council of Trent, the Catholic Church, with post-Reformation enthusiasm, insisted that marriages *must* be performed by a priest. Subsequent developments made the oversight of a deity optional according to locale: after the French Revolution, when religion was temporarily banned from French culture, marriage was decreed a secular event and to this day, the official conjoining of a French couple occurs at Town Hall. In bourgeois nineteenth-century French families, elaborate contracts were drawn up specifying financial arrangements between the couple's family, and a ceremony was made of the signing of these documents. The reception, or celebration of the marriage, was held on the night the contracts were signed, signaling that this was the most important element of the nuptial arrangement.

No matter what entity joins a man and a woman, weddings always involve ritual, a set of prescribed behaviors. The scholar John Gillis explains why in *For Better, for Worse: British Marriages 1600 to the Present:* "It is generally agreed that ritual is particularly endemic in situations of change at those times of an individual, group, or society when there is the greatest uncertainty and when people have difficulty in expressing their ideas and feelings in a more direct way. In fact, ritual is dynamic and creative, because it allows people to handle situations that are otherwise troubling and disruptive. Ritual not only brings order out of chaos, but relieves people's fears about their personal and collective futures." Ritual time is different from ordinary time: once you're launched into a ritual, you don't stop to answer the phone or because you've lost interest. You must go through all the motions. Most remaining rituals in American life cluster around religion and education, though military life (which frequently encounters "troubling and disruptive" situations) is full of them.

The moment of marriage is a stressful time of change for the couple and, to a lesser extent, their community, which must alter how it relates to them. It falls into a category that a French anthropologist, Arnold Van Gennep, labeled a "rite of passage." This is a ceremony that helps people negotiate the transition from one social condition to another. Van Gennep's definition outlined three distinct stages. First, the subject is separated from everyday life. The engagement can be seen as the separation phase, when two people draw away from their previous single life and prepare for their life together. Next, the people undergoing the rite are placed in a ceremonial location, where they are introduced to their new role, either in words or in actions. In wedding terms this is the ceremony itself, when the couple make their promises to each other. Often their hands are joined; at some Latin weddings a mantilla or a cord is draped around the pair; Hindu couples walk around a fire. Finally, they are reabsorbed into their community in their new guise. This part often involves feasting.

Hence the reception, which invariably includes food and drink, welcomes the couple as a unit into the community. In the days when weddings often involved strategic or military bonds between the families of the bride and groom, the meal was an essential part of expressing that bond, since breaking bread with someone implied a covenant of alliance.

One of the earliest of wedding historians, Edward Westermarck, points out that in many societies, wedding rituals have sprung up around superstition. A bride and groom, as they advance from one stage of life to another, are thought to be susceptible to interference from evil spirits. (The bad fairy at Sleeping Beauty's christening took advantage of a similar situation.) "There is a very general feeling or idea that the bride and bridegroom are in a state of danger, being particularly exposed to other persons' magical tricks or evil looks, or to the attacks of evil spirits . . . or to some impersonal mysterious cause of evil, and therefore stand in need of protection or purification." In Westermarck's view, some of the components of the wedding ritual evolved to provide this kind of protection. The traditional throwing of shoes at the bride and groom after the ceremony, for instance, could be an attempt to keep away evil spirits, while the strewing of flowers before the couple may provide defense against spirits below the ground.

We have to be careful, though, about how we assign the sources of our wedding rituals. Maybe the white runner drawn down the aisle before the bride's procession somehow expresses this ancient fear of bad things underground—and maybe it's just supposed to keep the bride's long white dress clean. Even when a tradition has clearly documented roots in the past, our use of it for weddings can never be traced back directly to the source. The bridal veil, for instance, does have a reliable precedent in Roman times—Ovid refers to "a bride, with a veil upon her face." But today's brides are not veiled in white because this lovely custom has been handed down from woman to woman over two thousand years. At some point early in the nineteenth century, when the fashions of the ancient world were being rediscovered, a clever woman put a length of sheer fabric over her head and thought it looked fabulous. The appearance of mystery and modesty linked with the important quality of chastity. Maybe the metaphor of the husband removing the veil and breaking his wife's hymen came into play.

The tradition certainly has its roots in the classical world, but it is an invented tradition, to use the words of scholar Eric Hobsbawm. Traditions (which may involve rituals) are self-conscious behaviors, often employing props or costumes discarded by the everyday world. A veil, to a Muslim woman, has an everyday use. To a Western woman it is out of the ordinary and thus becomes significant. Hobsbawm makes the distinction between custom, the everyday behaviors that come automatically to people, and tradition, in which we need to be instructed. What ritual is to individuals, tradition is to communities: a way of negotiating awkward, often disturbing change, by spotlighting continuity in a certain, limited context. Weddings are surrounded by traditions, but some of them are new. The unity candle ceremony, for instance, sprang up in the last twenty-five years, and has become particularly popular in the last ten. The tradition of the formal wedding in America—with the religious ritual, the bride in her white gown with attendants, the processions, the photographs, the reception, the cake—is fairly recent, too, as we shall see.

Introduction

The usual history of marriage begins with the theme of "marriage by capture." The myth of the earliest, pre-Christian Romans kidnapping the Sabine women would probably be the model here: primitive menfolk swoop down on a neighboring village to carry off wives. Deep emotional communion between individuals was not envisioned; this was a matter of sexual release, procreation, and someone to mind the cooking fire. Westermarck expresses some skepticism about this antecedent for our marriages, but most scholars give it credence. Written records describe the next phase of marriage, which was a kind of barter system. Women were traded to men, more or less as chattel, for cash or livestock. The woman's consent was a much later innovation of the lawmaking Roman Empire (as was divorce). This practical model held sway in principle right through the eighteenth century, though the blatantly commercial nature of the transaction receded into the background. Accustomed as we are to the omnipotence of personal inclination, it's difficult to imagine the pragmatism with which most couples paired off. Literature, it's true, has left us with great love stories from the classical era onward, but they hardly reflect the experience of the common man. Everyday romance is a luxury, possibly even an artifact of the industrial era, and it didn't cloud marriage decisions until well into the 1800s.

America's early history of weddings is as fragmented and various as the nature of the individual colonies. While Virginia planters might invite friends and relatives for weeklong house parties (and Virginia slaves be forbidden to marry at all), New England town-dwelling couples often married quietly in the presence of their families. When they came to church on the first Sunday after their wedding, it was traditional for the bride to wear her very best new clothes, and she might even stand in her pew and turn around slowly so that everyone present could examine her outfit, front and back.

By the 1820s and '30s, wealthy urban brides and grooms married in a fashion that recognizably prefigures the modern wedding. Once all the preparations for the marriage were made—the trousseau complete, the couple's new home furnished—the families could turn their attention to the wedding itself. As little as a week in advance, the bride's family sent out cards of invitation to a small group of friends and family, often for eight o'clock in the evening. The bride and groom, in handsome new outfits, were married, and after the short ceremony the new couple circulated among the guests. Sometimes a full meal was served; always an elaborate cake was prominently displayed and eaten, and a toast drunk to the bride and groom.

The development of this intimate celebration into today's elaborate formal wedding is recognizably an American process, one both driven by our history and reflective of it. When a social practice changes as little over the years as weddings have done, those alterations are significant. The way we get married in America shows us what we think—and what we have thought—about women, about marriage, about family, and about love itself.

CHAPTER 1

This Getting Married Is No Trifle!

MR. AND MRS. TOM THUMB • "THE GIRL MUST MARRY:
ELSE HOW LIVE?" • FROM GIRL TO WIFE • "BETWIXT A
RELIGIOUS CEREMONY AND A—PANTOMIME!" •
"THE CITY WEDDING IN NEW YORK"

The New York City union of Charles Stratton and Lavinia Warren is a good place to launch a discussion of the wedding in nineteenth-century America. The event, which took place in 1863, included all the elements of an urban upper-class marriage. The bride's white satin dress was created by New York's foremost couturiere, Madame Demorest, with a deep bertha and wide flounce of fifty-dollar-a-yard point lace. (Resemblance to Queen Victoria's wedding gown may not have been accidental.) Her tiny white satin slippers were embroidered with seed pearls, and her tulle-and-lace veil was held with an orange-blossom wreath. After the bride and groom had been formally joined by an Episcopal minister at fashionable Grace Church on lower Broadway, they processed back down the aisle to the famous "Wedding March" from Mendelssohn's *Midsummer Night's Dream*—a secular tune that had recently come into matrimonial vogue.

It was unusual in the 1860s for a wedding reception to be held in a hotel, but a lot of space was needed since Stratton and his bride were both public figures. As Tom Thumb, the three-foot-four Stratton was exhibited at P. T. Barnum's

A staged studio shot of Tom Thumb's wedding—the "church" backdrop is quite effective. The best man, Commodore Nutt, was another one of P. T. Barnum's performers who had also proposed to the bride.

American Museum on Broadway. Lavinia Warren, his bride, was a colleague; their attendants, Minnie Warren and George Nutt, were also little people employed by Barnum. The romance between the bride and groom was, by all accounts, genuine: Nutt had also proposed to Lavinia but she preferred Stratton. Their boss, Barnum, never so much as sneezed without considering the promotional angles, but he is said to have been genuinely fond of Stratton, whom he had practically adopted when Stratton was six. As he recalls in his memoirs, Barnum was determined to give his protégé "a genteel and graceful wedding." In 1863, that meant an event that mimicked the nuptials of New York's upper classes. At the reception, an eighty-pound cake was cut up, with dainty servings decoratively boxed to give the departing guests. The wedding gifts were on display, as they would have been at any Fifth Avenue mansion, and even some of the names on the donors' cards were the same: newspaper magnate James Gordon Bennett gave the couple a miniature silver tea set while President and Mrs. Lincoln sent a pair of Chinese fire screens. In an early example of product placement, the Singer company sent a sewing machine, while Lenox contributed a set of its own china. Perhaps the biggest departure from the norm was the fact that the bride and groom had to receive their guests standing on a piano, lest they be crushed in the crowd.

The degree of public interest in this wedding was also unusual, which is why we have such good records of it. *The New York Times* ran the story on its front page, going on for three and a half columns of very small type. The tone was disapproving, though. Barnum was thought to be exploiting his star employees. Certainly the days before they were married were profitable ones for the American Museum, as visitors by the hundreds paid to see the loving couple on exhibit. Lavinia's trousseau, displayed in the windows of Lord & Taylor, drew gawking crowds. *The New York Herald* sourly remarked in an editorial that, "There will be a crowd to see the little people married, and certainly there would be a greater crowd to see them encouched. . . ." which was a delicate way of referring to the consummation of the match.

The point was that weddings, in those days, were private. Barnum's lapse of taste was that he permitted too many people—and, worse yet, the press—to witness the ceremony and celebration by which Charles Stratton and Lavinia Warren became husband and wife. In the joining of a man and a woman there was too much at stake, and too much of it was intimate, for publicity to be seemly. The looming prospect of the couple's sexuality was only part of the issue. Lavinia and all of her fellow brides underwent, in marriage, an apotheosis that takes an effort of imagination for modern women to understand. Here Lavinia loses her usefulness as a prototypical Victorian bride, because her life had already been much more eventful than that of the average middle-class American girl. She was, after all, a working woman. Barnum might well have exploited her, but the fact remained that she earned her own income. This alone set her off from the other girls who married in 1863, who had neither careers nor aspirations to them. They would be nothing but wives, since in the nineteenth century, marriage was what women were for.

By midcentury, the United States was on its way to becoming the industrialized society we live in today. Nevertheless, the large majority of Americans still lived rural existences that had more in common with the seventeenth century than with the twentieth. Theirs was not a culture of plenty, but of *enough*. Unremitting physical labor to create the stuff of everyday life was the occupation of such families, for men and women and children, too. Work, of course, was divided: women took care of the house, managed the cleaning and cooking and laundry, and provided the family with clothes, often starting with the raw fiber. Women also raised the children, frequently a large brood. Birth control was primitive and children were a source of labor. The fertility rate (the average number of children borne by a woman) in America was 5.42 in 1850, dropping to 4.55 in 1870. That meant many pregnancies with no prenatal care and no anesthetics for delivery. It meant frightening childhood illnesses (nearly half of American children died before their fifth birthdays) and many mouths to feed.

It's no wonder, then, that girls thought of their futures with trepidation. Childhood was grueling, but the prospect of becoming a wife caused many a girl dismay. Mollie Dorsey, a girl in the Nebraska Territory in 1857, mused in her journal, "Will I be a happy beloved wife, with good husband, happy home, and small family, or an abused, deserted one, with eight or nine small children crying for their daily bread?" Tears at a wedding were expected in the mid-nineteenth century, and they weren't mere tears of sentiment. A bride was likely leaving her family for the first time. Roads were bad in rural America, travel was difficult, and if a girl was going far from home, she knew she might never see her loved ones again. She was stepping away from everything she knew into an awesome set of responsibilities, and facing the mystery of sexual life with little confidence (and, often, limited information).

But the anxious bride had no choice. As the feminist Charlotte Perkins Gilman wrote in her searing book *Women and Economics* (published in 1898), "The girl must marry: else how live?" Girls were educated to run a house and raise children. Respectable jobs for women were scarce and poorly paid. Very few women lived independently: if a woman did not marry, she would probably join the household of one of her relatives as a kind of unpaid auxiliary labor. Becoming a wife was the female calling.

And of course it had its consolations. Most important, girls chose their husbands. They might control very little else in their lives, but nineteenth-century America believed in the romantic marriage so strongly that any elements of coercion (as in the arranged marriages practiced by some European or Asian immigrants) were culturally discouraged. Courtship was left to the young, to manage as best they might. The paucity of eligible men was sometimes a problem, especially after the Civil War, but a capable girl in the wilder parts of the country stayed single only as long as she wanted to. Women were so scarce in the West, and men needed them so badly to keep house, that girls could take their choice. The government even took a keen interest in the nature of marriage and the health of this institution, which it saw as essential to the well-being of the republic. The married man, accustomed to responsibility and capable of functioning in a community, was the essential American citizen, and the family the building block of the nation. Furthermore, the crucial element of free will in American marriages reflected the outstanding characteristic of democracy. Spouses in America selected each other, as American citizens elected their leaders.

Above all, mercenary concerns were supposed to play no part in a match. Love and money never mingled. Of course anxious parents sought a husband who could support their daughter, but the frank financial negotiations of European families were looked on with distaste. This may be why the practice of giving a daughter a dowry never took hold in America—it certainly explains some of the misunderstandings that accompanied international marriages late in the nineteenth century. Adele Sloane (heiress to the W. & J. Sloane furniture fortune, and descended from the Vanderbilts on her mother's side) kept a diary during her debutante days, and commented harshly on a friend's breaking off an engagement: "from the first I knew she did not care for him, and was only going to marry him because he could give her everything she wanted and because it pleased her parents. But all along it seemed wrong to me and such an injustice to the man. . . ."

In Adele's view, affection was required for a successful match. Yet girls were still in the passive position. They were courted, and they might have inklings of a man's intentions, but they were not supposed to respond fully until a declaration was made. Girls could choose their husbands, but the wise girl did so based on fairly practical criteria. Comparing two beaux, Adele Sloane ruminated, "I could not love either, and for that reason Mr. Whitehouse would make me the happier; he would not be nearly so exacting, nor so jealous. He would believe in me absolutely and marry me because he loved me, and not because I loved him." Of her ultimately successful suitor, Jay Burden, she writes, "I am sure . . . that I could care for him enough to marry him. . . . We have the same tastes, and we both have our whole life before us, and I am quite sure that he could help me and I could help him." What a woman looked for was a man "to guide and sustain her, and breathe strength into her life," wrote Constance Cary Harrison, an etiquette writer and novelist, in *The Well-Bred Girl in Society* (1898). Marriage was a matter of reciprocal sacrifices and duties. Men would provide for a household, while women would keep house, raise children, and submit to their husbands' sexual urges.

Because there was no getting away from it. The moment you opened the Order of Matrimony in an Episcopal prayer book of the era, the text would warn that marriage should not be entered into "wantonly, to satisfy men's carnal lusts and appetites, like brute beasts that have no understanding." It would then go on to proclaim that the institution was "ordained for a remedy against sin, and to avoid fornication." Bearing children, and whatever led up to it, were clearly an important part of marriage. And being a virgin was an essential part of being a bride. It meant that there would never be any doubt as to the paternity of any children. It was assumed that, after marriage, women would be faithful to their husbands because it was assumed that women had no sexual feelings. Some scholars even suggest that men were supposed to limit their lovemaking to once or twice a month in order to channel their energies into the burgeoning U.S. economy. Whether they did so or not, it was the wife's role to comply, with no expectation of pleasure.

Virginity was not merely physical, however. Middle-class girls were also shielded from any knowledge of the sexual side of life. Ideally a mother delivered to a groom a girl who was perfectly ignorant. Prostitution, infidelity, even the milder forms of sexual titillation were unknown to her. In Edith Wharton's *The Age of Innocence* (written in 1920 but set in the 1870s) Newland Archer watches his fiancée May Welland at the opera as Faust woos the innocent Marguerite with only the worst of intentions. "'The darling!'" he thinks, "'She doesn't even guess what it's about.' And he contemplated her absorbed young face with a thrill of possessorship in which pride in his own masculine initiation was mingled with a tender reverence for her abysmal purity."

To protect this purity, upper-class betrothed couples were supervised strictly. While American girls often enjoyed a great deal of freedom to associate with the opposite sex, engagement was seen as a kind of danger zone. An affianced pair had to be chaperoned in public and never left alone at home. The bloom must remain on the rose until the wedding night. Some of the traditional strictures about who pays for a wedding probably have their origin in this heightened anxiety about protecting an engaged girl's evident virginity. If a groom or his family paid for anything beyond the bridal bouquet, the girl was under an obligation to him. And she only had one kind of currency with which to repay him.

Deflowering, however, was not the only change that awaited a girl once she was married. A girl, in the nineteenth century, was a child, under the authority of her parents. A wife, though she came under the authority of her husband, was in charge of their household, and in the nineteenth century, that was no insignificant realm.

The home provided evidence of a man's power to provide. At the most basic level, a man might construct a small house with his own hands, roofing it and digging a well and making a fence for the livestock. As the century went on and the middle class expanded, households grew more elaborate. Larger dwellings, more rooms, more and finer furnishings required a different kind of effort from the lady of the house. The farm-wife skills of baking, spinning, and weaving were often supplanted by administrative and supervisory skills. A housewife's morning of work might take place at her desk as she made up the menus and shopping lists, paid bills, or checked the linen inventory. If her husband could afford to pay a staff to take over basic housekeeping, a wife could divert some of her time to a kind of ceremonial housework—fine embroidery, flower arranging, and the kinds of arcane crafts like weaving jewelry out of hair that speak to us today of women with too much time on their hands. In fact, it was time well spent identifying their husbands as successful.

The nineteenth-century household was much more, though, than the embodiment of a man's prosperity. Its emotional significance was paramount. Industrialization did not come to America without a cost. Labor conditions could be harsh for the men and women and even children working in, for instance, the mills of Massachusetts. Even members of the new white-collar classes had to make the transition between producing tangibles and processing information, between independence and submission to a corporate goal. Competition drove the new workplace. Leonard Jerome, a stockbroker in New York after the Civil War, claimed that, "Wall Street is a jungle where men tear and claw."

Home was the respite from tearing and clawing. As late as 1927, *Gunn's New Family Physician,* a family health manual, stated that in order for a man "[t]o recover his equanimity and composure, home must be a place of repose, of peace, of cheerfulness, of comfort; then his soul renews its strength and will go forth, with fresh vigor, to encounter the labor and troubles of the world." It was a wife's responsibility to achieve peace, cheerfulness, and comfort for her husband, who must not be disturbed by a particle of domestic unrest. Unruly children were sequestered in the nursery, clumsy kitchenmaids fired, unsatisfactory butchers not mentioned.

But it wasn't enough for a wife simply to keep the household humming along attractively with no apparent effort. If men, in the nineteenth century, were the foot soldiers of capitalism, women were quite simply angels. Constance Cary Harrison wrote, "Every man's ideal of a wife . . . is a girl, who may be pretty, who might be brilliant, but who must be good." Women were pure. They were more gentle than men, more affectionate, more self-sacrificing. In women resided the emotions and the moral center of each household. Henry Ward Beecher's sentimental novel *Norwood* (1867) expresses some of this view of women in unself-conscious terms. The hero,

Barton Cathcart, is about to leave home and his beloved Rose for Amherst College. He tells himself "that Rose was the star of his life. And, alas! he bitterly felt that she was lifted up so far above him—was so noble and rich in nature—so sure to command those far more worthy of her love than he could ever expect to be, that one might as well follow a star in hopes of clasping it, as follow Rose through the coming years in expectation of winning her!"

Sex partner, housekeeper, star—the roles played by a wife were a far cry from those played by a girl in nineteenth-century America. At the more elevated levels of society, the difference was especially pronounced. Wives even dressed differently from girls: they wore brighter colors, more daring décolletage, more elaborate jewelry. They had liberties denied to unmarried women, most notably greater freedom of movement and access to a greater breadth of experience. Wives could read French novels or have tea with men who weren't their husbands. At the turn of the twentieth century, a group of society women took the bold step of dining in public, at a restaurant—an undertaking that would have tarnished the reputation and the chances for marriage of a girl. A matron had a social weight that a girl lacked—she was an individual of considerable authority in the latter half of the nineteenth century. Even the standards of beauty favored her: good looks, from the 1860s onward, were attributed to tall, strong-looking women with voluptuous, maternal figures.

No wonder girls awaiting their transformation felt somewhat awestruck. Nineteenth-century letters and journals record the mix of misgiving and eagerness, anxiety and anticipation that occupied girls in the days before they were married. On her wedding day in 1865, South Carolina bride

Eleanor Cohen wrote in her journal, "today I cease to be a girl, and enter on the duty of 'a wife'—God grant me strength to act correctly to make him happy & above all to live in the fear and love of God—Can it be that today maidenhood ceases Oh! This getting married is no trifle, but an event that gives use to *grave serious* thought. . . ." Even Constance Cary Harrison struck a portentous note as she described the proper formation of a wedding procession. The bride, she wrote, "is joined at the altar step by her fiancé, who takes her hand, and then she becomes his for life."

She became his for life. Over and over again, at weddings all over America, from cabins folded into the Colorado foothills to parlors in modest midwestern towns to grand new churches on wide new city streets, girls approached their husbands-to-be knowing full well that this was a momentous and irrevocable act. Mollie Dorsey, on the eve of her wedding, wrote, "I know this is a solemn step, one that involves a lifetime of happiness or misery. . . ." What helped these girls and their families (and, to a lesser extent, the grooms) negotiate this transition was the wedding itself. Its complexity, its formality, its invocation of both religious and civil authority, its multipart form and involvement of all the senses combined to form a ritual that satisfied both the individuals involved and the community that witnessed it.

Let's return to Lavinia Warren as she becomes Lavinia Stratton. Unlike the average American bride of 1863, Lavinia was a public personality. Her wedding was attended by some two thousand people, many of whom were not known to her. (Though P. T. Barnum proclaimed that he had not actually *sold* invitations to the wedding, they appear to have been transferable.) Much closer to the norm was the wedding of

Mollie Dorsey, quoted above. Mollie was a brave and resourceful girl who grew up in a pioneer family in what is now Nebraska. She was engaged to Byron Sanford, a kind and humorous young man with few practical prospects in the rugged West beyond what his physical strength and willingness to work could achieve. Their wedding was scheduled for February 14, 1860, but Byron had to travel several hours on horseback to the county seat to get the marriage license. Once there, he found the county clerk missing. Their ceremony had been scheduled for 2 P.M., to allow their handful of friends time to drive home before dark. Byron, however, didn't get back to the Dorsey cabin until after 8 P.M., by which time Mollie had heard all too many stories told "for my especial benefit . . . where the bridegrooms *never* came, and the brides ended their days in insane asylums." To tease their guests, Mollie and Byron secretly put on their wedding clothes and sneaked into the kitchen, and when the family was called for "prayers," the wedding ceremony took place instead.

Most weddings took place somewhere on the spectrum between Mollie Dorsey's and Lavinia Stratton's, though rather closer to Mollie's. Especially in the early part of the nineteenth century, the home wedding was the standard, for a complex web of reasons. Some of these were religious and went back as far as the Reformation. Most Protestants, including Episcopalians, were comfortable with what would now be called "low church" worship. This preference for unadorned church services (and indeed churches) made ritual pomp distasteful. Jane Carlyle, wife of the English historian Thomas Carlyle, wrote in 1862 about her first experience of a church wedding. "I had rather wished to see a marriage performed in a church with all the forms, the eight bridesmaids &c. &c. . . . it looked to me something betwixt a religious ceremony and a—pantomime!" Churchgoers are now happy to acknowledge the ties between religious ritual and drama, but Mrs. Carlyle was not alone in her aversion in the 1860s.

Weddings in America were also marked by logistical concerns that didn't trouble the English. Sometimes there simply wasn't a church to marry *in*. The newer settlements out West might be served by a minister who held services in a school or community hall. The most remote homes, like Mollie Dorsey's, wouldn't even have that option. This scarcity of public buildings may account for the nineteenth-century American concept of the parlor as a setting for ceremonial occasions. This has come to seem slightly ridiculous—why avoid a room except for a handful of uses a year?—but the practice was well understood 150 years ago. A parlor was almost a sacred space, lending significance to the events that occurred there. After death, corpses were laid out in a parlor; in fact, this is where the term *funeral parlor* comes from. In more prosperous homes that might contain two parlors, one of them would be reserved for significant formal occasions like funerals or weddings.

Finally, a strong tide of sentiment animated all of these practical, logistical reasons for marrying at home. When a girl was leaving her parents and the surroundings she'd grown up in, marrying on the spot had a deep emotional resonance. At the end of Henry Beecher's *Norwood*, Barton Cathcart finally marries Rose, his "star," under an elm tree on the lawn in front of her childhood home: "There, at length, stood Rose and her husband, under the very flickering shadows and checkered golden light that had amused her when a babe." In Louisa May Alcott's *Little Women* (1868), Meg's wedding is a model of simplicity. She and her fiancé, John, are married by her minister father beneath an arch of greenery—there is never any discussion of the ceremony taking place in a church: "There were to be no ceremonious performances, everything was to be as natural and homelike as possible." As late as 1913, Jessie Wilson, the daughter of the president of the United States, was married in the White House in spite of the Wilson family's strong religious background. In a 1966 interview, her husband, Frank Sayre, remembered, "we wanted our wedding to be where Jessie was living. It meant so much more than to have everyone going to an outside church. . . ."

The White House was hardly Jessie Wilson's childhood home. But by 1913, the church wedding was firmly the U.S. norm, so Sayre may have felt obliged to explain his bride's choice. Actually, as early as the 1860s and '70s, the more urban, wealthy families were moving weddings out of the house. The model for the church wedding may well have been English, since English couples were required to be married in an Anglican church. (Anglicanism was a state religion, after all.) In the earlier years of the nineteenth century, English manners would not have mattered to Americans, but by the 1870s, the U.S. interest in Europe as a cultural and social example was awakening.

Another contributory factor was the shifting understanding of the wedding itself. In the eighteenth century and earlier, marriages were usually arranged by parents and the extended community. If your son Joseph was strong and good-natured, while my daughter Abigail had become a skilled housekeeper, we would marry them to each other. The practical matters of who brought what to the match would be arranged ahead of time without consulting the young people.

Weddings were thus small, private affairs putting an official seal on an existing agreement. But in the nineteenth century, once the matchmaking process became private, confined to the couple involved, a large wedding served the important function of involving the rest of the community in witnessing and supporting the creation of another adult family unit.

The movement of weddings into churches and the expansion of the typical number of guests were symptomatic of a general social trend toward formality in America during the latter half of the nineteenth century. The middle class grew and grew, launching thousands of families into a new world of prosperity, comfort, and refinement—a concept dear to the Victorian heart. Refinement was the identifying characteristic of a lady or a gentleman, manifested in modest dress, controlled movements, a well-modulated voice, a carefully selected vocabulary, and avoidance of anything crude or unpleasant. After all, in a land where self-determination (or self-invention) was the national pastime, elites still had to be identified. American social history is littered with attempts to identify the chosen people, but one of the most reliable barometers over time has been the possession of conventional manners. The manners deemed acceptable in the late nineteenth century were elaborate—along with everything else about civilized life, from ladies' hats to cake decoration. As the 1860s became the 1870s, upper-class weddings began to lose the fresh simplicity of the parlor ceremony and took on the stately grandeur of the church event.

A church, as opposed to home, wedding meant not merely moving the religious service into a sacred space. The ritual became more intricate and added elements. In fact, one of the primary characteristics of the wedding emerges at this point: it is a cumulative tradition. As circumstances surround-

This photograph from the early 1860s appears to have been taken in a church, but it is probably a reenactment rather than the actual ceremony. The group is casually clumped together rather than arranged in what later became standard wedding formation.

ing it change, it responds by absorbing some new bit of business. Rarely is any portion of the celebration dropped or simplified.

Pacing down a long aisle between pews involves more drama than descending the stairs from your bedroom to your living room, and thatching the chancel of a church with palm trees is more of an effort than creating a bower of ferns in the bay window of the parlor. Most churches held more guests than most houses (though there were always plutocratic exceptions). Music, whether religious or not, is essential to accompany the procession. The number of bridesmaids that looked charming in a home setting might be lost in a church. The entire ceremony took on much more of the air of a pageant.

Producing a pageant requires more resources and more effort than producing even the most lavish tea party, which the smaller home weddings often resembled in the middle of the nineteenth century. Although a horseshoe (for good luck) or a wedding bell of wired flowers might be ordered from a local florist, other decoration was handled by the bride's mother and female relatives, using flowers from their gardens. Mollie Dorsey baked her own wedding cake, but that was often a mother's job. Refreshments could well be limited to cake and punch, but if other food was served it was usually prepared in-house as well. A bride's dress and, indeed, her entire trousseau were usually stitched at home; the advent of the sewing machine in the 1850s made quick work of the numerous sets of linens required for setting up housekeeping. A woman usually brought with her the goods to furnish a house, with help from her family, but not necessarily from each of the wedding guests. In the 1850s and '60s wedding gifts were just appearing, and they were usually decorative tokens like hand-embroidered handkerchiefs, not the *batterie de cuisine* a bride might expect one hundred years later.

In fact, the dawning professionalization of wedding preparations in the latter half of the nineteenth century reflects the early development of the consumer culture in America. At first, brides and their families would reach out to one or two "vendors" (as we know them now) for items that could be better produced by professional hands. Sewing a bridal gown and other trousseau elements were all in a day's work for a Victorian girl, but the elegant niceties—fans, stockings, bonnets—couldn't be made at home. And increasingly, middle-class girls wanted them. Items that had been purchased rather than made had novelty value and indicated membership in the middle class. Thus, while invitations for a small wedding had traditionally been written by hand, they were replaced by the engraved invitations still seen today. In the early twentieth century Montgomery Ward offered a set of a hundred "Wedding, Regret and Correspondence cards" for a mere $1.50. Wedding cakes that were baked at home could be sent out to a "confectioner" to be iced with artful swags and rosettes. Florists could produce arrangements far more ornate than the vases filled by the ladies of the house. Naturally, the food and decorations and even clothing produced by professionals were more elegant, more fashionable, more highly polished than those made at home. Expectations began to change. The "refinement" of a wedding with these elements became the standard in wealthy circles. In fact, Mary Elizabeth Sherwood's 1897 *Manners and Social Usages* states that, "The city wedding in New York is marked first by the arrival of the caterer, who comes to spread the wedding breakfast; and later on by the florist, who appears to decorate the rooms, to hang the floral bell, or to spread the floral umbrella, or to build a grotto of flowers in the bow-window where the happy couple shall stand."

Of course, very few people lived in the style Mrs. Sherwood liked to write about (though some did live even more grandly). Furthermore, not everyone embraced the new standards for fashionable weddings. Louisa May Alcott was something of a firebrand in her day, motivated by a slightly Puritanical streak. Fashion and materialism seemed to her not merely distasteful but positively dangerous. *Little Women* is full of jabs at high society, many of them embedded in the description of Meg March's wedding. Her family, though not rich, is educated and genteel. Alcott spends several pages of description on Meg's tiny new home, beautifully arranged by her mother and sisters, and adds, "People who hire all these things done for them never know what they lose, for the homeliest tasks get beautified if loving hands do them." Meg refuses most wedding finery: "Neither silk, nor lace, nor orange flowers would she have. 'I don't want to look strange or fixed up today,' she said. 'I don't want a fashionable wedding, but only those about me whom I love, and to them I wish to look and be my familiar self.'" Later, her highly social Aunt March reproves her for helping with last-minute preparations, saying, "'You oughtn't to be seen till the last minute, child.'

'I'm not a show, Aunty, and no one is coming to stare at me, to criticize my dress, or count the cost of my luncheon,'" retorts Meg. Alcott is voicing the discomfiture of America's more conservative citizens in the face of conspicuous wedding expenditure—a plaint that has continued, at various levels of volume, until this day. Is a wedding a sacrament, or is it a party? Is it a moment for private emotion, or an opportunity for exuberant display? The way these questions have been answered reveals a great deal about the preoccupations of American society at any given moment. In the late 1860s, new money and new standards of behavior were pointing the way toward what would later be called the Gilded Age. Alcott, with her jaundiced view of high society, made a strong case for simplicity and sentiment.

It is difficult to generalize about nineteenth-century American weddings when conditions across the country varied so widely. But there was a growing notion, as the century went on, of a standard middle-class wedding. Not every girl could afford it, and many didn't even aspire to it. A handful of brides could enjoy rituals far more expensive and elaborate. But by the end of the Civil War, there was an increasingly common idea of what a wedding should look like.

CHAPTER 2

Dear Fanny Must Be Married in White

A *LITTLE WOMEN* BRIDE • HER MAJESTY WEDS •
WHY WHITE? • THE BARGAIN OF MATRIMONY •
FLATWARE AND FURBELOWS • "COMPETING OR
OUTSHINING" • "A RECENT DAISY WEDDING" •
"THIS CAKE MUST BE JUST RIGHT"

For most of the nineteenth century, what we know as the "white" wedding was the prerogative of a rich girl. In *Little Women*, Louisa May Alcott derides the folly of the "fashionable" ritual and dramatizes her values in fictional Meg March's choice of simplicity over style. By the standards of 1870 America, though, her family was privileged. They lived in a sizable house with gardens. Meg was, to be sure, marrying an impecunious teacher, but he was able to provide her with a charming little home. Her family employed a faithful servant, Hannah, and her wedding gifts included "bridal china," a silver vase, and "a generous supply of house and table linen." For her ceremony Meg was attended by her sisters in "suits of thin silver gray, . . . with blush roses in hair and bosom." ("Suits" in this instance probably meant two-piece dresses with long sleeves and the full skirts of the era.) The guests were served "a plentiful lunch of cake and fruit, dressed with flowers." Just a few elements set Meg's wedding apart from an ordinary tea party or "at home": the sisters in matching outfits, the flowers, the wedding cake, the wedding gifts, and Meg's own dress.

Meg March's wedding dress was white. Today, marrying in a colored gown is so unusual as to require explanation, but wedding dresses have not always been white. The popular supposition that their color signifies virginity was not the primary reason for the adoption of nuptial pallor. Another common explanation—that brides wear white today because Queen Victoria started the fashion—is much closer to being accurate. But it is not complete. As with almost every feature of weddings, the tradition of the white dress has complicated roots.

They go back to the late Middle Ages in western Europe, and are largely aristocratic. Most documentation of long-ago marriages concerns royal pairings, so we know that Princess Philippa of England, marrying a Danish prince in 1406, was clad in an ermine-trimmed white satin tunic. Later royal brides, like Italian Catherine de Médicis or Mary, Queen of Scots, wore white with gold or silver brocade and lace. While some noble eighteenth-century brides followed suit and married in white and silver or white and gold, others wore yellow or blue—no particular distinction attached to the color white.

When fashions changed at the beginning of the nineteenth century, soft, pale fabrics came into style, especially for young girls. The formality and grandeur of the eighteenth century gave way to what historians sometimes call an "age of sentiment." The desirable look for women was one of fragility. Although the silhouettes of gowns changed in the first half of the nineteenth century from the Empire high-waisted column to the Victorian tight bodice and full skirt, light colors and floating fabrics maintained their popularity. Tarlatan, tulle, lawn, and organdy were in demand, with satin a very formal option. (The style can still be seen on the corps de ballet of *La*

Sylphide and *Giselle*—hardly surprising, since the costume conventions of romantic ballet became codified around the second quarter of the nineteenth century.)

Nevertheless, it was not axiomatic that Queen Victoria would wear girlish white when she married Prince Albert in 1840. The previous English royal bride, Princess Charlotte of Wales, had spoken her vows in silver brocade with a fur-trimmed purple velvet train. The situation of the royal family was different in 1840, though, from 1816, when Princess Charlotte had wed. And while there is no evidence that Victoria's wedding gown was chosen with an eye to its public effect, there is also no doubt that it, and she in it, presented an effective image of the new English royalty.

According to a popular story, when Princess Victoria realized at the age of eleven that she might inherit the throne of England, she said, "I will try to be good." A little goodness was sorely lacking in the royal family at that time. The monarchy's credibility was at an all-time low, thanks in part to the extramarital and financial shenanigans of William IV and George IV before him. (King George III's madness hadn't helped.) A pure young girl on the throne might be just what was needed to improve the public opinion of England's rulers.

It was one of those moments in English history when the reputation of the crown and the person who wore it mattered. The middle class in England was growing. The power of Parliament consistently encroached on the power of the throne— and Parliament was less and less controlled by an aristocracy tightly linked to the monarch. A cadre of educated, informed bourgeois voters was beginning to influence politics, and it was they who voted on the government appropriations to support the royal family. The royal family, it followed, must demonstrate that it was worth supporting.

The queen's engagement to Prince Albert was a very encouraging sign. Royal marriages were dynastic, that was a given. Spouses for the ethnically German Hanover clan had been drawn from the minor principalities of Germany for a century. Albert was no different, in that respect, from Caroline of Brandenburgh-Anspach, George II's consort. But Victoria *loved* him. This was, after all, the romantic era. The formality and occasional crudeness of the Baroque had given way to natural emotion. And the royal match was the real thing. Albert was deemed "handsome." The queen, while never pretty, had a youthful freshness. The imaginations of her subjects were captured by this match.

True love came to the monarch, and the monarch, in turn, went to the people. Because Victoria lived at Buckingham Palace, she had to travel in a coach to the Chapel Royal at St. James's Palace. (Previous royal brides, resident at St. James's, never had to set foot outside.) She thus showed herself on the streets of London, "very much cheered by the mob on the way to and from the chapel," as a diarist of the era recorded.

Even those many citizens who were not on the streets of London could share in the queen's happy day, thanks to the infant popular press. The newspapers devoted column after column to the event, and within weeks, engravings of the wedding were for sale in bookstores. So the average English subject found out exactly what the young queen wore to become a wife.

The dress was fashioned of heavy white satin, with a deep bertha and flounce of Honiton lace. ("White," until well into the twentieth century, actually meant "cream" since the chemicals required to bleach satin to a blue-white shade are a fairly recent development.) Both fabric and lace had been

Engravings like this one circulated widely after Queen Victoria's wedding.
Despite the very large diamonds of her necklace, she looks more the
maiden than the monarch.

manufactured in England, a politic nod to the British economy that most royal brides since have emulated. The long lace veil was anchored to the bride's head with a wreath of orange blossom, but the queen wore no tiara. Though lavish (the lace alone cost a thousand pounds in the currency of the day), the ensemble was quite simple. Every previous monarch who married while on the throne had worn a purple velvet and ermine mantle, the official regalia of royalty. Victoria eliminated that.

As a public relations move, it could not have been bettered. This was an occasion—one of the few in a monarch's life, in fact—that many of her subjects had also experienced, or would experience. And by dressing less like a queen than her predecessors, and more like any other wealthy young maiden, Victoria brought her wedding still closer to a purely domestic event. It was in actual fact more public than any previous royal wedding, yet the queen was presented to her people as, simply, a bride. Naturally her subjects could identify with that. Naturally they loved her. Naturally bridal white became the standard for those girls who could afford it.

The queen must have been very fond of the style of her wedding dress, with its flounce and bertha of lace, because portraits from 1842 and 1854 show her in nearly identical gowns with different styles of lace. There was no reason why she should not have worn her actual wedding dress again—it was standard practice in aristocratic circles to do so. In fact, many a noble bride wore her wedding gown when she was presented at court after her marriage. Court etiquette demanded that a woman wear a train. It seems possible that in England, a wedding dress with a train was a status symbol, suggesting that a bride anticipated a court appearance.

Of course very few American girls were presented at

court, but they, too, wore their dresses again. In fact, many bridal outfits for American girls were made with two separate bodices. The wedding bodice would have a high neck and long sleeves, as bridal modesty required. The alternative bodice, sleeveless and low-necked, could turn the wedding ensemble into a conventional evening gown to be worn after the honeymoon. Some brides went to the trouble of having dresses made over. In *The Age of Innocence,* Newland Archer suggests that his lovely young wife, May, wear her wedding dress on their honeymoon in London, but she can't: "'it's gone to Paris to be made over for next winter, and Worth hasn't sent it back.'" Because these gowns were expected to see several wearings, Worth and the other French couturiers routinely packed two sets of floral trimmings with the dresses: one of artificial orange blossom for the wedding, and one of silk roses for later.

Only the very wealthiest brides could aspire to wear Worth, whose prices were shockingly high. In fact, not all brides could aspire to wear white dresses at all. But during the latter two-thirds of the nineteenth century, the white wedding gown seems to have become a source of identity for a bride, or a class marker. In *To Love and To Cherish: Brides Remembered,* historian Linda Otto Lipsett tells the story of a New Orleans girl, Fanny Green, whose family prepared to escape the city as Union forces neared. Fanny's sweetheart, "the Captain," had been living with them, recuperating from a wound. Before fleeing together, the couple must be married, it was decreed. As the contents of the house were hastily packed, wedding plans were made for that very evening. But, according to Lipsett's source, "Dear Fanny must be married in white, so every one declared. Then ensued a ransacking of trunks and

This is a two-piece gown from Worth, shown with the low-necked, bead-trimmed evening bodice that turns it into a ball gown. For her wedding day, its owner, Clara Howard, would have worn the more modest long-sleeved matching bodice.

drawers for a pretty white lawn [gown] she had—somewhere! At length it was brought to light in a very crumpled condition, not having been worn since the winter." The family on the verge of flight couldn't spare the time to iron it, but at least Fanny wore her white dress.

Why was it so important to her, or to her family, that they took time from escaping an oncoming army to find the gown? What was it about the alternative—being married in some other color—that was unacceptable? Because in point of fact, many a bride in the nineteenth century was married in a color, and not all of these brides were poor. The Wadsworth Atheneum in Hartford possesses the wedding dress of a girl named Rachel Alonso Thill, who married between 1855 and 1860. Her father was an early industrialist—he owned the first canning factory in New Haven, Connecticut. Her gown is a gorgeous blue and beige brocade, with a deep collar lavishly trimmed with chenille fringe. Catherine Zimmerman's *The Bride's Book,* a history of American wedding fashion, abounds in examples of colored dresses worn in the nineteenth century. Brides chose them, it seems, for a number of reasons.

The first is the simple impracticality of white: in the creation of the dress, in its wearing, and ultimately, in its maintenance. Most women's clothes, until the very end of the century, were made at home. Although sewing machines (first effectively marketed in the early 1850s) made much home sewing easier, white is extremely difficult to work with because every error shows. Each pucker, each crooked seam, any flaw that would pass unnoticed in a dark or patterned fabric, becomes glaringly obvious in white. Not only that—the seamstress has to go to great lengths to keep the fabric clean while she works on it. This often involves draping her lap and the floor around her with a sheet to avoid picking up any kind of mark.

Even today we certainly grasp the difficulty of wearing white. But imagine how much damage can be done to a long, very full white skirt. Every bride who has had champagne spilled on her gown understands this. What's more, nineteenth-century roads were rarely paved, so pristine hems and trains risked being dragged in the dust or mud.

Finally, if a wedding dress was to be worn again, it had to be maintained, which was especially labor-intensive with pale, thin fabrics. Stains and marks had to be bleached out, and a smooth, crisp surface imparted to six yards of skirt, using a primitive iron heated on a stove. Dear Fanny Green, married in her crumpled white lawn dress, probably couldn't have ironed it herself even without the Union army marching ever nearer. In the last third of the century, heavier, more durable fabrics like duchesse satin and corded silk came into fashion, but so did elaborate constructions like fishtail trains, draped bustles, and the massive sleeves of the 1890s. The refined, lacy gowns of the 1900s were no easier to maintain. It was back to the bleaching and ironing, with an extra measure of mending tattered flounces. A white dress in pristine condition implied its wearer's employment of an expert laundress, seamstress, and ladies' maid—conspicuous consumption if ever there was.

It's natural enough for a woman to put extra care and expense into the dress she plans to marry in. That being the case, many nineteenth-century brides invested in dresses they could wear more often than a white gown. When Queen Victoria married in 1840, as we have seen, pale colors were the rage, but fashion is cyclical, and often technology-driven. In 1856 an eighteen-year-old chemist named William Henry

Perkin patented a dye called mauveine that worked beautifully on wool and silk, giving them rich purple hues. Until
then, dyes had all been vegetable-based, often imparting delicate and fairly fugitive tints. Perkin's innovation of chemical-
based colorants set the stage for a rainbow to take over
fashion. A mere six years later mauveine won major prizes at
the English Exposition Internationale and Queen Victoria
was seen in a mauveine-dyed dress. Other brilliant colors
soon followed: fuchsia, magenta, vivid greens and turquoises,
all chemically based, dyed fabrics for upholstery, curtains, and
of course, dresses. What may have made these hues all the
more appealing to a bride dreaming of a wedding gown was
the fact that, until marrying, she was not supposed to wear
them. Girlish colors were still pale. After eighteen years of
pink and butter yellow, who wouldn't dive headfirst into ma-
tronly kingfisher blue? Furthermore, darker colors would
wear better and, five years after the wedding, would not scream
"bride" to every dinner guest. Thus museum costume collec-
tions are full of nineteenth-century wedding dresses in large-
scale plaids (popular in the 1850s and '60s), jewel-toned
brocades, and artful combinations of rich-hued silk and velvet.

There was still one more reason to avoid bridal white,
one that is still valid today. It is a question of suitability. During the latter half of the nineteenth century, a white dress may
have demanded or implied a degree of formality that not
every bride wanted (or could afford) to adopt for her wedding. It may have been, to use a modern term, pretentious.
Certainly there was no shame attached to having what was
called "a quiet wedding" and wearing the smart but practical
traveling suit you had chosen for your honeymoon trip. Laura
Ingalls Wilder's *These Happy Golden Years* vividly describes

how Laura and Almanzo decide to have a small private ceremony. Neither family can afford a big church wedding, but
Almanzo's bossy sister, Eliza, plans to travel west from Minnesota "to take charge of our wedding," as he puts it. This is
unacceptable to the couple. As soon as Almanzo has com-
pleted construction on their tiny new house and Laura and
her mother have finished making her black cashmere dress,
they are married by Reverend Brown in the sitting room of his
house, without even her family present.

Though Laura Ingalls's mother disapproved faintly of
her wearing a black dress (an old saying runs, "married in
black, you'll wish yourself back"), many another Western
bride did so. Lots of girls possessed one good dress, which
was black for practical reasons (including the fact that it could
be worn for a funeral). Historical societies are full of stiff,
board-backed *carte de visite* photographs from the 1880s and
'90s, depicting solemn young couples in their bridal finery.
President Harry Truman's parents were married in Lamar,
Missouri, in 1881. His mother, a far-from-blushing twenty-
nine, gleamed in a jet-beaded black gown that would stand her
in good stead for her social life as a married woman. To make
it bridal, she had added a spreading white collar. Other brides
wore tulle veils or trimmed their sober dresses with sprays of
artificial orange blossom. In 1901, Sears, Roebuck advertised a
wreath of wax blossoms for eighty-five cents; a girl could get
an additional brooch and bouquet for another eighty cents.

Laura Ingalls Wilder and her family, like Mollie Dorsey
of Nebraska and many other settlers of the West, lived more
or less at subsistence level. In such a household, the expense
of time and money for a grand white wedding was unthinkable. As the middle class grew, though, and as more and more

Most nineteenth-century brides were simply married in their best dress, which was often black (durable and appropriate for inevitable funerals). The veil and flowers (probably artificial orange blossom) made it bridal.

Americans achieved a measure of prosperity, the trappings of the white wedding became more readily available. The full-blown "wedding industry" that turned brides into princesses in the 1950s was nowhere near development, but a first step was taken: white wedding dresses got easier and cheaper to obtain as the century went on.

Probably the first sign of this evolution came in the fashion supplements of the magazines like *Godey's Lady's Book,* which were eager to guide women toward correct wardrobe choices. In fact, they wanted to help women sew them: by 1865, readers could order patterns in standard sizes (an 1860 innovation) from *Godey's.* Around this time, department stores began developing areas where women could choose from a wide selection of fabrics. Philadelphia's Strawbridge and Clothier even had an "Evening Room" where women could examine samples in the lighting prevalent at evening parties (brighter than we're used to, since electric light was just being refined). "Wedding silks" were also mentioned in the advertising.

Mail order brought rural brides more than artificial orange blossom. If they couldn't select the perfect satin in a big-city department store, they could still order it from Sears, Roebuck or Montgomery Ward. And if a girl didn't trust her sewing skills or wanted a higher level of expertise than her mother could offer, she could assign the creation of her wedding gown to a local dressmaker. The cost need not be prohibitive. One frugal bride of 1900 in Rochester, New York, kept meticulous track of her wedding expenses in a notebook that survives today. She bought the fabric and two kinds of lace trim for her wedding dress and paid a dressmaker to stitch it together, for a total cost of $21.50 (around $450 today). She actually spent more on the ready-made traveling suit that she, like many brides, wore as a going-away outfit.

The dressmaker option was not necessarily the cheapest way to obtain a white wedding gown, though. Some dressmakers worked as itinerants, traveling from house to house and doing all of a family's sewing for a few weeks. They might be paid little more than room and board. But at the other end of the expense scale were businesswomen operating out of well-lit professional premises, where they sold fabrics and trimmings as well as cutting and sewing garments. They might employ a workroom of skilled seamstresses. Some, as a marketing ploy, even laid claim to French ancestry and called themselves "Madame." Department stores, too, had dressmaking departments, so that a bride could select the fabric for her gown at one counter, the braid and lace at another, and a pattern at a third. What all of these arrangements had in common was giving the bride some creative control over the finished outfit. Having a dress handmade requires a series of decisions about fabric, cut, and trim, as well as the real physical intimacy of the measuring and fitting process. Only the wealthiest brides experience those luxuries today.

Ready-to-wear gowns, which were widely available (even from mail-order houses) by the mid-1880s, lacked those advantages. What's more, the fashions of the era were close-fitting, and a garment made to a standard size might not match a bride's actual proportions. Some retailers offered mail-order gowns but nevertheless encouraged brides to visit their stores for alterations, to ensure a correct fit. Ready-to-wear was new enough so that a bride might balk at having her wedding gown be her first experience of a "boughten" garment. But by the second decade of the twentieth century, garments were cut considerably looser than they had been thirty years earlier. Styles were often simpler, with a high waist, a tubular skirt, and limited trim. It became much easier to buy off the rack, and department stores pressed their advantage. A ready-to-wear dress might lack cachet, but advertisements pointed out that the time and money saved on a bride's gown could be devoted to buying her a more complete trousseau. The gown was important, but it was only a small portion of a bride's equipment.

Poor Fanny Green, married in haste to her captain, may have wondered what elements of her trousseau made it into the jumble of trunks and baskets that accompanied her family to their country plantation. Certainly she would have had one, a collection of table linens, bedding, and underclothes that she had been amassing since girlhood. The trousseau was part of the bargain of matrimony. The groom provided the place to live and furnished it. Beds, tables, horses, carriage, and cookstove were his to build or purchase. The bride brought the soft goods: sheets, pillows, quilts, napkins and tablecloths, handkerchiefs and dresser scarves and antimacassars. Often these were the work of her own hands, sheets stitched from raw lengths of linen and trimmed with hand-crocheted lace. The quality and quantity of a girl's trousseau varied during the Victorian era as much as did the character of her wedding dress. On the frontier it might be limited to a few sets of bedding, a pair of tablecloths, and pillows hand-stuffed with feathers from the family chickens. This would still be enough to attract suitors: some men married simply to acquire a level of comfort they couldn't achieve on their own.

At the other end of the spectrum were the wealthy girls who were expected to bring to marriage the furnishings for a very large house—for life. Early in the nineteenth century, this could have meant twenty-four dozen sets of linen, all made from the finest damask and embroidered with a bride's initial or monogram. It sounds like an immense amount, but laundry was done much less frequently in those days, and the laundry process, involving as it did harsh bleaches and abrasion to remove stains, was extraordinarily hard on fibers. The quantities for a bride's personal linens would have been similar: chemises and corset covers, drawers and nightgowns, dozens and dozens of petticoats. A woman—who, after all, had no way of acquiring money besides being given it—was supposed to bring enough clothes to her marriage to last for at least the first year.

Even for a middle-class bride, the outlay was significant. A modest trousseau in the 1880s would have cost around two hundred dollars—close to four thousand dollars in today's money. However, as the century went on, the vast quantities of linens diminished. A mere two dozen sets of sheets (even as few as a dozen and a half) would suffice because laundry began to be done more often and more efficiently. Too, by the turn of the century fashions in women's clothes had begun to change so rapidly that the purchase of a dozen corset covers became incautious. In a mere twenty years, they—and the corsets themselves—would be obsolete.

In the first half of the nineteenth century gifts from outside the immediate families played no real part in equipping a young couple for housekeeping. Gradually the circle widened so that relatives and distant kin, then close friends and even affectionate well-wishers might give a couple a wedding present. There was no question of obligation, though, and gifts were often small tokens. Mollie Dorsey spent a few months before her wedding living in Nebraska City, sewing for a more well-to-do family. A married friend, to her surprise, gave her "some beautiful embroidered undersleeves and handkerchiefs for wedding presents." (Undersleeves were linen or cotton half-sleeves that peeked out from beneath the belled sleeves of the period's dresses. Like white linen collars and cuffs, they could be changed and laundered often, freshening up a dress.) A friend would not give a practical gift, because that might imply that the family was unable to furnish the bride with the proper necessities.

By the last quarter of the nineteenth century, scholars agree, the practice of giving wedding presents was very widespread, even in the smallest, least sophisticated communities. At the same time, as we shall see, the entire wedding ritual was becoming more standardized and more elaborate. Gift-giving was a way for family and friends to express their approval and support of a marriage. Although it is easy to see the materialism in the gift-giving practice (especially as it became inflated in the upper classes), it's important not to lose sight of its basic emotional impulse. A wedding welcomes a new unit of adults to the community and celebrates the establishment of a new household. A wedding present—whether a pressed-glass bud vase or a chest of silverware—not only demonstrates support for the new couple, it also allows friends and family to participate in a happy, optimistic event.

And as it happened, the late nineteenth century was an intoxicating time for gift-giving. Dozens of technological innovations ushered in an era of unprecedented material profusion. Happily for brides, many of these innovations made it possible to mechanically produce artifacts that had previously been made very expensively by hand. The jacquard loom wove a version of brocade. Pressed glass pretended to be hand-blown and cut. The transfer-ware process decorated ceramics without involving any fidgety paintbrushes. Best of all, scientists discovered how to apply a thin layer of silver to a metal alloy, frequently of nickel and copper. The result— silver plate—brought cutlery, teapots, even big pieces like trays and candelabra into the price range of many a middle-class family.

In the upper class, silver was a staple wedding present. Every bride set up housekeeping with "her silver," which meant her flatware, engraved with her maiden initials. Twelve place settings were adequate, but of course more was better in an era when a really well-to-do hostess boasted that she could entertain one hundred guests on two hours' notice without sending out for anything. The late Victorians loved to create objects that served only one highly specific purpose, so a place setting might include an oyster fork, a clear soup spoon, a fruit knife as well as a dinner knife, a fish fork as well as a dinner fork, and additional items for dessert. Serving pieces were so precisely differentiated that many still languish in antique stores, unidentified (and this is after the cheese scoop, the berry spoon, the fish slice, the ice cream spoon, the croquette server, the sugar shell, and the asparagus tongs have all been labeled). The U.S. Congress commissioned Tiffany & Company to create a special tea service for Nellie Wilson's 1914 wedding to William Gibbs McAdoo. The ornate "Chrysanthemum" pattern was selected, with special monogramming and extra engraving all over the surface of the heavy tray. In addition to the tray and teapot, the service included a coffee pot, a hot water kettle, a chocolate jug, a sugar bowl, a creamer, and a waste or slops bowl. Etiquette expert Mary Elizabeth Sherwood wrote in *Manners and Social Usages*

(1897), "The first thing which strikes the eye of the fortunate person who is invited to see the bridal gifts is the predominance of silver-ware. . . . Not only the coffee and tea sets, but the dinner sets and the whole furniture of the writing-table, and even brooms and brushes, are made with repoussé silver handles—the last, of course, for the toilette, as for dusting velvet, feathers, bonnets, etc."

And if a silver-handled brush for dusting velvet seemed too pragmatic or too cheap, there was always jewelry. Young girls were not supposed to wear much jewelry; a modest string of pearls was considered sufficient to adorn their freshness. Diamonds and colored gems were strictly reserved for married women. Indeed, a rich girl marrying a rich man would be expected to glitter at social events—and jewels could be considered something she'd really need. When Consuelo Vanderbilt married the Duke of Marlborough in 1895 she received astonishing jewels, among them a yard-long string of mammoth pearls that had belonged to Catherine the Great. However, it was her pearl-tipped diamond tiara that really came in handy when she went to England and took her place at court as a duchess. Some brides were so thrilled by their new baubles that they piled them on for the wedding itself; a diamond star in the veil, pearls with a diamond clasp, and a diamond brooch might well sparkle their way up the aisle. Even Queen Victoria, downplaying the nuptial grandeur, wore a necklace of sizable diamonds and, pinned to her bodice, a large sapphire surrounded by diamonds from "dear Albert."

At the most elevated stratum of society one did reach the dilemma of what to get a girl who clearly had everything—the puzzle that sends poor Charlotte Stant to find the golden bowl in Henry James's 1904 novel of that title. As Charlotte

Grace Moon married Stewart McDonald in St. Louis in 1907. The diamond brooch at her throat was most likely a wedding gift, worn for the first time on her bridal gown. The form of the orange-blossom wreath had not changed much from Queen Victoria's day.

tells the groom, "it isn't a question of anything expensive, gorged with treasure as Maggie is; it isn't a question of competing or outshining. What, naturally, in the way of the priceless, *hasn't* she got?" You couldn't give silver forks to a millionaire's daughter who was marrying an Italian prince. If the bride's mother has bought her Catherine the Great's pearls, what does that leave for the poor guest? The indefatigable Mrs. Sherwood had some suggestions: "articles somewhat out of the common" like "old Louis Treize silver boxes of curious design" or "little silver canoes and other devices to hold cigarettes and ashes." Nellie Grant, the cherished daughter of the president, married Englishman Algernon Sartoris in 1874 and amid the flood of silver and jewelry came a poem from Walt Whitman. Another president's daughter, Alice Roosevelt, was married in the White House in 1906 and received a box of snakes from a snake collector—someone who was sharing what he loved best, perhaps.

When Charlotte Stant speaks about "competing or outshining," she means it literally, for this was the era when the practice flourished of displaying wedding gifts for the guests to examine. It was standard procedure to devote one room in the bride's house to the presentation, with linen-covered tablecloths and flowers set around to relieve the glitter of silver and crystal. Reed and Barton, the silver manufacturer, had a full-service shop in New York at the turn of the century. In addition to offering the usual silver, stationery, and luxury goods, the employees performed services like arranging the exhibition of wedding gifts. Not surprisingly, writers often compared the spectacle to the aisles of the better kind of store.

Actually, the finer sensibilities shrank at the commercial,

competitive aura of the gift display. As early as the 1870s, charismatic Brooklyn preacher Henry Ward Beecher wrote a piece in *Godey's Lady's Book* denouncing the practice, which he felt encouraged ostentation. *Godey's* went on a little crusade against wedding gifts, once claiming that wedding invitations were frequently sent bearing the phrase "No presents received." Mrs. Sherwood stated in 1897 that "many persons of refined minds hesitate to show the presents." Not surprisingly, though, persons of refined minds seemed to be in the distinct minority at the turn of the century.

Much more common was the attitude remarked by economist Thorstein Veblen in his groundbreaking *Theory of the Leisure Class,* published in 1899. It was Veblen who coined the phrase "conspicuous consumption," and Veblen who pointed out that, in the upper reaches of society, women functioned primarily as status symbols for their menfolk. Men slaved to earn, while women, through their public and unnecessary spending, attested to their mates' success in the marketplace. The array of gifts at a wedding was a case in point. The goods on view were so lavish and so ostentatious in their inutility that they brilliantly telegraphed the essential point: how immensely rich everyone was.

Gift-giving was not the only opportunity for grandiose display in the late nineteenth-century wedding. This was the era when more was more, and aesthetic moderation appeared dingy or unfinished. To current taste, that is nowhere more obvious than in the floral decorations for weddings.

They were not outrageous to begin with. Accounts of weddings before the 1860s don't mention them at all. Orange blossom, of course, was used to trim the bride's dress. It had long been the favored bridal flower because of a botanical peculiarity: citrus trees like orange and lemon are capable of yielding bud, fruit, and bloom all at once. What a perfect symbol of fertility! If a practical girl was wearing her best black wool, she might baste sprigs of artificial orange blossom to her bodice or work them into her hair, as Queen Victoria had. Her Majesty had the real flower, which was expensive beyond the average girl's reach, but fine facsimiles were available. In 1872, *Harper's Bazaar* even published directions for creating your own orange blossom wreath, using five reels of wire and 360 sprigs of the artificial flowers.

Formal wedding photographs from the mid-nineteenth century sometimes portray grooms decked similarly to the brides, with a sizable spray of flowers—lily of the valley or the conventional orange—and perhaps a white ribbon fixed to their lapels. Our modern descendant is the boutonniere, and the predecessor is the "wedding favor" as it was known in the eighteenth to mid-nineteenth centuries. Engravings of the Prince of Wales's marriage in 1863 show that the prince (like his father before him) wore large white bows attached somewhat incongruously to the epaulets of his dress uniform. These were wedding favors, and in earlier years all the guests at a wedding had worn them. They might be more or less elaborate, sometimes including silver leaves or flowers, sometimes forming a fat white rosette. Even the horses pulling the bridal carriage wore favors on their bridles.

Curiously enough, one of the staple elements of the wedding that seems Victorian on the face of it is actually a slightly later development. Though brides since the ancient Greeks had carried bouquets of herbs or flowers, Queen Victoria did not and neither did most of her daughters. The queen merely held a handkerchief. Many brides of the mid-nineteenth century did the same, though some clasped a prayer book covered in white leather or silk. It was not until the mid-1870s that fashionable brides began to add tight nosegays of flowers to their bridal regalia, though their dresses were often liberally trimmed with wreaths or knots of orange blossom. (In a rare 1862 photograph, Queen Victoria's daughter Princess Alice, in her bridal finery, clasps her hands in an awkward pose; at least the bouquet did away with that problem.) In fashion illustrations of the 1880s and '90s, sometimes bridesmaids carry bouquets while brides do not, though by the mid-1890s bouquets seem to have been standard for at least the richest brides. Consuelo Vanderbilt recalled in her memoir *The Glitter and the Gold* that, "A bouquet of orchids that was to come from Blenheim did not arrive," but news accounts record her carrying a three-foot-wide bunch of white flowers, so a backup must have been on order.

It's hard to imagine Consuelo tossing that massive bouquet to her attendants, and accounts of nineteenth-century weddings don't include mention of this tradition. Yet a photograph in the collection of the New York State Historical Association shows a bride of 1908 standing on the upstairs porch of her house, arm raised to hurl her flowers to a cluster of young women. It is a moment of startling informality, and it's easy to imagine that most stately, refined weddings avoided such jollity. Actually, this pretty custom has its roots in exactly the kind of coarse proceeding the Victorians deplored. In the late Middle Ages, public celebration of a wedding followed the bride and groom into the bedroom. A kind of ritual disrobing followed—bits of the bride's clothes like sleeves, lacings, and garters were snatched at by the guests. It's a short step from the guests snatching to brides, in self-defense, tossing items. Bedding the bride fell out of favor by the eighteenth century and the mere mention of a lady's "nether limbs"—let alone the clothes that covered them, like garters—became taboo by the mid-nineteenth century. When the custom of the bride tossing something to her guests revived, it was her bouquet that she relinquished, aiming it at the crowd of her bridesmaids and other unmarried female guests. While the recipient of the garter was deemed lucky, the new tradition said that the girl who caught the bouquet would be next to marry.

What a modern observer would probably find strangest about the late-nineteenth-century wedding is the profusion and elaboration of the floral decorations, which were very much what Veblen called "conspicuous consumption." What could be a more obvious way to spend money than to decorate a large space with the most evanescent of nature's creations? And to deck it, furthermore, so thoroughly that sometimes you could hardly see stone or wood in a church interior! There really isn't that much apparent difference between today's bridal procession and that of a hundred years ago until you get to the background: a bower of ferns or a grotto of chrysanthemum-studded palms strikes the eye as something from another era.

Not that floral wedding decor was that elaborate in the early Victorian years. *Little Women*'s Meg March was married beneath a simple arch of greenery, and the average home wedding saw the house prettified just with vases of flowers from the family and friends' gardens. To mark the occasion, a wired creation might be ordered from a florist: a bell, a dove, a horseshoe, or even a wishbone, suspended from the ceiling, marked the spot where the officiant and the couple were to

The participants in this ceremony, lined up in the classic wedding choreography, are almost hidden by the profusion of potted palms. This photograph, from the turn of the century, was probably taken for a set of stereopticon views.

stand. Grace Lumpkin's *The Wedding,* written in 1939 but set in the South in 1909, contains a long passage in which the brother of the bride takes a wagon out to gather moss and smilax that the family will twine into ropes. They are hung, tent-fashion, from the corners of the parlor to the chandeliers for a festive effect.

As early as 1874, remarkable floral effects were seen at the grandest weddings. Nellie Grant's White House nuptials eclipsed many another Washington social event that year. Below a window in the East Room, where the ceremony took place, a platform had been built that was banked with ferns, vines, roses, and lilies. A massive wedding bell of white rosebuds was suspended above the platform, while wreaths on either side spelled out the initials of the bride and groom: NWG and ACFS. The columns of the room, in a patriotic touch, were wrapped with red, white, and blue blossoms, while the chandeliers were so heavily festooned that the scent, according to one reporter, was "almost oppressive."

The cost of this kind of display could easily run into the hundreds of dollars, but the last quarter of the nineteenth century saw no diminution in the enthusiasm for astonishing floral decoration. In fact, it got downright silly. When Frances Folsom married President Grover Cleveland in 1886 (and this was a quiet wedding owing to the discrepancy in their ages and the fact that she, an orphan, had been his legal ward), a plaque of dark pansies was suspended from the mantel with "June 2, 1886" spelled out in paler blossoms, while the centerpiece of the bridal table was a sailing craft identified by the newspapers as "the good ship Hymen," complete with white flags, a bridal monogram, shoals, and rocks—all made of flowers.

By the turn of the century, florists and mothers of the bride were clearly reaching for originality—enough with the thousands of orchids or American Beauty roses! Mrs. Sherwood's invaluable 1897 *Manners and Social Usages* offers some insights and suggestions, like the unifying floral theme, where one single flower is used for all of the wedding decor. "So well has this been carried out," she says, "that at a recent daisy wedding the bride's lace and diamond ornaments bore the daisy pattern, and each bridesmaid received a daisy pin with diamond centre." For a fall wedding she offers a cunning notion: a tapestry of autumn leaves as a backdrop for the bride and groom. An artist draws a design on canvas and "earnest and unselfish girl friends" stitch on the leaves in different hues. Mrs. Sherwood proposes cultured but depressing themes like Romeo and Juliet, Hamlet and Ophelia, or Tristan and Isolde. (This is the point at which one suspects the author of a sense of humor unusual in etiquette writers.) At her most outlandish, Sherwood recounts attending a wedding where a small house had been built of light wood and completely covered with roses. "If someone had not suggested 'bathing house,' as he looked at this floral door to matrimony, it would have been perfect. It also looks a little like a confessional."

If the decorations of a late-nineteenth-century wedding are the aspect of the ritual that have changed most, the cake is probably the one that has changed least. Like so many other elements of our wedding ceremonial, it took on its emblematic form between 1850 and 1900. Curiously, although American wedding customs follow English ones in most respects, we do not agree on wedding cakes. By the early nineteenth century, a strong tradition of white cakes had grown up here, and they gradually became adapted for the wedding, so that while the English wedding cake is traditionally a dark fruit-cake, its U.S. counterpart is both pale in color and light in texture. White icing had long borne the connotation of purity and refinement, since brown sugar was the kitchen staple, but English wedding cakes have usually been iced with a rolled sugar preparation while American cakes are decked with buttercream or another soft frosting. English cakes also usually contain a layer of marzipan between the cake layer and the icing, making for an altogether more durable confection than what is seen at American weddings.

In fact, English cakes more closely resemble their predecessors, the dense, highly spiced cakes of the Renaissance. Simon Charsley's *Wedding Cakes and Social History* traces the decorative, ceremonial appearance of wedding cakes to late medieval "subtleties," elaborate constructions of sugar, wax, paste, and paint that, molded into allegorical shapes like lambs or angels and surrounded with inscriptions, were served with the courses of a banquet. Charsley suggests that the sharing of a cake at a wedding probably dates back even further to the Christian practice of breaking and sharing bread as an important element of worship. Many modern experts on wedding symbolism also mention the practice of "cake-breaking," in which unleavened oat or shortcakes were broken over the bride's head as she entered a dwelling after she had been married; guests were supposed to eat a piece of the broken cake. This custom could be the origin of the old tradition of giving away tiny boxes of wedding cake to guests. Girls who slept with the cake beneath their pillows were supposed to dream of their future husbands—a bit of traditional lore that was still current in the 1970s.

Whatever its origin, the wedding cake was essential to

getting married. Brides marrying in the most modest fashion imaginable marked the ceremony with a cake, probably because it was the least expensive component of what was becoming the standard wedding. Laura Ingalls Wilder tells of her mother making a "big, white cake" for her extremely simple wedding. "'This cake must be just right,' Ma insisted. 'If you can't have a wedding party, at least you shall have a wedding dinner at home, and a wedding cake.'" The fact that Laura had to beat egg whites until her arm ached suggests that it may have been a light cake like a Lady Baltimore.

Naturally, some wedding cakes were more elaborate than others. As with other components of the wedding, they became more complicated later in the nineteenth century. Queen Victoria's wedding cake, for instance, was flat—a single (though massive) layer. The practice of baking individual tiers of cake and layering them separated by columns developed in the 1850s, and when Victoria's eldest child, the Princess Royal, married in 1858, the cake rose six or seven feet in the air. There were three elements, only the bottom of which was actual, edible cake, though the two upper "compartments," as they were called, had been crafted out of sugar. The formation of the decorations had probably been rendered possible by the invention, around 1840, of the piping bag with a metal funnel. Filled with icing, tipped with various circular or star-shaped tips, the pastry bag permitted bakers to achieve hitherto unthinkably ostentatious effects. (The technology has yet to be improved, as any moderately ambitious baker knows.)

In cake decorating, as in fashion or furniture design, technology spurred aesthetic developments. What *could* be done *was* done, and cakes were piped, swagged, and festooned until barely a flat surface remained. While a vase of flowers was a traditional topmost ornament for a cake, figures made of sugar paste also began to appear. Queen Victoria's cake was decorated with figures of herself and Prince Albert, clad, for obscure reasons, in classical Roman costume. A dog at the groom's feet and a pair of doves at the queen's referred to fidelity. Flowers, cornucopias, cupids, and lovebirds, all rendered in white sugar, were standard motifs.

Over the last half of the nineteenth century the wedding cake's purpose was transformed along with its appearance. The modest cake, made at home, possibly decorated with fresh flowers, was clearly food, meant to be eaten. Even the highly social Mrs. Sherwood instructed her readers that wedding cake and punch, sherry, or tea were a perfectly appropriate menu for a reception. But as confectioners' techniques made decorating a cake increasingly important, its role at the reception shifted. Two layers of the Princess Royal's wedding cake were purely for display, not for consumption. Bit by bit, the cake, like other elements of the wedding, became more opulent. Once a routine though festive dessert, it became a showpiece that required the professional touch. By the turn of the century, the wedding cake at a middle-class wedding was generally produced in a commercial baker's establishment.

As it gained height and elaboration, the wedding cake also gained a new significance in the wedding feast. Though it was apparently the bride's duty to cut the cake, this process did not take on a ceremonial aura until around 1880. In England, the bride was to slice a wedge from the cake (sometimes employing a saw: the layers of sugar paste icing, marzipan, and fruitcake did not yield easily), which she would then divide into morsels for each guest. American etiquette experts

Once bakers learned to separate the layers of wedding cakes with columns, there was no limit to their height, and they became less food than decoration. Only one or two layers would have been edible.

occasionally derided the wedding cake in the last quarter of the nineteenth century, claiming that nobody really liked to eat it. Yet public sentiment refused to abandon this piece of elaborate confectionery: whether or not the cake was eaten, it needed to be present at the reception, it needed to be publicly cut by the bride, and guests needed to take home little white boxes of it "to dream on."

CHAPTER 3

The Etiquette at a Grand Wedding
Is Always the Same

MATRIMONIAL MANNERS • THE AGE OF THE PLUTOCRAT •
AMERICAN HEIRESSES AND ENGLISH LORDS •
THE BRIDE GOES PUBLIC • THE AMERICAN GIRL •
WHITE HOUSE WEDDINGS

While the development of the United States as a nation was undeniably impressive, American society was slow to acquire what Europeans thought of as good manners. Historian Arthur Schlesinger explains why in *Learning How to Behave: A Historical Study of American Etiquette Books* (1946). To begin with, our population of former immigrants tended to come from the lower classes (else why emigrate?) and brought little with them in terms of courteous customs. The lack of a native aristocracy prevented elegant habits from trickling down to the populace. What's more, the very nature of our big, brash, untamed country made development of a code of manners a low priority. Who could be bothered sorting out calling cards when a forest had to be cleared? The constant influx of immigrants speaking foreign languages delayed the development of courtesies of speech: it is very hard to be polite to someone without a common vocabulary. Finally, Schlesinger points out, the relatively small population of women (whom he calls "guardians of decorum") meant that there was little demand for social niceties.

By the last third of the nineteenth century, though, these conditions had been overcome by the preoccupations of a new middle class. The brawny virtues of the individual who had tamed the physical landscape looked clumsy next to those of the citizen who knew his place and did his duty without disturbing his neighbors. At the simplest level, residential density demanded some conventions. If you see a lady every day as you leave the house for your office, how do you demonstrate your friendly respect—without missing the trolley? Throughout the latter half of the nineteenth century, the citizenry of the United States was subjected to an ever-increasing stream of etiquette books. Historian Ellen Rothman points out that "life was becoming more highly structured on every front"—in banking, in transport, in culture. To give just one example, the country was organized into standard time zones in 1883, to facilitate scheduling the passage of trains that by then traveled all the way across the country. With life's new structures came a new level of formality that served, perhaps, to put a comforting distance and control into most social encounters, from the mundane to the extraordinary. One of the primary preoccupations of nineteenth-century etiquette concerns individuals' access to each other. In rural or village settings, this was not an important issue; neighbors were important for survival. In cities, though, you had to select your circle of acquaintance. Etiquette provided ways to regulate this process, so that the wives of bankers could properly snub the wives of shopkeepers, and the wives of shopkeepers avoid association with the wives of laborers. Class became important.

And in this land of self-determination, social aspiration followed hard on the heels of class consciousness. Hence the proliferation of advice literature: manners are one of the outward signs of class. If you want to move a rung up the social ladder, you must learn how to behave the way they do who live up there.

Weddings were an important topic to etiquette writers. Nobody needed to be told how to serve a simple homemade cake to a dozen people in a log cabin, but prosperity complicated matters. Wealth combined with urban sophistication complicated them further: John H. Young's *Our Deportment,* published in 1879, devotes a mere thirteen pages to weddings, but Mrs. Sherwood's 1897 *Manners and Social Usages* goes on for fifty pages, discussing fashions, menus, and the arcana of leaving calling cards after a wedding. Airily, she states that, "No book can tell the truth with sufficient emphasis, that the etiquette at a grand wedding is always the same." If so, she managed to make it sound terribly daunting.

Putting on a "grand wedding" wasn't just an opportunity for the newly bourgeois family to hint at its ample discretionary income with lavish flowers, an ornate cake, and a white satin dress for the bride. A wedding was also (and has remained to this day) the occasion for a family to display its command of the intricate planning and execution of a ceremonial social event. The correct taste, as exhibited in dress, food, flowers, music, right down to the decoration of the cake, proclaimed membership in the elite. Taste, of course, is a moving target. It can't function to sort parvenus from arrivistes unless it is constantly changing—hence the importance of the wise guides, whose life work was to shepherd their readers through the wedding process.

It was important to get all of the details right because a wedding was a public occasion. Bride, groom, and their families were the center of communal attention, and the details of their behavior were noted with an alertness and an eagerness for missteps that reflect rather poorly on human nature. In Edith Wharton's *The Age of Innocence,* the engaged couple,

Newland Archer and May Welland, are launched into the unblinking scrutiny of New York society the moment their engagement is announced. Newland, invited by the Countess Olenska to visit her, thinks "she ought to know that a man who's just engaged doesn't spend his time calling on married women." When he presses May to shorten their engagement, she protests that "her mother would not understand their wanting to do things so differently." She suggests to her eager suitor, "that kind of thing is rather—vulgar, isn't it?"

As Wharton, writing from the vantage point of 1920, knew, New York in the early 1870s had seen *nothing* in the way of vulgarity, compared to what it would shortly witness. In the decade after the Civil War the city was just emerging from its drowsy provincial past to become the mighty financial center of the nation. The habits of its social leaders were those of a comfortable tribe with little need to impress. They lived in modest row houses, entertained at formal dinner parties, went to church twice on Sundays, and married their children off to each other in discreet domestic ceremonies.

But the financial structure that had produced substantial wealth for Schermerhorns and Stuyvesants had changed. Farming, real estate, even wholesale merchandising were being replaced in the 1870s by much bigger operations, and by a more complex economy that made some new men rich on an unprecedented scale. Railroads, streetcars, utilities, oil, shipping, retailing, and finance provided millions and millions of dollars to men with names like Astor, Whitney, and Vanderbilt. The new people wanted to be accepted by the social leadership of New York, but they weren't prepared to wait politely with their hands in their laps. They didn't understand why you had to live in a poky little brownstone on

Gramercy Park when, by building just a few blocks north, you could get a wider lot and spread out a little bit. Why move the furniture and roll back the rugs every time you wanted to dance? Why not just build a ballroom? Why *not* serve champagne and play cards on Sunday night? Well-bred New York ladies of the 1870s ordered their clothes in Paris, but wouldn't dream of wearing them right away—they shunned the ostentation. But the moment Mrs. August Belmont's dresses had cleared customs, she was parading them up and down Fifth Avenue in that showy carriage her husband had bought her. Vulgar? Possibly—but so much fun!

The Old New Yorkers with their quiet ways didn't manage to hold out for very long. By the mid-1880s, Gotham social life was firmly in the hands of the nouveaux riches. Fifth Avenue was gradually lined with copies of European castles and servants were forced to don velvet liveries like English footmen. Unfamiliar faces appeared constantly at the opera (in the new, opulent Metropolitan Opera House) and when they were identified in a whisper, the source of their money was always included ("Lorillard—tobacco, you know"). The men vied against each other in business and in spending, ably seconded by their wives. Second and third houses sprang up in Newport, Rhode Island, and Lenox, Massachusetts. Yachts were built and raced. Europe was plundered for paintings and paneling as connoisseurship became a competition. Dances became balls and balls became costume masquerades. Sons and daughters were raised like royalty, with governesses and tutors and footmen to bring the nursery meals up from the kitchen many floors below.

But one way in which Americans differed from the European aristocracy they so strenuously admired was in their attitude toward their daughters. An English or a French girl was a mild disappointment at birth, an afterthought in the family budget, and an expense to marry off. The American girl, though, was something else entirely. She was the earliest celebrity this country produced, famous for being famous. Every town had its belles, the prettiest and most celebrated unmarried women whose every social success was glorified. Rich American girls were prettier, more poised, better groomed, better educated, and infinitely better dressed than their European counterparts. What's more, the American mania for European travel (satirized by Mark Twain and mulled over by Henry James) provided plenty of opportunities for comparison.

And European men compared. In particular, English men compared. To be entirely specific, English aristocrats took note of these attractive and wealthy young ladies. The times that had been so good for industrialists across the Atlantic had been very bad for those English families whose fortunes were produced by land. A severe agricultural depression beginning in the 1870s reduced income on many estates by as much as 50 percent. Furthermore, the aristocracy functioned as a kind of rarefied welfare state: the mark of a gentleman was that he did not work. He lived on an allowance made to him by his family. If he was the eldest son and heir to an estate, he learned how to manage his lands; younger sons went into the poorly remunerated fields of the military, the church, politics, or the civil service. No one expected to live on his salary. This system had worked in the palmy days of English agriculture, and it still worked for those fortunate peers whose green fields covered seams of coal or could be converted into urban housing. The Duke of Westminster, who owned large tracts of central London, had no need of an American heiress to balance his books. The debt-ridden Duke of Marlborough, however, who owned the only private palace in England, needed a "dollar princess" quite badly.

So English aristocrats began marrying American heiresses. They did so in a trickle at first, quite accidentally. Lovely dark-haired Jennie Jerome, daughter of a Wall Street stock speculator, fell madly in love with Lord Randolph Churchill, the son of the seventh Duke of Marlborough, and married him in Paris in 1874. Two years later, social New York was shocked by the Grace Church wedding of Consuelo Yznaga, a southern girl, to Viscount Mandeville, whose father was the Duke of Manchester. Consuelo had been snubbed by the stiffest New York matrons because her manners were unconventional—she played the banjo and sang minstrel songs in public. But she was going to be a duchess!

Soon enough, rich girls from midwestern cities caught on to the phenomenon. A lovely Ohioan named Jeannie Chamberlain took a steamship to Europe and got some fine Parisian dresses. She met the Prince of Wales in a German spa and entranced him. By the time her European itinerary brought her to London, she had bagged an invitation to the prince's country house, Sandringham. London society was thrilled to meet her and she married a courtier. Jennie Jerome's sisters married Englishmen, as did Consuelo Yznaga's. In fact, Consuelo Yznaga's son (yes, she did become a duchess and her son was the ninth Duke of Manchester) married another girl from Ohio. The eighth Duke of Marlborough, divorced and desperate with debts, came to New York and snared a rich widow in 1888. A mere seven years later his son returned with a similar transaction on his mind.

Jennie Jerome was one of the earliest and loveliest American heiresses to marry an English aristocrat (in 1874). Here, some ten years later, she wears a turquoise velvet gown she had made to match the gems in the medal on her shoulder.

It was 1895, a year the social historian Dixon Wecter called the *annus mirabilis* or "year of miracles" for Anglo-American marriages. In April, Washington beauty Mary Leiter (whose father had been one of Marshall Field's original business partners in Chicago) married diplomat George Curzon, son of Viscount Curzon. Jeannie Chamberlain's sister married a landowner from Lancashire, and a doctor's daughter from New Jersey, Elizabeth LaRoche, married Sir Howland Roberts. But the climax of the year came in November, with the marriages of two of New York's biggest heiresses.

These were families that did everything on a large scale. Consuelo Vanderbilt's father, William Kissam Vanderbilt, worked in the family business—the New York Central Railway. Pauline Whitney's father, William Collins Whitney, had earned more than $40 million in just over five years as a founder of New York's Metropolitan Transit. Pauline's husband, Almeric Paget, was considerably the lesser catch, since he was only the grandson of a marquess. Consuelo, however, hit the jackpot by reeling in the ninth Duke of Marlborough, owner of glorious Blenheim Palace—and unfortunate son of the poverty-stricken eighth duke.

Consuelo, in fact, had been maneuvered into marriage by her ambitious mother, Alva. Marlborough desperately needed money to keep a roof (four acres of it) on Blenheim. Alva had raised Consuelo impeccably—she was sophisticated enough to shine in any society, fluent in French and German, accustomed to a life of astounding formality. Marlborough felt that Consuelo would be a fit chatelaine for Blenheim, and if the girl had other notions, her mother overlooked them. Her wedding was little short of a coronation.

It had to be planned with some dispatch. The Duke had met Consuelo in London, invited her to visit Blenheim, then accepted an invitation to visit the Vanderbilts in Newport in August. It was not until September that he actually popped the question and Consuelo, cowed by her mother, accepted him. The next two months were a flurry of financial negotiation (he got $2.5 million in railway stock) and wedding preparations.

Alva had made some plans in advance. Six months earlier, when Consuelo was being fitted for summer clothes in Paris, Alva had commissioned Worth to create a wedding gown, without even consulting her daughter. Charles Worth was the couturier of choice to rich American girls, a wizard dressmaker whose astronomical prices ensured exclusivity. The Vanderbilt family traditionally worshipped at St. Bartholomew's Church, but the sanctuary of that building wasn't large enough for the musical resources Alva required—symphony conductor Walter Damrosch plus fifty orchestral musicians and sixty choir members. So Alva booked St. Thomas's Church on Fifth Avenue for her daughter's nuptials on November 6.

This brought Consuelo's wedding into direct competition with Pauline Whitney's, which had been announced in July and was scheduled for just six days later at the same church. Pauline's smaller orchestra was to be led by Nathan Franko, but opera stars Edouard de Reszke and Lillian Nordica would perform. Pauline, like Consuelo, wore a Worth dress with a five-yard train. It took five clergymen to marry Consuelo and her duke, while a mere three united Pauline and her commoner. For Consuelo's wedding six ropes of flowers were suspended from the dome of the church, roses spanned the chancel in arches, the balcony was hung with orchids, and the altar rail was smothered with lily of the valley and roses. Pauline's wedding featured four triple Gothic arches of orange leaves and pompom chrysanthemums, while

Consuelo Vanderbilt married the Duke of Marlborough in 1895. This sketch of the recessional hints at the ostentation of the wedding—the floral decorations almost obscure the church interior.

the steps to the chancel were marked by an open gate of dahlias and more mums. Consuelo's wedding required more policemen to keep the crowds in order (300 to Pauline's 250), but the Vanderbilt clan all went to Pauline's wedding rather than to hers. That was because Alva had divorced her husband earlier in the summer, and Alva bore a grudge, even insisting that Consuelo return any gifts from her father's side of the family.

In fact, in terms of American social prestige, Pauline Whitney's wedding was the superior event. Probably because of her mother's scandalous divorce, Consuelo's guest list was not very grand (and included no one from the groom's family). The church was better filled for Pauline's wedding, and among her guests were many dignitaries including Anglo-American couples such as the Earl and Countess of Essex and George and Mary Curzon, and English diplomat Michael Herbert and English politician Joseph Chamberlain, both of whom had American wives. But the most distinguished guest of all was President Grover Cleveland, who kept the crowd at the reception until well after the grand luncheon was over, since he was enjoying himself so much and protocol dictated that no one could leave before him.

These two weddings were covered in thorough detail by the newspapers of the day. Pauline and Consuelo, as the daughters of two of America's richest men, were famous even before they got engaged. But their families'—and the public's—attitudes toward their weddings make a remarkable contrast to the way weddings were thought of earlier in the century.

White House weddings have always attracted public curiosity, but in 1832, when the president's son Lucius Polk married Mary Eastin, little information about the event seeped out beyond the guest list. Washington's newspaper of the day, the *Globe,* carried a three-line announcement three days after the event. Wilbur Cross and Ann Novotny, authors of *White House Weddings,* say, "It was considered indelicate to pry into the details of a matter so private in nature as a wedding and then to air them to the public at large." In 1844, when the widowed President Tyler married Julia Gardiner, the daughter of his late secretary of state, the families plotted to maintain secrecy (both because of Tyler's unpopularity and because of the thirty-year age difference between bride and groom). The couple were wed in New York, and only the carriage with four white horses that drove the bride to the church hinted to passers-by that a wedding was afoot. Nonetheless, word spread quickly, and after the wedding breakfast, when the newlyweds drove downtown to take a ship to Washington, every vessel in the harbor was dressed with flags of congratulation. But overall, as Julia's brother wrote to her later, the families had been adept at "preserving at once the President's dignity, and our own feelings, from all avoidable sacrifice." Another glimpse of this attitude appears in *The Age of Innocence,* when the arrangements for May Welland's wedding are discussed. Her wealthy but invalid aunt wishes to attend the wedding, but her wheelchair is too wide to fit between the uprights that support the awning running from church door to curb. "The idea of doing away with this awning, and revealing the bride to the mob of dressmakers and newspaper reporters who stood outside fighting to get near the joints of the canvas," is horrifying to May's family. "'Why, they might take a photograph of my child *and put it in the papers!*' Mrs. Welland exclaimed. . . . and from this unthinkable indecency the clan recoiled with a collective shudder."

By this time that instinct for privacy was one of the few distinctions between America's old monied class and the nouveaux riches. The public gaze was an offense against sensibility, that relic of the Romantic age that caused the truly well bred to shrink from powerful stimuli. In the eighteenth century, when matchmaking was quite pragmatic, weddings tended to be open to the community and frequently, in the lower classes, included some kind of bedding ceremony. Bawdiness was not to be avoided. But once the age of sentiment was reached and marriage for love became the norm, a damper was put on the sexual innuendo. It was almost as if, once actual sexual attraction had entered the matchmaking equation, the whole situation was too combustible. Allusions to the wedding night were shunned, except in the robust language of the Episcopal prayer book (all the more reason to keep the ceremony exclusive). Potential exposure to the suggestive commentary or appraising glances of the lower orders was avoided at all costs—hence the awning.

Yet not every bride's family was as protective as the Wellands. In the days before their marriage, Tom Thumb and Lavinia Warren attracted hordes to the American Museum, which was soon taking in three thousand dollars a day as the curious lined up to see the little fiancés. P. T. Barnum, operating more as impresario than in loco parentis, let it be known that he had offered Miss Warren fifteen thousand dollars to delay her wedding (as a married woman, she would of course retire from her career). Miss Warren responded that she wouldn't accept one hundred thousand dollars to put off her union with her intended! Unstated but understood: the little people burned for each other. Consequently the museum receipts flourished.

By the last quarter of the nineteenth century, some wealthy

families acknowledged that a wedding was a quasi-public affair. Ida Honoré was the daughter of a wealthy Chicagoan, and when she married Colonel Frederick Grant in 1874, the pageantry of the event was pitched, in part, to the populace. Why else would Grant (the president's eldest son) arrive for his wedding in a wagon drawn by four army mules? Why else would the Grand Western Light Guard be engaged to provide a concert for the crowd outside the house?

But that was in the West, where society had a more free-wheeling attitude. Back in New York the difficulty was to keep the crowds at bay. This became more and more of a problem as the century went on. Guest lists for weddings swelled; often hundreds of people were invited to the church, but only a fraction of those were invited to the reception. (This is probably the origin of the classic wedding invitation's configuration: a large card inviting guests to the church with a smaller card added for the reception.) Gradually it became necessary to send tickets to the church along with the invitations. The ushers' role was transformed. At a small home wedding, a "best man" stood up with the groom as his supporter and witness. As weddings moved into churches and the number of bridesmaids grew, symmetry required more "groomsmen" to balance the maids. At the same time, they took on the ceremonial task of showing guests to their seats—but at the most fashionable weddings, the ushers' job assumed some of the aspects of a bouncer's. Mrs. Sherwood's etiquette book suggests that in some wedding recessionals the ushers precede the bride and groom "to be ready to cloak the bride, open the doors, keep back the people, and generally preserve order."

Some families let the ushers remain purely decorative and called in the law. Neither Brown professor Franklin

Jameson nor music teacher Sara Elwell was remotely famous, but when they married at Brooklyn's Grace Church in 1893, six hundred people were invited to the ceremony and police officers were hired to check the invitations at the door. Heiress Cornelia Martin would have done well to follow suit. Raised largely in London by her ambitious mother, Cornelia was engaged before the age of seventeen to the Earl of Craven. Her parents returned to New York for the wedding out of loyalty to their native shores. This sentiment must have been sorely tested when, at the conclusion of the marriage ceremony in Manhattan's Grace Church, the crowd outside overwhelmed the ushers as they opened the church doors. They stampeded inside, trapping the bride and groom, and stripping the church of every bloom and leaf. Twenty policemen had been stationed in front of the church beforehand to check invitations, but reinforcements had to be called in.

By 1893, American heiresses had long captured the public imagination. The potent combination of the American girl's charm and her father's wealth made her an object of fantasy at many levels of society. At the same time, the figure of the bride had emerged definitively from the mist of privacy that surrounded her earlier in the century. One marker of this drift toward publicity comes from England, where Princess May of Teck (she became "Mary" on her husband's coronation) married Prince George of York in 1893. George, as eldest surviving son of the Prince of Wales, was second in line to the throne. May, a kind of royal cousin, had previously been engaged to his elder brother. When Albert Victor, the Duke of York, died of influenza a month before the wedding, May mourned. Her emotions had recovered sufficiently by July 1893 for her to accept the hand of Prince George. This

Princess May of Teck (later Queen Mary) became Duchess of York in 1893. The floral trim on her dress was beginning to go out of style, but the pale tint of the bridesmaids' gowns was still fashionable.

time around, English subjects' feelings were aroused not only by the spectacle of a royal marriage, but of a tragic and brave bride as well. It was, as Ann Monsarrat points out in *And the Bride Wore . . .*, the most public royal wedding to date. The general populace was invited to view the wedding gifts— some thirty-five hundred items worth around three hundred thousand pounds. A garden party at Buckingham Palace allowed five thousand guests to gawk not only at the English royal family and the bridal party, but also at the many royal visitors from all over Europe. The wedding procession was sent from Buckingham Palace to the Chapel Royal by a long and circuitous route for the benefit of spectators, and the elderly Queen Victoria rode in a brand-new carriage with extra-large windows to allow the people a better view of Her Majesty.

Not only was the public allowed to witness the festivities: so was the press. In fact, the attitude toward publicizing details of a wedding had changed completely in both England and America since Lucius Polk's White House wedding in 1832. The last two-thirds of the nineteenth century were marked by many social changes, one of which was the development of the popular press and its powerful influence on popular culture.

Technological innovations came first. The production of paper from wood pulp rather than linen fibers sharply reduced publishers' costs. The cylinder press, which rolled type over paper rather than individually stamping sheet after sheet, sped production drastically, especially once these presses were powered by steam. Soon the paper was fed through the presses in rolls rather than sheets, further accelerating the process. These high-speed presses could have papered America to public indifference, however, without a corresponding post–Civil War phenomenon: the creation of a large reading audience. School attendance laws were tightened and the average school-leaving age advanced, resulting in a much more educated citizenry than America had known before.

Of course no American innovation really takes root unless it somehow produces money. Advertising was the final piece in the puzzle that allowed press barons to get rich. Newspapers had to be sold for mere pennies, which barely covered the cost of their production. But the columns upon columns of advertisements leavening the reportage made the publication of a newspaper or a magazine a profitable enterprise. In magazine publishing, the advertising subsidized higher production costs, allowing the price to drop from the relatively expensive thirty-five cents a copy that limited readership to the upper class, to as low as a nickel by the end of the century. Circulation climbed, as did the number of publications. Some sources suggest that nearly three thousand three hundred magazines were produced in the United States during the 1890s. Magazine publishing even came to have an influence on newspapers. Earlier in the century, newspapers were not produced on Sunday, which was still considered a day of rest. Beginning in the 1880s, though, newspapers realized that they were missing an opportunity. Working men who did not have time to read a paper during the week could spend an hour or so with one on Sunday. Newspaper publishers added more pictures and more news analysis, and sold many more ads in these Sunday editions, which increasingly resembled the magazines they competed with.

The pictures, of course, were crucial, and like the rest of the innovations in periodical publishing, they were made possible by technology. In the 1840s woodcuts provided the only way to insert pictures into columns of type, and they were confined mainly to small ads. Engravings on copper or steel plates allowed much more scope for detail, but cost as much as a thousand dollars per plate to produce. *Frank Leslie's Illustrated Newspaper,* which was founded in 1855, relied heavily on engravings, as did its English predecessor, the *Illustrated*

London News. These were not cheap publications: *Leslie's* cost ten cents a copy, but it was so popular that by 1858 it had a circulation of one hundred thousand readers. With the development of electrotyping and, later, halftone printing, it was possible by 1890 to reproduce photographs and line illustrations inexpensively and accurately, both in newspapers and in magazines.

Like any mass audience, the readership of the late nineteenth century had an appetite for what entertained it. The illustrated magazines and Sunday newspaper supplements offered up an enticing mix of crime coverage, sexual titillation (very restrained by our standards), and society news. This last was not the sedate record of births, deaths, and marriages that the upper class was used to: now it was lively eyewitness coverage of the doings of America's rich. When Alva Vanderbilt opened her grand Fifth Avenue palace with a costume ball in 1883, *Leslie's* sent a sketch artist so that its readers could feel they'd been there. A New York gossip paper called *Town Topics* barely kept on the right side of the law with its detail-laden innuendos about life in high society. In 1892 a consortium of wealthy backers with names like Astor and Stuyvesant founded a magazine called *Vogue* that was devoted to fashion, culture, and manners, while *Munsey's Magazine,* for a more modestly situated reader, specialized in a kind of strike-it-rich aspirational literature. A century ago as now, America's wealthiest families were news.

This nascent cult of the celebrity tracked not only the Rich Man; another favorite character for the press was the American Girl, that delicious young protocelebrity. Writers ever since Hawthorne and Poe had focused on her as a kind of metaphor for the country itself. Her youth and innocence reflected the new, optimistic foundations of America, while her fresh, natural beauty had its parallel in the untouched landscape. At the same time, as industry laid its mark on the cities and people of the United States, a pretty, frivolous young lady provided a charming contrast in her complete inutility. Women, because of their scarcity, were historically treated well in this country; visitors frequently remarked on the rough-hewn chivalry that allowed females to travel alone and unmolested as they could not have done in Europe. The American Girl appeared in the press as a favorite daughter of the entire nation, with her image admired and her exploits proudly shared among her relatives. (Henry James's Daisy Miller is the most artful fictional example of this media creation.) An heiress like Jeannie Chamberlain, traveling to Europe and winning the admiration of the Prince of Wales, reflected glory on all of her kind. Meanwhile, back home in St. Louis or Wichita, a homegrown belle was twitching her train and flirting her fan and providing the social columns with solid inches of material.

Part of the resonance of the figure of the American Girl was potential. She mirrored the possibilities of America, hinting at a glorious future. But while the country's fate was still being worked out, the future of a young girl could only be one thing: marriage. She was, after all, a nineteenth-century woman. To become a wife would be her crowning moment. This was the ever-satisfying culmination of her narrative, and it was detailed in the newspapers as lovingly as any of her previous exploits.

Or more so. When Nellie Grant married Algernon Sartoris in 1874, the New York *Graphic,* a predecessor of the tabloid, published a twelve-page pictorial "Wedding Number."

It was available across the country for ten cents and it sold out. How do you fill twelve pages of a newspaper with wedding coverage? Detail. Details of the flowers, the gifts, the bride's gown, the bridesmaids' gowns, the bridesmaids' genealogies. Sartoris was English, so there was a lot of explaining to do about his exact position in the British Legation in Washington, and his exact position in British society back home. (His chronic alcoholism was a detail the papers ignored.) Sketch artists provided portraits of bride and groom, as well as of the president, in case anyone had forgotten what he looked like.

But where did the information come from? Not so many years earlier, it had been "indelicate" to air domestic concerns in public. Now, the press reported that the Grant/Sartoris wedding breakfast was consumed with gilded cutlery and the dishes included chicken croquettes, lamb cutlets, soft-shell crabs, woodcock, and snipe on toast. (Grant was a famous trencherman, and this menu was relatively restrained.) In all likelihood an enterprising reporter suborned a departing guest to get a glance at the gold-engraved white satin menu that each one took home as a memento. But how did reporters find out about the tiny flagstaff jutting forth from Nellie Grant's pink-and-white bouquet? Could anyone get close enough to read the banner it flew? The message was "LOVE." When *Harper's Bazaar* described the White House floral decorations in every particular ("waving in feathery sprays from the tops of the tall and slender gilt tripods"), had a writer actually been there? Was this secondhand information from a guest? Or had there been a press conference?

It was, after all, the White House, and there must have been some mechanism for feeding appropriate information to

This sketch of Nellie Grant's wedding appeared in the New York *Graphic*, which sent an artist to record the event. Note the floral wedding bell, twined columns, and hanging plaques with the couple's initials.

the newshounds. But what was appropriate? Nellie Grant's wedding was a private occasion, as opposed to a state one. It was even quite small by the standards of the day: only two hundred people witnessed the vows. Yet it seems likely that someone on the White House staff was briefing reporters. Even in 1874, the press was a force to be reckoned with. They wouldn't go away. They had their columns to fill. They might as well fill them correctly, however indelicate the process. By 1878, when Rutherford Hayes's niece Emily Platt was married at the White House, media management seems to have been considered a necessary evil. It was a quiet wedding, since Emily was an orphan of twenty-eight marrying a forty-two-year-old widower. Mrs. Hayes, stepping in for the bride's mother, forbade the newspapers to mention the gifts or the trousseau. She felt that brides, knowing their wardrobe details would be made public, were inclined to spend more than they could afford to.

Mrs. Hayes was fighting a losing battle, though. By the 1890s the wedding coverage for America's most famous brides was astoundingly thorough. A reporter could easily devote 250 words to the cut and trim of a bridesmaid's gown ("blush pink corded silk . . . princess-cut basque . . . Elizabethan chiffon puffs . . . silver passementerie . . . high neck trimmed with real lace . . . long, loose sleeves, narrowing at the wrist in a frill"). When Consuelo Vanderbilt married the Duke of Marlborough in 1895, ten days before the wedding *The New York Times* devoted a column and a half on the third page of the paper to descriptions of her underwear: fourteen sets of cambric corset covers trimmed with real Valenciennes lace and "Consuelo" embroidered on the ribbons, etc., etc. Although Consuelo herself, in her memoir *The Glitter and the Gold,* mentions her shock at the vulgarity of the story, a later writer claims that artists from *Vogue* were permitted to sketch her trousseau for publication. (Cornelius Vanderbilt, her uncle, was a stockholder of the magazine.)

There was gossip at the time, in fact, that Alva Vanderbilt, Consuelo's mother, was using a press agent. If true, it would have been shocking, for the pretense still existed that a wedding was a private affair. To the extent that one cooperated with the press, it was reluctantly. Actively managing the newspaper coverage of one's daughter's wedding would have been remarkably vulgar.

Yet if there was a woman in New York who needed the help of public opinion, it was Alva. Not six months earlier, she had taken the then-astounding step of divorcing her husband, William K. Vanderbilt. This earned her the enmity of the entire powerful Vanderbilt clan and created a rift in New York society, for Alva did not meekly creep away into seclusion the way divorced wives were supposed to. She wanted to have her cake (her divorce) and eat it, too (maintain her position as a social grande dame). Obtaining a duke as a son-in-law was a good step—or so it had seemed at first.

The problem was that by 1895, the American fascination with European aristocrats was waning. Too many poor peers had steamed over to America, snatched up fresh young American girls with big dowries, and swept them back to England or the Continent. Stories were trickling back, rumors of young wives unhappy with the looser morals of the decadent aristocracy. Why should all those hard-earned American dollars stream over to Europe to subsidize some playboy who didn't even work? Why should the Duke of Marlborough, the very picture of an effete aristocrat, waltz back to his drafty palace with lovely dark-haired Consuelo at his side and a substantial amount of railroad stock in his pocket? The newspapers nipped at his heels ceaselessly in the days before the wedding, and he could do no right. He skipped the wedding rehearsal but showed up to sign financial documents. He was stopped by police in Central Park for "coasting" on a bicycle. He was shorter than his bride. When asked about the upcoming marriage, he said it had been "arranged." He never said he loved her. So in the end, despite all the column inches and the sketches and the Worth dresses and the pearls, Consuelo Vanderbilt's wedding to the Duke of Marlborough left a funny taste in the mouth. When Consuelo's cousin Gertrude (even richer) married the boy next door, Harry Payne Whitney, the wedding itself was much smaller, as the Vanderbilt family was then in mourning. Yet America rejoiced—this time the dollars were staying at home.

The same rhetoric animated the wedding coverage in 1906 of America's next full-fledged princess to marry: Alice Roosevelt. Heiresses were still marrying English lords, but nobody paid much attention. Alice Roosevelt, though, the gorgeous headstrong daughter of President Theodore Roosevelt, had been news for years. She smoked. She had a tart tongue. She did whatever she wanted, and if that meant traveling halfway around the world with Congressman Nicholas Longworth, loosely chaperoned as part of the secretary of war's goodwill tour—nobody could stop her. One can imagine a sigh of relief echoing through the White House when she finally announced her engagement, and a date was set a mere two months later. It was an almost imperial wedding, with thousands of gifts from all over the world, a New York trousseau, and seven hundred guests. (No bridesmaids: Alice felt a bridesmaids' procession was "peculiar.")

The whole event was carried off with the panache that

seemed to cling to those Roosevelts—so the next White House wedding must have seemed awfully muted in comparison. Woodrow Wilson never was good copy, and his daughter Jessie, twenty-five in 1913, was a scholarly college graduate with a strong interest in social work. Just before her father was elected president she got engaged to Francis Bowes Sayre, a Harvard Law School graduate just as high-minded as she was. The wedding was as quiet as a White House wedding could be, with a private ceremony and no news releases. Gifts were actually discouraged. Apparently thousands of Alice Roosevelt Longworth's presents were still languishing in storage somewhere, and the Wilsons didn't like the idea of waste. Every item in Jessie's trousseau was bought ready-made and her all-American dress had been made in New York from silk woven in Paterson, New Jersey. The entire event seemed as intentionally middle-class as was possible at 1600 Pennsylvania Avenue.

And in this instance, the Wilson family was perhaps in tune with the times. Just as the antiaristocratic backlash had caught the Vanderbilt/Marlborough wedding, a kind of revulsion toward grandiose robber baron weddings had begun to tinge the press coverage. In fact, the robber barons themselves were looked on askance as the century turned. Labor abuses, outlandish extravagance, and financial chicanery tarnished the reputations of many plutocrats. Blind worship of the almighty dollar was replaced by soberer concerns as the reform era gathered steam. Extravagance—lionized in the 1880s and '90s—was characterized as un-American, a betrayal of Puritan principles of thrift and industry.

By 1900, the media were starting to promote the simple wedding. A magazine put out by the Boston Cooking School ran a story on a girl who defied her mother's desire for a grand church event and was married in her parents' parlor, with homemade decorations. It occurred to more than one writer that the emotional heart of a wedding—the daring pledge of two young people to spend their lives together—could be obscured by thousands of red carnations and ten bridesmaids. There was also some slightly patronizing concern expressed on behalf of middle-class families overreaching to provide grand weddings for their daughters. Caterers could provide the perfect simulacrum of a society wedding breakfast, supplying silver, china, and servants in houses that possessed none. Even a middle-class bride and her family could, for the duration of her wedding day, adopt the lifestyle of the really rich.

This practice has been the norm for most of the twentieth century. Most families that hold a wedding reception are entertaining more people more formally than their normal life has the capacity for. We make nothing of this, but at the turn of the twentieth century, it was a kind of flash point. The grand white wedding with hundreds of roses, gray horses drawing the carriages, a full choir, a white satin gown for the bride, an elaborate multicourse wedding breakfast with champagne, and tables laden with silver and crystal for the young couple to start their new life with—this form of marriage was considered the prerogative of the upper-class bride.

A magazine called *Suburban Life* (America's short-lived answer to the English *Country Life*) ran a story in 1912 called "The Evil of Elaborate and Showy Weddings." The subtitle announced: "Money lavished on ostentatious display—sacredness of marriage forgotten in the preparation of a gorgeous, extravagant pageant." The author, Margaret Woodward, told the story of a middle-class neighbor whose daughter, Edith, demanded a showy wedding. She overspent on her trousseau; she insisted on an imported wedding dress with real lace. The neighbor mortgaged his house to build terraces and a conservatory for the wedding day. The poor man's ultimate fate was left unclear (unlike that of a man described in a 1904 *Ladies' Home Journal* editorial, who bankrupted himself to pay for his daughter's elaborate wedding). Woodward went on instead to castigate first the very rich for their ostentatious displays. Next she turned her ire on the poor: "At their pitifully cheap festivities, they squander their hard-won earnings." Even the middle class couldn't please her, quick as they were to "ape" the style of their social betters. It was, she felt, a "serious evil" to take on debt merely "to satisfy some extravagant desire."

Margaret Woodward didn't state, in her screed, how she would have liked to see her neighbor's daughter married. Her point was merely that Edith and too many girls like her were laying claim to the prerogative of the upper class. It was unseemly for brides from a middling background to be married with the pomp that was the right of the rich. She was not alone in feeling this. For most of the next century, the authorities on etiquette and weddings would repeat their formula: a wedding should match the social circumstances of the bride. If you weren't a rich girl you shouldn't aspire to the grandest kind of wedding. A modest informal wedding could be *just lovely.*

But the etiquette experts were drawing a line in the sand, trying to maintain the privilege of a grand wedding for a limited upper class. The members of that group may like to believe their ranks are complete, but in America this is simply never true. And the first step toward entering the elite is to behave as if you belong. As the nineteenth century became the twentieth, standards of living were rising. More Americans had more of everything. The prerogatives of the rich were increasingly accessible, and they included a grand white wedding for a cherished daughter.

CHAPTER 4

The Last Gown of Virginity

As the twentieth century matured, more families could imagine marrying off their daughters in high style; the challenge, though, was getting the girls appropriately matched up in the first place. It was a dizzying time of changes; while the world of 1910 would be alien to us, the world of 1928 would be fundamentally familiar. The car, the radio, the telephone, indoor plumbing, limited workweeks, paid vacations, women's suffrage, and dozens of other innovations rolled across the country in the years after World War I. The war itself, and America's participation in it, shook the confidence and optimism of the generation that saw service. The result was a decade of turmoil that transformed most kinds of social interaction, ushering in a new era of informality.

One of its most striking avatars was the New Girl. To begin with, she wore so many fewer clothes than her mother! Her short skirts—previously the uniform of small girls—were only part of the story. From the skin out, she was barely covered by skimpy, slinky garments that skimmed her slender figure. Her hair, sliced off in a bob, exposed the nape of her neck. Instead of the womanly softness cherished by the men of the nineteenth century, the sleek racing model of the 1920s exhibited a glossy, hard, highly colored finish.

It was bad enough that she looked, to adult eyes, like a woman of ill repute, with her scarlet lips and her plainly visible knees gleaming in silk stockings. Her behavior was, if anything, worse. Gone was the demure debutante whose patent ignorance was her greatest selling point. It wasn't so much that the flapper smoked and drank. By the mid-twenties, so did everyone. (Prohibition, voted into law in 1920, had the paradoxical effect of promoting public intoxication.) The problem was her independence: she simply didn't seem to care what her parents thought.

The real problem for a conservative parent was that the grown-ups had lost control. The root of this phenomenon was probably the increasing emphasis on education in America. The newly complex economy of the United States required a highly educated citizenry. Young people thus spent more time than ever before in school, finishing high school and, in greater numbers, going to college. The physical needs of youth were met: Ma and Pa still provided a bed, a roof, three hot meals, and warm clothes. Yet the teenager's responsibilities were limited—all she had to do was go to classes and keep up with her schoolwork. Furthermore, she was not alone — she moved through this unfettered stage of life with her cohorts, the other young people of her age and circumstances. Naturally enough, she began to look to them for approval, discounting her parents' values and opinions. If nineteenth-century teenagers seem oddly mature to us, earnestly stitching on their trousseau sheets or taking on a shift in Pa's tobacco store, the teenagers of the 1920s are the ones we still live with today.

Their social life certainly took on a more familiar form. Youngsters in the nineteenth century courted, but their children went on "dates." Courtship was a sincere process of discovery, in which each potential partner attempted to discern the qualities of the other's character in carefully supervised one-on-one encounters like walks or visits in the parlor. Dates, however, took couples *out*. They left their homes and went to public places of amusement like restaurants or dances, where they would encounter other young people on dates. And though dating was the first step in the process of finding a mate, there was nothing in the least binding about it. You could date dozens of people with nothing more in mind than a good time.

A good time, though, was important. Maybe the underlying purpose of dating was experimenting with different candidates for eventual marriage—but nobody was going to make the cut unless he was fun. Fun meant up-to-date, well dressed, energetic. Flirting was essential and so, for the first time, was sex appeal. While virginal charm distinguished the maiden of 1910, with her clear blush and her downcast eyes, the girl of fifteen years later would lean toward you and wink as you lit her cigarette.

Sex was in the air. It was in the movies and the books and the dances and the conversations and the backs of cars. Especially the cars, which provided young couples with something unprecedented—privacy. You couldn't get very far with a girl on her front porch as long as her mother was in the parlor "reading," but in the back of a car, parked in a quiet lane, it was easy to steam up the windows. Again, the rules had changed completely. The announcement of an engagement might have warranted the intimacy of a good-night kiss for the girl of the nineteenth century. The flapper went considerably farther than that based on nothing more than a whim—and perhaps the shared contents of a hip flask.

What's more, her reputation didn't suffer. That chaste bloom, so highly prized in an earlier era, no longer mattered; nobody would *want* a girl who was sexually ignorant. Sexual experimentation was part of the mating process. How else could you tell if you and your fella were really compatible? You had to have that spark. And as Phyllis Blanchard and Carlyn Manasses said in *New Girls for Old* (1930), a girl "would certainly prefer to give the impression that she is a 'hot number' rather than a 'flat tire.'"

In the nineteenth century, sex had been about duty; women had submitted to their husbands' desires and children were the result. But by the second decade of the twentieth century, birth control was both more reliable and more widely available. Couples could choose from a wide array of devices, effectively limiting pregnancy as the inevitable corollary of sex, which could then become purely recreational within the bounds of marriage. It was also much more widely discussed; the popular magazines ran almost twice as many sex-related articles between 1910 and 1914 as they had in the previous five years. Popular entertainment kept pace: Edith Hull's lurid romance *The Sheik* was a bestseller when it was published in 1921, but it was quickly eclipsed by the film version which made Rudolph Valentino a household word.

Oh, yes—the movies, another harbinger of moral decay. The experience of sitting in the dark watching exotic and thrilling action on the screen drew most young people to theaters at least weekly. And what were they seeing? Slapstick comedies, aristocratic romances, sensational adventures—

films like *The Sheik,* in which Valentino played Sheik Ahmed ben Hassan, a dark-eyed chieftain who encounters an appealing English girl in the desert and sweeps her off to his tent to have his way with her. Women filled movie theaters again and again, overcome by Valentino's potent appeal.

The Sheik may have been unusually titillating, but it just represented an extreme version of what was on view most days of the week. One movie critic in the 1920s estimated that the average film contained 5.5 love scenes. Given the frequency of film viewing in the 1920s, audiences were positively saturated with the notion of sexual attraction as the motive force of the ideal relationship. When groundbreaking sociologists Robert and Helen Lynd reported on the city of Muncie, Indiana (calling it *Middletown*), in 1929, they wrote, "Theoretically, it is the mysterious attraction of two young people for each other and that alone that brings about a marriage, and actually most of Middletown stumbles upon its partners in marriage guided chiefly by 'romance.'"

In fact, the young people of the 1920s did not merely arrive at marriage in a different way from their parents—they also expected something quite revolutionary from the relationship. Abandoned was the Victorian model of patriarchy. Women wanted, according to Blanchard and Manasses, "a new kind of marriage ... a perfect consummation of both personalities that will involve every phase of mutual living." Sexual satisfaction, companionship, compatible interests, and congenial personalities were to be part of the new marital bargain. Marriage was no longer a sober undertaking in which both parties wittingly assumed the responsibilities of adulthood. It was a continuation of the perpetual party of adolescence. The glittering figure of F. Scott Fitzgerald provides an example. The handsome young novelist, whose *This Side of Paradise,* published in 1920, made him both rich and famous, married Alabama belle Zelda Sayre that same year. His fiction and her life had been full, until then, of drinking and dancing and wild car rides, all madcap gaiety with no hangover. Their marriage did not change this pattern. The madcap gaiety continued, merely doubled, and the press adored them. They were young, modern, madly in love, and their marriage seemed to embody that "perfect consummation of both personalities" that Blanchard and Manasses's subjects sought.

Yet even as the young generation looked for the sun, the moon, and the stars in their marriages, they were willing to provide an escape route if reality did not live up to their glowing expectations. Divorce, a scandalous proceeding to their parents' generation, was ever more widely accepted in the interwar years. Although divorce rates had been creeping up through the nineteenth century (and were dramatically higher in the Western states that had short residency requirements and lenient laws), they soared in the early years of the twentieth century.

Historian Elaine Tyler May studied Los Angeles divorce cases in the late nineteenth century and in the 1920s, and reported the results in *Great Expectations: Marriage and Divorce in Post-Victorian America.* She asserts that between 1867 and 1929, the population of the United States tripled. During that time the number of marriages quadrupled—but the divorce rate increased by 2,000 percent. "By the end of the 1920s," she says, "more than one in every six marriages terminated in court."

The nature of the marriage contract had changed, along with the negotiations leading up to it. There could be few reasons to terminate a marriage when its terms were essentially pragmatic, a matter of duties and obligations. Indeed, most states granted divorces only when one spouse or another was guilty of adultery, intemperance, insanity, or other grievous faults. But in California, May shows, in the 1920s, expectations of marriage were much higher—and consequently, more frequently disappointed. "Husbands," she says, "were torn by desires for both excitement and purity; and few women could satisfy both. . . . [T]he consistent theme was the desire for the new vitality and the old morality to coexist within the home." The difficulty was that very few mortals could pull off this balancing act. Glamorous Zelda Fitzgerald, for instance, made the world's most exciting fiancée, but a very unsatisfactory wife.

As expectations for the marriage itself were changing, the means of celebrating it altered, too—but subtly. One of the most striking qualities of the formal wedding is its imperturbable resilience. In the face of radical social change, this set of preindustrial rituals has tended to absorb new elements without appearing to change much at all. The most obvious difference between a wedding of 1910 and a wedding of 1925 was the bridal gown.

As we have seen, nineteenth-century brides wore gowns styled in the fashion of the day, and they wore white if they could afford it. Starting in the 1920s, though, many wedding dresses took a step out of the mainstream. While they generally followed fashion in the matters of cut and hem length, at the upper echelon of society they were thought about in a different way. In a 1928 interview, French couturier Jean Worth (son of the great Charles Worth) called the wedding dress "the last gown of virginity. It is the gown that marks the girl's departure from the family hearth to take her place at her own hearth. It is a sacred gown; it is a gown of ritual."

This is a departure from the earlier attitude, when women often got married in the best dress their closets afforded. A gown of ritual, by its very definition, is exempt from everyday usage. Graduation gowns are the best modern example, resembling quite closely their medieval antecedents. A gown of ritual sets the wearer apart as a participant in an extraordinary event. To do this, it must not resemble everyday clothing, and often this means being explicitly out of style. So what we see, beginning in the 1920s, is that wedding gowns resisted the extremes of style. Bridal costumes ordered from Charles Worth in the 1870s were perfectly à la mode, down to the last ruffle on the train. Even the most stylish gowns from fifty years later, though, are often more conservative than their nonbridal counterparts. True, they follow the general outlines of evening wear for their period. But fashion had lopped off sleeves and scooped out necklines to an extent that simply wasn't acceptable in most houses of worship—a bride couldn't show as much skin as she would in a stylish evening dress. In fact, dresses from the mid to late twenties often exhibit a kind of schizophrenia. Fashionable brides wanted knee-length gowns, but they also wanted trains, which were normally graceful extensions of long skirts. The dilemma was solved in various ways, with a train attached at the shoulders or a hemline that dipped drastically from knees in front to train behind, but to modern eyes the result is graceless. The dresses, with their bold modern fronts and their old-fashioned backs, seem to be facing in two directions at once. No wonder—they were.

The conflict between modern and conservative even played itself out in the materials. Mrs. John Alexander King published *Weddings: Modes, Manners & Customs* in 1927, largely describing high society's grand, conservative nuptial traditions. She says, "For the handsome, important wedding

In 1928, when Carol McDonald married Dozier Gardner, skirts were very short. Even the hem of the wedding gown rises almost to the knee in front, though it dips into a train in back. The maids' gowns, with their scoop necks and split sleeves, are also quite revealing.

gown, wedding satin, with its elegance, its dignity, its grace and stateliness, is the Queen of Fabrics." She adds that wedding satin, a special heavy grade of silk, used to be stiff enough to stand on its own. Unfortunately, by 1927 the most fashionable fabrics were fine enough to crumple into a liquid heap and matte-finished materials like crepe and chiffon were as stylish as lustrous charmeuse. Stiff heavy satin, like the train itself, was something of a throwback—yet brides still wore it.

Of course many brides in the interwar era did stay at the forefront of fashion. Mary E. Lewis, in *The Marriage of Diamonds and Dolls* (1947), remembers that "many American brides wore Vionnet crepe gowns with cowl neckline and a short skirt." Other brides, especially as the twenties became the thirties, wore gowns that kept more or less abreast of the times. One way to do this was with color. Pale pink, ice blue, even lavender dresses were advertised and illustrated in the fashion magazines. Frequently these colored dresses were intended for informal weddings, but Jeanette MacDonald married Gene Raymond in 1937 in a grand church wedding, wearing a rose-pink organza gown confected by Hollywood costume designer Adrian. Silver and gold lamé were worn by some aristocratic brides on either side of the Atlantic. There was even, in 1933, a minuscule editorial flurry of excitement about black wedding gowns, with which the ultrastreamlined bride would carry a stark sheaf of white calla lilies. It seems unlikely that this fad penetrated much beyond the fashion fringe, but it demonstrates that brides did have some latitude in their choice of color.

In fact, in the 1930s a relative realism entered the wedding picture. The Depression trained almost every American to think twice about waste and extravagance. Wedding dresses might be ritual garments, but they had not yet become simply costumes for one remarkable event. Mary E. Lewis remembers that in the late teens "any girl who wanted to re-use her dress for summer dances, as was the custom, chose Georgette, . . ." the slightly crinkled, sheer fabric that was so practical. One fashion motif that started to influence wedding gowns in the interwar years was revivalism. Designers applied motifs from earlier eras to modern gowns. A medieval revival (known coyly as the *moyen age* style) resulted in long tight sleeves pointed in a V over the back of the hand. The *robe de style,* literally "gown of fashion," was another briefly popular look; in the late 1920s Jeanne Lanvin and other designers showed gowns with full skirts, puffed out at the hips over gathered petticoats. They were thought to be reminiscent of eighteenth-century paniered dresses. These options flirted with the effect of costumes, and as the wedding gown neared that status itself, revival styles seemed appropriate. But as even the patrician Mrs. King pointed out, if a wedding dress had to "serve later as an evening dress or dinner dress," it was wiser to wear a more "modernistic" garment. Modern, that is to say, like the bride herself

There were plenty of options. In the summer 1935 issue of *Bride's* magazine, almost one-third of the dresses advertised or featured in the editorial pages exhibited features that made them eligible to be worn again. A short jacket could be removed, revealing a bare-backed evening gown, or lace sleeves could be detached. As late as 1939, *Bride's* ran an editorial feature on "budget" wedding dresses. After a mid-thirties fondness for gleaming satin, fashion cycled around again to favor matte fabrics, so lace, muslin, and a special favorite, marquisette, were all the rage. These cotton fabrics, pointed out the magazine, "are serviceable, as the dresses may be worn for several seasons as dance dresses and they are also washable." During the late 1930s, *Bride's* was quite sensitive to the girl getting married with a small bankroll and continually featured modestly priced wedding gowns. In the winter of 1935, the least expensive dress they showed cost $29.95, and there were several options at around $40, less than a third of the price of the gowns for girls "who needn't budget."

Bride's, of course, wanted to pull them all in—the magazine had a vested interest in promoting the traditional white wedding to girls of every class. Its real interest, though, was in the high rollers, a bias it made plain by running photographs of society brides in every issue. Most of the dresses featured in the editorial and advertising pages fell into the higher-priced range; in the fall issue of 1940, The Blum Store in Philadelphia advertised a gown that cost a whopping one thousand dollars. High fashion was certainly more fun than practicality: what editor wouldn't give more play to French-designed slipper satin than to a wear-again dinner dress in ivory crepe? The magazine had a field day in 1935, when the two younger sons of George V of England found themselves brides. "Nothing has perhaps given more impetus to the glittering costume of the Bride than Princess Marina's silver lamé wedding dress," enthused the magazine. "For a stately girl with a lovely figure— lamé sets off her every fine point." The royal tie-in was made again in 1938: "Fashion is favoring lace for bridal dresses, perhaps due to the fact that the royal Brides of Egypt and Albania both chose exquisite gowns of lace earlier in the year." Well, perhaps. Neither nameless bride was the fashion plate that Marina, Duchess of Kent, became. But the avid public focus on royal nuptials points up another telling shift in the way weddings were viewed between the wars.

The change we see beginning as early as the 1890s is the sense of the wedding as a pageant, full of color and symmetry. Period illustrations of earlier royal weddings and even the few examples of photographs illustrating wedding parties (created using models, for sale as stereopticon views) show a confusing welter of people. Though the players can be identified, the stark, graphic choreography of today's wedding ceremony is completely missing. But in the early twentieth century a kind of self-consciousness steals over the planning of the ceremony. The wedding is not just a sacred event joining a man and a woman for life: it is also a *tableau vivant,* planned and designed for its visual impact. And the first hint we have of this new attitude is in the role played by the bridesmaids.

Since the Middle Ages, the church (and later the state) has required that weddings be witnessed by at least two people. This precaution both provided objective proof that the ceremony did take place, and ensured that it was voluntary. Earlier still, in the bad old days of marriage by capture, young men seeking a bride were accompanied by a posse of other young men. Raids on neighboring communities might provide several wives for several men, since young women banded together for their own safety. The actual source of the bridesmaids' tradition can't be pinned down exactly, but it can safely be attributed to the fact that bride and groom alike, as they go from the single to the married state, are thought to require support from friends. Some sources even speculate that the old tradition of dressing bridesmaids like the bride was a safety measure: any spirits wishing to do the bride ill in her vulnerable liminal state would be confused by a bevy of young ladies in similar dresses.

In the high Victorian era, maids were usually younger than the bride, always unmarried (the pregnant bridesmaids of today would have been shocking), and costumed in white. As late as 1910, they sometimes wore veils like the bride herself. In a home wedding there might be as many as four maids, but one attendant or two sufficed. The most important duty of the maid of honor was to hold the bride's bouquet at the moment when the groom placed the ring on her finger, just as it was the best man's job to actually produce the ring.

Gradually color eased into the maids' costumes; often pink was chosen, sometimes in a sash or an underskirt, but eventually in the entire dress. Bridesmaids carried bouquets even before the bride herself did. As the grand weddings of the late nineteenth century got more elaborate, the number of bridesmaids swelled until Mrs. Sherwood could say, in *Manners and Social Usages* (1897), that "eight is the number of fashion." She also mentioned that they wore "elaborately trimmed bonnets" to match their gowns. Newspaper coverage was already talking about the beguiling picture made by a bevy of maidens surrounding the bride in "glistening white."

Jessie Wilson, married in 1913 to Frank Sayre from the White House, went a step further in costuming her maids. She had only four, but she evidently had a vision of how they should look. Each wore a gown of pink satin over a silver petticoat, but the pinks varied in shade from a shell tint to deep rose. The bouquets also varied in tone, and the headdresses— well, for decades bridesmaids complained about their hideous headdresses, and these girls can have been no different. Jessie's vision involved rose velvet draped around the crown of the head and an upstanding ruff of silver lace, wired into points. It may have looked wonderful on paper—it may even have looked wonderful in 1913, but today in photographs the unfortunate girls look like jokers from a deck of cards. The "shading" motif hung on, though: in Eudora Welty's *Delta Wedding* (published in 1946 but set in 1923), Mississippi plantation bride Dabney Fairchild crows about her creative concept for the attendants. "'I'm going to have my bridesmaids start off in American Beauty and fade on out,' said Dabney, turning around. 'Two bridesmaids of each color, getting paler and paler, and then Shelley in flesh. She's my maid of honor.'"

In fact the strong tradition of making bridesmaids suffer to create a picture has its roots in the 1910s and 1920s. The bouquets were sometimes replaced by decorative props like fans or chiffon muffs or shepherd's crooks wreathed in flowers. In Grace Lumpkin's *The Wedding* (published in 1939 but set thirty years earlier), a wealthy southern girl is planning a big church ceremony. Her maids are to wear white point d'esprit and carry, instead of bouquets, tiny Confederate flags. (The Yankee rector forbids this plan, provoking much resentment.) Color schemes became more elaborate and sophisticated: when Cathleen Vanderbilt, reprobate Reginald's daughter, married Harry Cushing in 1923, the maids wore peach chiffon with sand-colored straw hats wrapped in matching fabric; the maid of honor sported sand chiffon in the same style. All the attendants carried flame-colored gladioli, which were also used to decorate the hotel ballroom where the wedding took place. As Mrs. King opined in her *Weddings: Modes, Manners & Customs,* "although the social reason for having bridesmaids is the desire of the bride that she shall be attended by her friends, the artistic presentation requires that the attendants, like the lesser jewels of a perfect setting, should enhance the prominence and the beauty of the perfect gem." Speaking more generally of planning a wedding, Mrs. King went even further: "The ideal bride is the bride who combines a deep spiritual appreciation of the significance and beauty of the wedding sacrament with the power to plan a beautiful wedding picture. . . . The bride of taste will know the beauty and

Jessie Wilson's bridesmaids' hats were made of wired silver lace following her own design. Her sister Nellie, center, the maid of honor, was distinguished by extra tinsel on hers.

value of a perfect wedding procession, and she will organize her pageant with that in mind. But she will not allow her procession to become merely a fashion show." Readers could be forgiven for receiving the impression that Mrs. King found the "pageant" at least as important as the "sacrament." By the 1930s the sacrament seems to have taken something of a backseat to theater: in a Carson, Pirie Scott ad for a grand gown shown with a "monk's cap and tiny muff" trimmed with ermine, the copy praised the "drama that gives you, without question, the leading role." The concept of bride as star of her own production was forming already.

Of course you can't have a production without an audience. If you want an audience you have to ask a lot of people to the wedding. And if you're going to ask a lot of people to the wedding you can't have it in your living room unless you're someone like Cornelia Vanderbilt in 1924 and you're marrying at Biltmore, the prodigious mansion in Asheville, North Carolina. Biltmore had a formal banquet hall, in addition to what *The New York Times* called the "massive reception hall" and the "circular palm room," which held the bridal table for the wedding breakfast. But few brides occupied Cornelia Vanderbilt's place in society, which imposed very real obligations on the bride and her family to invite large numbers of guests. There were still, in the 1920s and '30s, many reasons for a bride to prefer a quiet wedding. Mrs. King suggests that the girl might be "the kind of person who dislikes publicity, who shuns ceremonious function, who holds simplicity in high regard . . ." A death or illness in the family might put brakes on plans for a lavish wedding. Certainly many brides still responded to the appeal of a simple ceremony held at home in the midst of an intimate group. And financial constraints often made the choice for a couple, especially during the dark days of the Depression. As *Bride's* pointed out in a 1935 article on modest nuptials, "we can't all have magnificence in our wedding receptions."

Shortly after the First World War, brides' assumptions about where they would get married seem to have been quite variable and to have depended on their circumstances and their tastes. In 1919 the young Harry Truman came back from France and urged his fiancée, Bess Wallace, to meet him in New York to marry. Bess insisted on being married at home, though, so Harry made the trip to Independence, Missouri, where he and Bess had grown up. Six weeks later, the ceremony took place at Trinity Episcopal Church, the reception in Bess's grandparents' big white house a block away. Bess had wanted the white dress, her two cousins for bridesmaids, and the sense of her family around her. Zelda Sayre, on the other hand, did travel to New York to wed Scott Fitzgerald in the rectory at St. Patrick's Cathedral. Zelda's three sisters were present and she wore a navy suit with a matching hat. The only bridal touch was her bouquet of white orchids.

Zelda's biographer Nancy Milford suggests that the New York marriage avoided the thorny prospect of a Catholic wedding (Fitzgerald's faith) in the bride's hometown of Montgomery. Ultimately, local practices and prejudices still had paramount influence on how a couple got married. Historian Katherine Jellison discusses the nuptial traditions of three generations of a farm family from western Nebraska in an article published in 1995. Many of the rural communities in the Midwest maintained strong cultural ties to their German or Czech origins. A wedding is an inherently conservative event and, Jellison says, it was tradition for these first- or second-generation immigrants not to attend "'English' wedding celebrations or invite members of the English-speaking community to their own." The first wedding Jellison describes is that of Sophie Bischoff, who married in a Lutheran church in 1927 before the members of her immediate family. After the ceremony came the wedding dance for some hundred guests at the family farm, for which Sophie, her mother, and her sisters had prepared all the food. As was customary, the party featured homemade beer and music provided by the guests on the violin and organ. Sophie baked her own wedding cake. Sophie's sister Ella married in 1930, by which time her family had moved into the village of Culbertson. Like Sophie, Ella had bought her gown in the town of McCook (sixty miles from the farm but only eighteen miles from Culbertson), but Ella also bought her cake and her wedding flowers there. Since the Bischoff family didn't want to disturb their village neighbors, the reception included neither dancing nor drinking as Sophie's wedding had. Jellison's article puts a face on the research carried out by sociologist John Modell and presented in *Into One's Own: From Youth to Adulthood in the United States, 1920–1975.* Modell examined wedding announcements from Minnesota newspapers covering the 1920s to 1950s. He looked at three different locales: St. Paul, the town of Albert Lea, and the even smaller Thief River Falls. He found that in the years covered by his study, weddings changed in several ways. In the 1920s, at least 90 percent of the wedding receptions Modell read about took place in the home of the bride or groom, but by the late 1940s, they had moved out of the house. In the smaller towns, receptions were generally held in what he called "church-related buildings" like a parish house or a parlor, while in St. Paul they were moved into restaurants, clubs, or meeting halls.

In the Minnesota weddings that Modell considered, the reception became a steadily more important element of getting married. In this respect, they moved in the opposite direction from the weddings Jellison wrote about. But Sophie and Ella Bischoff's weddings were remnants of an insular immigrant culture: the polkas and beer-drinking of the German "wedding dance" were a far cry from the sedate event that the urban middle class knew as a wedding reception.

Actually, dancing had been an important feature of the frontier wedding. In small remote communities, a wedding was a rare opportunity for socializing, and all the guests required to dance was a fiddler, a caller, and a level patch of ground. The concerns for privacy and decorum that marked urban weddings in the nineteenth century had no place in an environment where neighbors relied on each other for survival and saw each marriage as a vital step toward building a strong community. The tight-knit immigrant communities of the late nineteenth century functioned in much the same way, with an ethic of interdependence within the group and an insistence on retaining the cultural practices of home. A Jewish or Italian wedding on New York's Lower East Side was most likely held in one of the community halls that flourished in the 1910s and 1920s. The importance of hospitality and cultural cohesion were very much to the fore in these events, which often featured dancing and music that seemed raucous or disorderly to the uninitiated. The same is true of African American weddings. As displaced people, living in communities whose values were sometimes at odds with the white mainstream of American culture, black couples married in ways that both mirrored that culture and departed from it. The most striking departure is the gleeful exaggeration of the pageant aspect of the wedding. Although the traditions of African American weddings have not been widely studied by scholars, the legendary Harlem photographer James Van der Zee captured many wedding parties striking for the number of attendants and the exuberance of their finery.

Because weddings look backward as well as forward, they retain anachronisms with a strong grip. New, stricter limits on immigration in the 1920s contributed to an immigrant population that was assimilating, but as Jellison's research shows, even an assimilated population cherishes the wedding practices of its country of origin. Nevertheless, exposure to other traditions, social aspirations, even logistics like the Bischoff family's move into town gradually eroded robust ethnic practices like dancing as middle-class habits of nuptial restraint reached into the immigrant working class. Yet as the punch bowl replaced the beer keg for families aspiring to a middle-class decorum, at the grandest weddings, the guests were taking to the dance floor again.

Dancing had been an option since the late nineteenth century, but only at evening weddings. It simply wasn't "done" to dance in the day. Mrs. Sherwood, in *Manners and Social Usages,* says, "It is not . . . very customary for a bride to dance, or for dancing to occur at an evening wedding, but it is not a bad old custom." She gives procedures for those who wish to revive the practice: the dancing begins with a quadrille, the bride partnered by her husband's best man and the maid of honor partnered by the groom. This is a stately, showy, very formal dance related to the eighteenth-century minuet. It has none of the suppressed sexuality and overt sentiment of the current dancing configuration, when the bride dances first with her new husband, then with her father, who cuts in.

Even in 1897, the quadrille was a pretty artifact of a gracious past, and it was about to be buried in an avalanche of disturbing new dances like the shimmy, the toddle, the turkey trot, and the bunny hug. Like so many of the more threatening products of the twentieth century, these new dances came bubbling up from the lower classes. The music—jazz, or at least jazz-derived—was driven by African American musical conventions. It was driven, actually, by the beat, which was remarkably *insistent*. Partners danced close, much too close, with their torsos in contact. Even a waltz, the previous standard for dance-floor intimacy, mandated a generous space between partners. The new dances, with their snug holds and waggling hips, were widely seen as lewd. The media were up in arms, attempts were made to bottle up the new dancing styles, but there was no stopping them. They raced across the country.

It was one of those situations (so common in the 1920s) when the elder generation entirely misread the significance of a cultural innovation popular among the young. The new dances were so sexual, so wanton. The people who played the music were often black; they lived in marginal neighborhoods and led irregular lives. Surely all of this amounted to a general corruption of youth. In fact, it didn't. Dancing was good clean fun, as Vernon and Irene Castle were the first to prove. A pair of pleasant, penniless American actors honeymooning in Paris, they accepted an engagement to dance at the Café de Paris. They were attractive and well mannered, and they demonstrated how the raunchy rhythms of the new music could provide the impetus for a graceful, creative dancing style. The Castles were soon the rage in high society, and everyone had to learn the new dances. Dancing became an important element of social life and that all-American experience, the high school dance, came into being. High schools had to offer dances to keep their students out of public dance halls and roadhouses. Robert and Helen Lynd remarked, in

Middletown, on "the elaborate formality of club, fraternity, and sorority dances in hotels" and "a highly competitive series of smartly appointed affairs by high school clubs." Dancing, in fact, was what young people *did* when they got together.

Naturally they wanted to do it at weddings, too: evidence of that came as early as 1913, at Jessie Wilson's White House marriage to Frank Sayre. After about an hour of doing her duty in the receiving line, the bride's madcap younger sister Nellie organized some more animated fun. The Marine Corps Band, at her request, moved its drums and music stands into the East Room, the rugs were rolled back, and America's foremost providers of military music played the tango and the grizzly bear for the spirited young guests. When Nellie herself was married six months later, even though her wedding was billed as "small" and "quiet," the dancing was built into the plans. In fact, by the 1920s dancing was commonplace at the more lavish weddings. When Consuelo Vanderbilt (a niece of the Consuelo Vanderbilt who became Duchess of Marlborough) married in 1926, dancing was a significant feature of the reception, though the ceremony had been held at four o'clock. By 1927, Mrs. King's *Weddings: Modes, Manners & Customs* declared that "[d]uring the reception there is usually music, and usually too there is dancing."

Of course dancing took up space, both for the band and for the dance floor, which probably accelerated the trend of moving the wedding reception out of the bride's house. Only the wealthiest families could accommodate a hundred or more guests twirling around the floor. But another innovation of the 1920s spread quickly through every class, because it was affordable and because it rendered the wedding day permanent: the development of wedding photography.

Brides and grooms had been photographed for years. A wedding is such an important event that even when photography was costly, cumbersome, and not very satisfying, people sat to have the moment immortalized. Few wedding pictures from before 1870 exist, even though cities like New York were full of photographic studios. Logistics may have played a part in this: a photo sitting was a lengthy and arduous enterprise in those days of film with ASA speeds as low as 12 or 14 (all-purpose film today is rated at 200 or 400 ASA). In fact, the lighting requirements for studio photography determined the format for wedding pictures until the turn of the century. Flash photography involved cumbersome chemical explosions timed to the click of the shutter, so most photo studios relied on natural light streaming in through banks of large windows. They were also furnished with various backgrounds and props that would suggest grand environments for their sitters: marble staircases or heavy velvet curtains, Oriental rugs, elaborately carved chairs, and large potted palms hinted at lives of stability and comfort. Couples were usually posed together, often standing, against one of these backgrounds. The focus is usually remarkably sharp, the expressions somber and earnest.

Charles Wesley Lewis, in a Ph.D. thesis, suggests that one reason so few brides were photographed before the last quarter of the nineteenth century was that taking the picture of a respectable young girl dressed in her bridal gown amounted to putting her on display, which was in poor taste. Being "on display" in those days came perilously close to earning a living with your looks, which was the next worst thing to earning a living with your body. Knowing this makes Mathew Brady's photographs of Tom Thumb's wedding all the more remarkable. Clearly P. T. Barnum scheduled a photo sitting at Brady's studio in advance of the actual event. Thus bride, groom, best man, and maid of honor all saw each other in their wedding finery before the great day, flouting an old superstition. What's more, the photographs made a liar of Barnum, who kept protesting that he wasn't commercializing his friend's wedding. In fact, pictures of the Thumb wedding were made into stereopticon views and sold by the thousands, to be gaped at along with pictures of the Grand Canyon and the great monuments of Europe.

The stereopticon was perhaps the nineteenth century's version of a television. It was a device that used an eyepiece to combine two identical photographs so that the viewer saw them in three dimensions. As photography developed, sets of "views" were sold to middle-class families, who would sit in their parlors and eagerly gaze at "The Statesmen of Europe" or "Civil War Generals." By the 1890s, photographers were costuming models and posing them to create a narrative: the ancestor of the moving picture show. "The Wedding Day" was one of the stories told in stereo views, with each step of a fictional couple's nuptial day recorded, from "The Bride on Her Wedding Day" (posing in her gown amid potted palms) to "The Wedding March" (same palms, addition of bridesmaids) to the suggestive "Alone, at Last Alone" (bride and groom fully dressed, embracing in front of a single bed).

It would be decades, though, before the average couple could hope to have their own wedding procession immortalized. Through the 1920s, most couples were satisfied with a session at the photography studio, often squeezed in between wedding ceremony and reception. The proceedings had been accelerated by innovations like arc lights and floodlights.

Charles Lewis says that the records of Minnesota photo studios show that wedding parties were often scheduled for hourly sessions on busy days. In that time, the photographer would shoot twelve to eighteen photographs, usually using an eight-by-ten-inch view camera, of the bride, the groom, and their wedding party. Shots of the bride were the most important, especially since they might appear in the society section of the newspaper. So eager to market this service were photographers that one studio bought a luxurious car and offered it as part of the package to prospective grooms: "Our ENCLOSED MOTOR CAR is at your service for your WEDDING PHOTOGRAPHS." The sales pitch went on, "Bridal portraits and groupings are considered an essential part of the wedding ceremony and to neglect them will surely cause regret." The rhetoric was predictive: if they said it often enough, surely it would become true.

In the late 1920s and early 1930s, photographers started to take their huge, unwieldy cameras on location, though the results were not always happy. The necessary arc lights drew so much power that they frequently blew fuses, and the cumbersome nature of the cameras themselves meant that pictures had to be limited to static groupings. The staircase or fireplace in the background would be the bride's own rather than the studio's, but the formally composed pictures did not look much different from studio shots.

News photographers were using the new thirty-five-millimeter cameras to cover crimes and sports and even the doings of high society, but the resulting small negatives didn't enlarge well enough to be very satisfactory for wedding photography. However, New York society photographer David Berns had made an important innovation in 1929, when he

James Van der Zee was Harlem's premier studio photographer in the interwar years. This backdrop lends some old-fashioned grandeur to the young bride and groom. The child with the doll was the photographer's later addition, an allusion to the couple's future offspring.

took both an eight-by-ten-inch camera and a smaller, lighter, five-by-seven-inch Graphlex to a wedding. He took all the portraits with the big camera while his assistant roved around the wedding reception with the smaller one, shooting informal action shots or "candids." Berns showed the resulting images to the society magazine *Town & Country,* which ran them, and successive clients requested the same service.

It made perfect sense; by the 1930s, everyone in America was used to seeing candid photographs. The liveliness of the arrested moment promised an honesty or authenticity that seemed to bring the subjects of such pictures right into the viewer's life. Candid photography both reflected and captured the new speed and informality of the modern era.

CHAPTER 5

Her Big Moment

JAZZ AGE JOURNALISM · HOLLYWOOD WEDDINGS, OFFSCREEN
AND ON · MAKING MONEY ON BRIDES · "THE HONOUR OF
YOUR PRESENCE" · FROM "HINT LIST" TO BRIDAL REGISTRY ·
SO YOU'RE GOING TO BE MARRIED

The invention of candid photography had a profound effect on our culture in myriad ways. It ushered in the shift, so pronounced in the last half of the twentieth century, from a verbal to a visual culture. It also contributed indirectly to the demystification of authority that crescendoed in the 1970s. As long as images of leaders were formal and iconic, it was easy to think of them as superhuman; once they were caught by the lens in an undignified or even emotional situation, they lost some of their grandeur.

Curiously enough, though, the increased informality of everyday life did not affect weddings. By the 1930s, the accretion of traditions we know as the white wedding had survived for nearly three quarters of a century. It had gone from a patrician custom, available only to wealthy girls in well-settled areas of the United States, to a kind of template for a celebration, a deluxe option that most brides and their families could adopt if they wished. One of the reasons the wedding had survived for so long was that it was both multipartite and infinitely adaptable. The religious ceremony alone, with its procession, music, floral decorations, and supporting personnel, retains its identity even when elements are omitted or altered from the Victorian original. Particularly during the interwar years, as the cultural ideal of the white wedding became ever more widely accepted, brides could aspire to as many of its components as they chose. Most brides elected to wear a white dress, but they didn't all wear white satin. Most brides had a reception, but they didn't all serve a full meal.

The cumulative nature of the formal wedding tradition has also contributed to its longevity. Elements are rarely dropped, but frequently added to the set of rituals that make up a wedding celebration. We start to see this very clearly in the mid-twentieth century, as what was once optional becomes obligatory. John Modell's research into Minnesota weddings shows that wedding receptions, frequently omitted in the 1920s, were always held by the 1950s. Bridal showers, likewise, first appeared in the 1920s, and were de rigueur in thirty years. So, too, with photography: candid photographs augmented formal shots but did not replace them.

If the series of formal portraits, unchanged in format since the 1880s, linked interwar weddings with their dignified antecedents, the candids linked them with the future. They aren't *un*dignified: the pictures that ran in the national magazines captured sedate moments like the bride and groom leaving the church or greeting guests in the receiving line. But they injected into the wedding proceedings an ingredient that had hitherto been considered with some ambivalence—publicity. Candid photography was news photography. Charles Lewis even suggests that some of the earliest wedding candids (David Berns's innovations aside) were taken when news photographers haunted churches on summer Saturdays, snapping shots of couples emerging from the wedding canopy that they would later try to sell both to the couples themselves and to the society sections of local newspapers. Long gone were the days when a protective matron, like Edith Wharton's Mrs. Welland, felt faint at the notion of her daughter's face appearing in a newspaper for anyone to see. The 1930s mother of the bride was more likely to angle for better placement and a larger image.

The media-savvy mother wasn't really being pushy. She was simply responding to a cultural shift that made the press a much more significant feature in Americans' daily lives after World War I. As usual, many conditions combined to produce this result. One of them was the journalistic coverage of the war itself, which introduced an unprecedented note of urgency to front pages of newspapers. Vivid photographs from the front communicated as no words could, and whetted the popular desire for more pictures and more exciting news coverage. The development of the tabloid newspaper in the United States was a logical result.

Tabloids were a departure from previous newspaper coverage in that they were aimed squarely at the working class. They were printed on paper half the size of the existing high-brow journals (the "broadsheets") and written to permit instant comprehension of the contents of a page. Telegraphic (if superficial) accounts of major news stories were leavened by plentiful large photographs and lighter fare like beauty contests and popular fiction. The emphasis fell at all times on the personal. The first issue of the *New York Daily News,* dated June 26, 1919, bore a large photograph of the Prince of Wales on its cover, accompanied by the news that he was planning to visit Newport, Rhode Island.

The tabloid format was immensely successful and spread rapidly across the country, while its innovations affected even the more traditional publications. One development was the addition of "rotogravure" sections to the Sunday supplements. The name referred to the printing process, which permitted more detailed reproduction of photographs, and the sections featured the kind of material that the broadsheets couldn't quite bring themselves to include during the week: recipes, photo features, and a tame kind of gossip.

For the genuine lowdown on celebrities' private lives, though, you still had to read the tabloids. In the very first issue of the *Daily News,* an introductory editorial stated, "Because the doings of the very fortunate are always of interest we shall print them as interestingly as possible in our society column." It was in their handling of high society's doings that the tabloid gossip columns broke the mold.

The broadsheets like *The New York Times* had always covered the most visible and formal events of the city's social leaders, in a somewhat dry factual manner: who, what, where, when, why. The balls and weddings of New York society were treated as news. Photographs began to appear in the 1920s, but they were generally very formal, often studio portraits, and only of the most newsworthy brides like the younger Consuelo Vanderbilt or silver-mining heiress Ellin Mackay (who married songwriter Irving Berlin). The innovation of the tabloids was to hire dedicated gossip columnists to ferret out information and present it in a lively manner. Gossip wasn't news as much as it was narrative, and one of the very best of the gossip columnists/storytellers was a clever, portly bachelor named Maury Paul. He began writing gossip for a small-town paper and by 1919 was producing columns for several different New York papers, under different noms de plume. Then William Randolph Hearst hired him to write exclusively as "Cholly Knickerbocker" for the *New York Journal American.*

Cholly's beat was society. Every night Maury Paul put on his white tie and tails, tucked an orchid into his buttonhole, and pattered off to watch and to listen. He wasn't going to get much joy from the dowagers, ladies like Mrs. Oliver Belmont or Mrs. Stuyvesant Fish or Mrs. Cornelius Vanderbilt, whose idea of a good time was a seven-course dinner with a footman behind each chair. But their sons and daughters—this was the 1920s, after all—were considerably livelier. Gioia Diliberto, author of *Debutante,* Brenda Frazier's biography, talks about the types developed by gossip columnists to categorize their subjects: the "Society Heroine" or the "Flapper Deb" or the "Girl of the Year," the latter a debutante who was acknowledged to have the most "oomph." The doings of these girls—their attendance at parties, their dancing partners, their clothes—were fascinating, but still, their great achievement was always marriage. And the gossip columnists' coverage of the big society weddings was relentlessly thorough. Maury Paul's biographer was Mary Nichols, writing under her pseudonym of Eve Brown. She had been his longtime assistant, and after his death wrote the exasperated but affectionate *Champagne Cholly: The Life and Times of Maury Paul.* She describes his efforts to cover weddings in the 1920s: "Maury glued himself to the third phone, and sweated out from the families every scrap of information about these great events. Prenuptial parties, honeymoon destinations, descriptions of wedding presents—these items he pulled like teeth from the principals." His style was breezy, conversational, and above all personal. Writing about Mabel Gerry's wedding to Englishman Francis Drury, Paul gushes, "When I say Miss Mabel was the most elaborately attired bride I have feasted my optics on in many, many moons, I do not exaggerate. She was resplendent—gorgeous! Her wedding gown of shimmering silver brocade tissue, draped in a princess effect with long silver lace sleeves and trimmed with a band of the late Mrs. Gerry's priceless Brussels lace, had a full panel court train of silver brocade. . . ." And on and on.

This is all riveting, especially when Paul gets to the strings and strings of pearls, but even more compelling is the large wedding photograph run by *The New York Times*. Cholly Knickerbocker's column was fresh and lively, but some decorum still reigned in newsrooms so it simply wasn't possible to say in words that Mabel Gerry was well past thirty and looked an awful lot like a horse. A photograph made these facts instantly plain. Pictures could also show you, as no amount of description would ever do, just how grand all these society weddings actually were. "Silver tissue" sounds lavish but until you see how it reflects the light, the effect is unimaginable. The luster of Mabel Gerry's pearls, the delicacy of Consuelo Vanderbilt's silk shoes, the size of her bouquet, the fineness of her veil, all these expensive details were, by the 1920s, available for the working class to appreciate. This, then, was what a really splendid white wedding looked like. Not that a girl could afford that herself—but she could approximate the effect, couldn't she?

Throughout the 1920s and 1930s the burgeoning gossip columns and popular picture press continued to make much of the elaborate weddings of the upper classes all across the country, so images of the grandest weddings became familiar to readers. The new candid photographs caught brides and grooms toasting each other with champagne, cutting towering cakes, lined up in their receiving lines with six girls carrying bouquets the size of cocker spaniels. Gossip columns filled in further details: the sterling silver coffee service and Baccarat glasses among the wedding presents; the name dance band playing at the reception; the Hollywood costume designer who'd made the bride's gown. These heady insights into the grandest weddings offered average brides ample sources of fantasy, especially as the Depression brought a drab tinge to so much of life. High life was well represented in the popular media—but then, in the mid-1930s, a different format began to present a mirror to the common man and show him, in the glossy pages of the new photo magazines, what his *own* life looked like.

The original, of course, was *Life* magazine, the brainchild of *Time*'s founder Henry Luce. As the prospectus stated, the reading public had become a *looking* public by 1935—"Thus to see, and to be shown, is now the will and new expectancy of half mankind." What *Life* would do was use photography to tell stories. It was an instantaneous and unprecedented success. The magazine covered everything from affairs of state to family affairs, from the Potsdam Conference to a parent-teacher conference. Weddings appeared, of course, but not necessarily the weddings of the rich and glamorous; in the pages of *Life* you might find a postman's daughter marrying a sales clerk, and the event would be reported and photographed with the same kind of avid interest lavished on a movie star's wedding.

Life and its competitor *Look* introduced a notion that later informed the hugely successful *People:* the momentary elevation of the commonplace citizen to a celebrity. The winner of a rodeo contest—or the loser, for that matter; the littlest angel in a Christmas pageant; the victim of a crime or performer of a good deed could step briefly into the floodlight of fame through the agency of these magazines. For a few days, a week, they might be recognized, congratulated, made much of. They would be, within their own communities, famous. And this was a good thing. Private life had lost its aura of the sacrosanct; publicity was a boon.

Getting married had always meant stepping into the spotlight to some extent. It is not enough for the bride and groom to agree to take each other for life: they must be *seen* to do so. The bourgeois appreciation of decorum and privacy that formed in the nineteenth century shrouded the wedding, like other intimacies, in a veil of exclusivity so that vows and celebration took place within the confines of the immediate community.

By the end of the nineteenth century, though, as the public was getting curious about the lives of the rich, social climbers were discovering the use of the press. By leaking information about their doings to reporters they often achieved flattering coverage. America's oldest families might preserve an aloof attitude and attempt to carry out their lives in seclusion, but the nouveaux riches tended to go public. It was rumored that when Mrs. George Gould married off her plain, hirsute sister-in-law to French Count Boni de Castellane, she hired a press agent to help her put the match in the best light. Likewise in 1923 when roué Reggie Vanderbilt fell hard for party girl Gloria Morgan, a debutante his daughter's age, the pair presented their case privately to Maury Paul. By giving "Cholly Knickerbocker" the exclusive right to announce their engagement, they ensured themselves some positive press. Soon enough, even families who didn't need a social boost from the newspapers were capitulating to newshounds' pestering. It was probably easier to accept the inevitable and give the papers a list of the wedding presents than to have guests physically removed from the reception when they turned out to be reporters.

And weddings were always good copy. When *Look* magazine debuted in 1937 its cover gave a clue about the preoccupations of the reading public in those days. The largest photograph showed the Duke and Duchess of Windsor, the duke wearing lederhosen. In a band along the right margin were four small square pictures with one- and two-word captions: "Heroes," "Brides," "Brave Beauty," and "Snow White." Brides sold. People liked to look at pretty girls; they liked to examine the gowns, read details about the menu at the reception, try to discern from the portraits whether the groom would treat his wife well. It was a far cry from the days when Consuelo Vanderbilt "wondered how I should live down such vulgarities" as seeing the details of her wedding trousseau appear in *The New York Times.* By the 1930s brides were no longer secluded virgins; they were becoming momentary celebrities.

In fact, so popular were brides that Hollywood studios, when promoting a new starlet, would often dress her up in a white satin gown with a veil and release the photo to the press. It wasn't that she was appearing in a movie involving a wedding, nor was she getting married herself: it was simply that the iconic white outfit caught the eye and could net these girls the coverage the studio was after. Jean Arthur barely registered in the public's consciousness until a 1930 portrait by Eugene Robert Richee showed her pensively cradling a sheaf of white lilies, her head shrouded in white tulle, pearls gleaming against the modest neckline of a white satin gown.

If there was one thing Hollywood knew how to do, it was put on a wedding. Sandy Schreier, author of *Hollywood Gets*

Married, points out that several of the founders of the original film companies had garment-industry backgrounds: "Zukor was a furrier, Goldwyn a glove manufacturer, Fox a dress manufacturer, Mayer an antique and button dealer and Carl Laemmle a haberdasher. When these men came to Hollywood, they didn't know how to make a movie, but they knew everything about the production and marketing of beautiful clothes." These were the days when movies relied on visual spectacle, and costumes were a crucial element.

They were also the days when studios had a hand in every aspect of their actors' lives; costume designers made their clothes, set designers decorated their houses—and the studios produced their weddings. When Hungarian silent film star Vilma Banky and actor Rod LaRocque got engaged in June 1927, their plans for a quiet wedding at the Santa Barbara Mission were swiftly revised when MGM stepped in. As LaRocque recalled years later, "Sam [Goldwyn, their boss] would have been terribly offended if we had not complied with their wishes." The couple cooperated with good humor: what choice did they have? The studio convened a photo call when the bride and groom obtained their marriage license at the County Clerk's office: Banky and LaRocque patiently posed, holding up the essential document so the cameras could read it: "Certificate of Marriage." The wedding itself took place at the Church of the Good Shepherd in Beverly Hills. The seven bridesmaids, in excruciatingly fashionable dresses with full, tiered tulle skirts, carried immense bouquets of roses and wore wide-brimmed straw hats—among their number were actresses Constance Talmadge, Bebe Daniels, and Mildred Davis. (It seems likely that some of these bridesmaids were not actually close friends, but merely other studio players who could benefit from the exposure.) The ushers included Ronald Colman, Harold Lloyd, and Donald Crisp, while LaRocque's best man was Cecil B. DeMille. Like De-Mille's films, it was an extravaganza: LaRocque remembered that "Tom Mix drove up in a coach and four. Everybody was there." Cameras rolled from every angle. At the Beverly Hills Hotel reception, the studio entertained between fifteen hundred and two thousand guests—"all our friends with all *their* friends," as LaRocque put it. The unforgettable detail was that amid all the hundreds of platters of turkey, salads, lobster, and shrimp at the massive buffet, there were two papier-mâché turkeys, "because of the lights," noted LaRocque. The real food was consumed and replaced but the fake turkeys sat there unblemished.

The studio heads didn't hesitate to avail themselves of all the talent they employed when it came time to marry off their daughters, either. Edith Mayer, daughter of Louis B. Mayer, was married in 1930 wearing a white duchesse satin gown created by costumier Adrian. It had long sleeves and a train that pooled in front of her in the formal photographs, covered with a rose point lace veil. Apparently the design was successful, since Adrian repeated it for her sister Irene, who married a little more than a month later. Three years earlier Irving Thalberg, a powerful producer at MGM, had married Norma Shearer in the backyard of his mother's house. MGM production designer Cedric Gibbons created a floral arbor for the ceremony; a plane flew over afterward and dropped rose petals on the assembled group. Marion Davies was a bridesmaid for both Norma Shearer and Edith Mayer, while Louis B. Mayer was Irving Thalberg's best man. Hollywood was a very small town in those days.

Small though the moviemaking community was, its influence was vast. Millions of Americans went to the movies

This gorgeous bride is silent-film star Vilma Banky—but it's not her wedding day.
She is costumed for *Dark Angel* (1925). The veil worn low on the brow with
flower earmuffs rarely looked as elegant as it did on Banky.

weekly to participate, however briefly, in lives more interesting than their own. The pageantry on the screen had nothing to do with realism, everything to do with aspiration. Weddings were a regular feature, in part because marriage was deemed the natural culmination of romance. But, as Sandy Schreier points out, "[M]ost of the early silent films and 'talkies' had brides and beautiful wedding scenes, whether or not it [*sic*] was called for in the story lines." No expense was wasted in making these brides lovely, either—Pola Negri's wedding gown in *The Cheat* (1923) set the studio back a hundred thousand dollars.

If movie audiences wanted escape during the 1920s, by the 1930s they *needed* it. Film technology had added naturalistic speech so characters and plots could become more complex, comedy more subtle. One of the classic film weddings of this period occurs at the end of *It Happened One Night*. Headstrong runaway heiress Ellie Andrews (Claudette Colbert) has fallen in love with dashing reporter Peter Warne (Clark Gable). When she believes he has deserted her, she goes back to her father and agrees to remarry her first husband, aviator/playboy King Westley (Jameson Thomas). Their first wedding was an elopement but the second time around, unconventionally, Ellie insists on a church wedding. (Until quite recently the formal white wedding was the prerogative only of the first-time bride.) Much is made of this in the film— the preparations are shown in considerable detail, right down to the huddle of cameramen on a rooftop, a reference to the massive press coverage of Barbara Hutton's wedding to playboy Prince Mdivani the same year. The film was released in 1934, just five years after the stock market crash, and the magnificence of the wedding is hammered home. The neckline of

Claudette Colbert, as heiress Ellie Andrews, is about to bolt from her grand formal wedding to playboy King Westley (Jameson Thomas) in *It Happened One Night*. The details of satin dress, kid gloves, and gardenias at the wedding gown's neckline signaled wealth to Depression-era audiences.

Ellie's form-fitting white satin gown is bordered in (expensive) gardenias. Westley lands on the broad lawn of the Andrews estate in his plane. The crowd of guests are all dressed formally, with men in morning coats and women in long gowns. The long procession, filing out of the house to the altar set up on the lawn, is accompanied by a huge choir, harp, and strings. The altar is draped with lace and backed by massive floral structures. Eight ushers and eight bridesmaids, along with a maid of honor and a flower girl, add drama to the procession. Ellie, having betrayed her nerves before the wedding by tossing down cocktails and nervously lighting cigarettes (very unmaidenly behavior), is somber as she paces along on her father's arm.

And then—she bolts. Informed by her father that Peter Warne is waiting in a car beyond the gates of the estate, she hikes up her satin skirt and races across the lawn, with her tulle veil streaming in the air behind her. As Elizabeth Kendall points out in *The Runaway Bride: Hollywood Romantic Comedy of the 1930s,* the grandeur and expense of the wedding is emphasized to impress on audiences the gravity of what Ellie is throwing away by bolting. The waste! But Ellie is running to join her soul mate. The satisfied filmgoer could only dream of the splendor of the Andrews lifestyle, but every girl could hope for love.

While the movies in the 1920s and '30s offered an escapist vision of romance, they were also educating their viewers. Gossip columns and their accompanying photographs brought the doings of the rich to the attention of the masses, but the movies gave a much richer, more detailed insight into the pleasures and privileges of high life, from breakfast in bed to the wee hours at a nightclub. As the Lynds wrote in *Middletown:* "Week after week at the movies people in all walks of life enter, often with an intensity of emotion that is apparently one of the most potent means of reconditioning habits, into the intimacies of Fifth Avenue drawing rooms and English country houses, watching the habitual activities of a different cultural level."

At the same time as motion pictures were exposing viewers to a lavish standard of living, American society itself was undergoing a sea change that brought it closer to the world we live in. Domestic standards of living rose sharply: indoor plumbing, central heating, telephones, radios, and cars became standard possessions for middle-class families. The big corporations so familiar in today's landscape were already doing business, cranking out nationally branded consumer goods that were available from sea to shining sea. The great American consumer economy—consecrated to selling its citizens items they might not need but could be made to want—took its form in the 1920s and '30s. Advertising, on the radio and in nationally distributed magazines like *Life,* became ever more adept at playing on the aspirations and emotions of its audiences. The attitudes of restraint and self-denial, of using up and making do, natural to the nineteenth-century culture of the formative republic, gave way gradually to an expectation that material desires would be fulfilled sooner rather than later. The home, from being a haven of moral purity, began to turn into a primary locus for consumption. Even lack of funds didn't stand in the way of purchasing, as banks discovered the enormous potential for profit in consumer lending. You no longer had to save for months to buy a car or a house or a hygienic-looking white-enameled stove to replace the black coal-burning monster; you could make a down payment, bring home what you wanted, and pay it off a few dollars at a time. Needs, desires, even whims could be satisfied on the spot. Saving and doing without, from the vantage point of the interwar years, wasn't modern.

As the standard of living rose in the middle-class home, so did the standard of dress. A leveling in the way the classes looked was one of the most revolutionary aspects of the 1920s and '30s. Of course there were, and still are, distinctions marking expensive clothes from cheap. But the startling new simplicity of women's clothes in particular made it much easier for a poor girl to dress like a rich one. The sheer elaboration of luxurious nineteenth-century clothes had vanished as everyone went about their business in plainly cut dresses and close-fitting simple hats. This sartorial equalization was just one aspect of a trend toward a national homogeneity and democratization. Advertising, movies, national publications, the radio, and packaged goods assured that, from Tallahassee to Sacramento, Americans had similar experiences and possessions and expectations. Local and ethnic differences diminished, especially as the young traveled away to school and "married out." They wanted to behave like each other, not like their parents—they wanted to look and dress and dance and be married the way everybody else did.

In the 1920s and '30s various newly powerful media may have showed Americans how the upper classes got married, but some of the sumptuary restraint of the nineteenth century did still linger. Dorothy Dix was a hugely popular advice columnist, syndicated in papers across the country and noted for her acerbic, commonsense attitude. Her book of counsel published in 1926 (*Dorothy Dix—Her Book: Every-Day Help for Every-Day People*) includes a chapter entitled "The Show Wedding." Dorothy was dead set against it. "[B]y the time she is ten years old the average girl has begun planning her wedding and deciding whether she will have a big church affair, with ushers and flower girls and ring-bearers and maids and matrons of honor and bridesmaids and a white satin dress and a real lace veil, and all the other flub-dubs, or whether she will be married at home under a floral canopy, with an admiring audience fenced off from her by white ribbons. And to realize this ten-minute splurge she is ready to ruthlessly ruin her family and half kill herself. If she doesn't get it, she goes through life feeling that she has missed her big moment." Dix felt that marrying is too important to be overwhelmed by the frivolous circus of an expensive and showy formal wedding, and that it would be much wiser for couples simply to "slip around to the parson and make their vows at the altar." But she held a minority opinion. The days of the modest bride and the intimate ceremony, like Meg's in *Little Women,* were long gone, and brides now insisted on their "big moment" if it was at all possible.

Increasingly, it was, as various businesses found that they could make money on brides. The first step was the professional assumption of tasks that had previously been performed by the bride or her family: cooking, baking, sewing, decorating. We have seen how some brides from the turn of the century onward turned to caterers, florists, seamstresses, and even department stores to meet their requirements. What was different starting in the late 1920s was that businesses began to regard brides as potential profit centers.

One of the earliest manifestations of this change was the introduction of separate bridal departments in the bigger stores. B. Altman's in New York City had one of the first, headed by Marie Coudert Brenning, who took it from a single fitting room to an area that encompassed trousseau shopping as well as the outfit for the big day. Since the body-skimming cut of the straight '20s silhouettes required little in the way of custom fitting, purchasing a wedding gown "off the rack" became a more appealing option. Elementary merchandising suggested offering a bride-to-be a host of other necessities: veils, shoes, stockings, and gloves, all in one location. It was far more canny, though, to draw her eye also to monogrammed bed linens, artful nightgowns and undergarments, even stylish and practical clothes for the first year of married life. This was the task of the bridal department staff or the bridal secretary, half saleswoman, half wedding planner. The bridal secretary could recommend, with equal authority, a bridesmaids' gown, a caterer, or a style of engraving for the wedding invitations. Julietta Arthur, in a 1939 article called "Here Comes the Bride's Business" (published in a short-lived magazine, *Independent Woman*), introduces would-be professional women to the metier of a bridal secretary. The career, she points out, has "developed only within the last twelve years or so." Bridal secretaries generally worked in either department stores or the new "brides' specialty shops." Arthur comes quickly to the point: "It is your business to send away the little bride so satisfied that she'll be a charge customer in your store for life."

Department stores would go to great lengths in order to meet the requirements of these "little brides." In the fall 1934 debut issue of *Bride's* magazine, Lord & Taylor's ad croons, "Let us fuss over all the wrinkly details for you—invitations, bridesmaids' presents, photographs, announcements and so on." Arthur claims that by 1939, Lord & Taylor was "supervising" about one thousand weddings a year. Some stores, scenting endless potential sales, offered to guide the bride through the entire wedding process, from sending out the invitations to furnishing her new home—from their own furniture departments, of course.

It wasn't merely the department stores that profited from weddings, though. Jewelers were also important consumer resources. At the very least, even if the only other outlay was the cost of a marriage license, a groom had to buy his wife a wedding band. Perhaps he bought an engagement ring. She might buy him a wedding present like a watch. In addition, jewelers in the 1920s and '30s also carried engraved stationery, flatware, china, and crystal. Naturally the principal purchasers of these items were young couples on their way to the altar. Despite some early hesitation about the tastefulness of targeting bridal customers, by the early 1930s jewelers grasped that the wedding market was essential to their survival. They began to focus on it consciously, first by advertising heavily in the traditional bridal month of June. They offered services like addressing and mailing wedding invitations. Some store owners scanned the engagement announcements in local newspapers and mailed to future brides booklets of wedding etiquette tips as a "gift." These booklets often contained spaces for brides to keep track of their wedding presents—many of which, it was hoped, would come from that very shop.

Twenty years earlier, the mother of a bride would have had no need of etiquette tips and might even have been insulted by them. Of course she knew how to plan a wedding—hadn't she been to dozens? Didn't she entertain frequently? Couldn't she create a wedding breakfast menu without the slightest strain? But there were brides in the 1920s and '30s whose mothers had not been married in white satin and real lace. They did not know exactly how to arrange a wedding procession, or how to word a formal invitation. They needed help, and the smooth salesmen behind the silver counter were eager to guide them.

The invitation is an especially telling bit of business. To this day, the most conservative brides trot off to Tiffany or their local equivalent and order the standard: a stiff ivory card or folded sheet, engraved with black ink in an arcane third-person formula. It reads "Mr. and Mrs. Bride's Parents / request the honour of your presence / at the marriage of their daughter / Faith Priscilla . . ." And so on, spelling out the groom's name and the location, date, and time. The English spelling of "honour" is not optional. Neither, strictly speaking, is the separate reception card or the inner envelope. (The small squares of tissue enclosed with the invitation were originally intended to prevent the slow-drying ink from smearing.)

Why are traditional wedding invitations so archaic? Consuelo Vanderbilt's wedding invitation, sent in 1895, looked exactly like this. The formal wedding is an innately backward-looking set of rituals, even though reception menus have changed, fashions have changed, and brides rarely go to the church in a horse and carriage. The answer is that in the 1920s and '30s, the period of swift social change, canny retailers appointed themselves custodians of wedding traditions. In addition to the expected services of selling dessert plates and engagement rings, they threw in their directives about how things should be done. Which was, naturally, in the most expensive way possible, and the way they always *had* been done. Invitations? Oh, engraved, ma'am, on a card—let me show you.

If there was a moment when weddings could have broken away from the yoke of the past, the interwar era was probably it. A general yearning for "modernity," new entrants to the middle class, a breezy informality permeating social life in general—all these elements were in place to wrest the form of the wedding into the present. It is true that the very solemnity and importance of embarking on marriage calls for something outside of normal behavior. It is also true that weddings were, in those days, usually planned and paid for by parents, a notoriously conservative group. But it is also worth considering that at a moment when so much social behavior was up for grabs, it was businesses that claimed authority over the wedding formula, and hauled it safely (and expensively) back to the nineteenth century. In fact, from the mid-thirties on, it was businesses that dictated—via shop windows or advertising or merchandising—what a wedding looked like.

They were not always successful in their attempt. Vicki Jo Howard, in her Ph.D. thesis, notes that in the 1920s, the jewelry trade made a concerted effort to sell engagement rings for men. Through advertising on the radio and in print, they tried to establish that this was an old tradition and one worth reviving. This ploy failed, but jewelers made another foray in the 1950s and '60s, successfully persuading many grooms to wear gold wedding bands like their wives.

In addition to appointing themselves custodians of tradition, retailers were also prepared to innovate. One of the logistically difficult issues of a large wedding was the handling of gifts. By this period, a guest's presence at a wedding implied the obligation to send a present to the couple. Duplications abounded, and the bridal ambition of completing sets of china or flatware could be thwarted all too easily by guests relying on their own tastes. Howard says that some jewelers in the late 1920s and early '30s kept informal card files as a service to their customers, tracking brides' and grooms' choices of patterns and what had been bought for them. In 1929, the *Ladies' Home Journal* issued a call to department stores to invent what Howard quotes as a "wedding-gift consulting bureau," but the notion still seemed both crude and mercenary. To take advantage of such a "bureau" might make the bride's family feel that they were placing orders for presents from their friends.

In the summer of 1939, though, a little flurry of advertising and editorial material in *Bride's* magazine suggests that retailers were finally willing to take the bull by the horns. The magazine's editors, deploring the number of "white elephants" that brides traditionally received as presents, offered a list of useful potential gifts and suggested that brides use the pages "as 'hint' lists for your present-giving relatives and friends." That suggestion actually seems a little more barefaced than the services offered in ads for Chicago department store Carson, Pirie Scott and the midwestern chain Halle Brothers. In Carson's "Bridal Room" a girl could register her patterns "for the benefit of inquiring friends," while at Halle Brothers, "[Gifts] for the bride will be carefully recorded to avoid duplication." Right through the 1940s, advertising for what came to be called bridal registries often explained how they worked, as if the notion was slow to catch on.

Bride's promoted its mission as serving the thousands of young women who married each year, but its business agenda was to sell ads. A similar profit motive is exposed clearly in Marisa Keller and Mike Mashon's *TV Weddings: An Illustrated Guide to Prime-Time Nuptials.* They tell how radio serials in the 1930s became popular vehicles for advertisers. Corporations had discovered that loyal audiences actually bought the brands they heard about on their favorite shows. In 1930, a writer named Irma Phillips tried to sell a radio soap called *Painted Dreams,* which would feature the engagement and wedding of one of the female leads. The drama was to include not only the wedding itself, but also endless shopping for the trousseau, furnishings for the new home, and all the trappings of the event itself. Phillips pitched the show to Montgomery Ward, pointing out that "this plan opens up an avenue to merchandize [*sic*] any article which may be sold by mail order or through other retail outlets of Montgomery Ward & Company."

Painted Dreams didn't make it to the air, perhaps because shopping on the air sounded so terribly dull, but Irma Phillips's sense of brides as potentially big business was accurate. Julietta Arthur, author of the article "Here Comes the Bride's Business," says that in 1936, Macy's bridal secretary Kathleen Blackburn appeared on a weekly radio show discussing "what the up-to-date bride should do—and buy." According to Vicki Jo Howard, *House Beautiful* magazine, in a labor-intensive cross-promotion, sent to its subscribers festive white-and-gold boxes full of brochures from department stores, photographers, and other potential wedding suppliers. The giant in the business, though, was *Bride's* magazine.

The first issue appeared in the fall of 1934, entitled *So You're Going to Be Married*. The canny publisher was Wells Drorbaugh, who sent his magazine free to a select group of girls on the East Coast whose engagements had been announced in their hometown newspapers. It was a clever idea: only the daughters of prominent families were noticed in the social columns of such papers, so Drorbaugh's advertisers were guaranteed a choice audience. The editorial mix confirmed this slant: one of the articles punctuating the photographs of satin gowns and monogrammed linens was a piece on how to manage your servants. The magazine assumed that its Brides (the word was always capitalized, well into the

1960s) would be married formally, go on an expensive honeymoon, then keep house and entertain. Despite the fact that the country was just pulling out of the Depression, only the formal white wedding was consistently viewed as the real thing. In the spring of 1935 the publication changed its name to *Bride's* and thereafter simply went from strength to strength, accumulating advertising pages, increasing in frequency, and helping to define the iconic American wedding. The template had been set in the years after World War I, when the wedding ceased to be a homemade celebration and became something you bought. In the years to come, more brides would simply buy more as getting married went from a transition to a kind of apotheosis.

CHAPTER 6

Tra-La-Tra-La . . . We've Got Our Men!

"MARRIAGES . . . A PUBLIC NECESSITY WORTH FIGHTING FOR" •
BRIDES AT THE BARRACKS • THE GIRLISH BRIDE •
"CAREFREE DAYS ARE PAST" • "IT'S WHAT EVERY GIRL
DREAMS OF" • WEDDINGS ON TELEVISION •
BRIDAL BARBIE

Before the great efflorescence of the wedding industry came the war. The effect of World War II on weddings was much more striking than that of the Great War a generation earlier. The bombing of Pearl Harbor, the duration of America's involvement in combat, and the sheer number of citizens involved permeated American life with awareness of the conflict. Young people rushed into marriage at an unprecedented rate: between 1940 and 1943, one million more couples wed than the prewar rate would have predicted. Suddenly, under the threat of Axis aggression, America's freedoms looked especially sweet. Not since the Victorian era, when the family was considered the building block of the Republic, had domestic arrangements had such significance. As Nancy Cott writes in *Public Vows: A History of Marriage and the Nation,* "Marriages and the families they created were private experiences so precious that they amounted to a public necessity worth fighting for." And the embryonic bridal industry seized upon the stirring rhetoric of the times. By the end of the war, a bride could be forgiven for believing that it was her patriotic duty to insist on a formal wedding, white satin and all.

Of course there were often pressing reasons why this could not be managed, most of them having to do with the availability of the groom. *Bride's* magazine claimed, in 1943, that as many as 80 percent of grooms were in the armed forces. Eager as these young men were to claim their wives, nuptial planning had to be squeezed in around the military agenda. The resulting ceremonies were often a matter of resourceful improvisation. Civil weddings, necessitating small casts of characters and little lead time, were very popular. The bride would wear a pretty suit or a dress, accessorized with a hat, gloves, and always flowers to mark the occasion. The groom could simply wear his uniform: for the duration of the war, any man in uniform was considered appropriately dressed for any occasion. The reception, if any, was short: what man would consent to stand around drinking punch instead of seizing the opportunity to have as much sex as possible before returning to the barracks?

And then, sometimes the wedding took place *at* the barracks. In 1942, *Life* ran a photo feature covering a group ceremony at Fort Bliss in El Paso, Texas. The USO organized the event, rounding up chaplains of several Christian denominations and decorating the gym at the YMCA with a canopy of white crepe paper streamers. The altar was decked with candles, white calla lilies, and flags. Each of the seven brides wore, with a street dress, a corsage of white roses provided by the wife of the commanding officer at the base. The cake (also courtesy of the USO) was cut by the new wife of the highest-ranking groom, First Lieutenant William Debelak. Later that year, the magazine covered a wedding at Schofield Barracks in Hawaii. What is striking about the photographs is the good-natured improvisation that cobbled together festive ritual from unpromising materials. The getaway car was a military half-track laden with machine guns and decorated with chalked-on slogans (including, on the driver's side bumper, "Big nite tonight"). Toasts to the newlyweds were drunk with a bourbon and soda concoction served up in a glass coffeepot.

The wedding industry was not willing, of course, to forego trying to sell *something* to these brides. An ad for a Richmond department store in the fall 1943 issue of *Bride's* touts the merits of "The New Wedding Suit," a wool number in "Bridal Blue," dressed up with a peplum and sequin trim and quite expensive at $98.95. In the spring 1942 issue (the first issue of the magazine to be published after the attack on Pearl Harbor), an ad for the Franklin Simon department store claims that, "Not even satin and orange blossoms could be more glamorous than the costumes we do for army and navy wives-to-be."

Still, the white dress hovered as the standard to be achieved if possible. Modifications were necessary, of course. The first thing to go was silk—it was required for parachutes. Fortunately, textile mills had been turning out synthetics for several years and a variety of rayon satins were pressed into service for wedding gowns. The full skirts and gathered bodices of the late 1930s were replaced by narrow princess lines, and fabric-wasting features like cuffs and full sleeves vanished. The bride's train had to be limited to two yards and foregoing a veil meant conserving even further. Many a gown was worn by more than one bride. Even with these limitations, American women were much more fortunate than their English counterparts, who could not get wedding gowns at all. Several informal aid programs, one headed by Eleanor Roosevelt, collected wedding gowns and sent them to Britain for the use of Allied brides.

Seven couples got hitched at this 1942 group wedding in an El Paso, Texas, army barracks. The USO provided the wedding cake, which the highest-ranking newlyweds cut. White rose corsages supplied the bridal touch on the women's street dresses.

Mrs. Roosevelt was not the only person who understood the morale-raising value of brides feeling like the genuine article. In the fall issue of 1943, a *Bride's* editorial gushed about the importance of "Brides in traditional wedding dresses and veils. These Brides are fulfilling their own dreams of white weddings, and granting their Grooms' wishes for weddings to remember." Also at issue, for bridal gown manufacturers at least, were dreams of profit. It was the War Production Board (WPB) that put into place limitations on fabric use in general, originally intending to ration the amount of material made available to the makers of wedding gowns. The Bridal and Bridesmaids Apparel Association (BBAA) organized to lobby the WPB and Congress with the following eloquent argument: "American boys are going off to war and what are they fighting for, except the privilege of getting married in a traditional way?" The ideals of democracy apparently embraced white satin along with more abstract notions like freedom of speech or due process. In any event, the BBAA was successful, and throughout the war, brides with enough time and money to plan a traditional wedding could be sure they would find plenty of choices available to them. A June 22, 1942, article in *Life* magazine even stated that the bridal industry had seen a 50 percent increase in sales over the previous year, though weddings were only up by 10 percent. The magazine's cover for that issue showed a bride whose bouquet was created from white fabric leaves and war stamps.

In fact, if the advertisers in *Bride's* were to be believed, insisting on a big formal wedding and wearing a white dress were patriotic acts. "Be the Romantic Picture He'll Cherish in His Heart Forever," urged Meier and Frank's. Franklin Simon ruminated about "an hour's beauty to remember for a lifetime" and a memory for the groom "to carry to the ends of the earth." The St. Louis department store Scruggs, Vandervoort and Barney proclaimed that "The Bride's Shop feels its task is more meaningful than ever."

The garment industry was not the only one to be affected by War Production Board dictates; the industries that produced those tables full of wedding presents—crystal, porcelain, and especially silver—were diverted to military tasks. They proudly advertised this fact in *Bride's,* pointing out that it was a young wife's patriotic duty to "think of other brides who want sterling silver just as much as you do . . . and share with them for the duration by starting your silver service with just the *minimum* number of place settings." This was Gorham, manufacturing armaments instead of teaspoons; Wallace stated that "[M]any of the skilled hands that crafted Wallace Sterling are making war materials today, so that you may enjoy your complete service tomorrow in the freedom that alone makes beauty meaningful."

It wasn't long, though, before a different anxiety made itself felt among America's brides-to-be. By 1945 they were no longer worried about not being able to buy enough silver: they were worried about their demobilized fiancés. Suddenly the nation had to reabsorb the sixteen million men who had served in the armed forces. There weren't enough homes for them. Women who had gone to work during the war were urged to give up their jobs so that veterans could find employment. The GI Bill offered substantial benefits like a full year's unemployment pay, job training, pensions, and low-cost mortgages, but there was really no telling how successfully all these soldiers would be reintegrated into society. Women were urged to be patient and agreeable, to pamper their menfolk, to listen and make them comfortable, build up their egos, affirm their decisions.

This anxiety about assimilating GIs back into domestic life does not entirely explain the cultural climate of the 1950s, but it was a factor. So was the sheer relief at the end of the war: America could go back to normal, and normalcy had never looked so good: Mom, Dad, Buddy, and Sis in a ranch-style house with a station wagon parked out in front. It was the heyday of the suburbs. The baby boomers got born. Fears about Communism and the Cold War made the domestic verities look even more precious. Marriage rates were at an all-time high; ages at marriage at an all-time low. In 1956, the average woman marrying was just over twenty years old, and the fashion sections of *Bride's* stressed this youth with breathless commentary about "girlish" and "ingenuous" gowns on "dewy" and "flower-fresh" brides. (The American publication of *Lolita* in 1958 shed light on an extreme version of this preoccupation.)

It was an oddly neo-Victorian world those young women were marrying into. A wave of feminist agitation in the 1920s had brought about substantial reforms in women's education and career prospects, in addition to winning females the right to vote. But by the 1950s feminism had retreated and the strict separation of spheres that had dictated family roles fifty or seventy years earlier was once again in vogue. Men would work in the threatening outside world, while their wives would run the home and bring up their children. A widely read treatise published in 1947 by Ferdinand Lundberg and Marynia Farnham, *Modern Woman: The Lost Sex,* called for women to resume the roles their grandmothers filled so well: passive, submissive, feminine. Even women who worked—

and in 1960, that was between 30 percent and 40 percent of them, depending on your source—were under pressure to conform to the ideal of the compliant female. In the mid-1960s, *Bride's* ran a regular feature by a young married man named Peter Hunsaker, who aired his views of what men really desired from their wives. In April/May 1967, he addressed working women, saying, "You must also keep in mind that your first responsibility is to your home and husband. Don't let your job become more important than his. . . ." A few months later, he weighed in with a list of directives for keeping a husband happy. Among them: "Don't appear to be more intelligent than he is—even if you are." "Don't appear to be domineering." And finally: "Appear to be frugal. . . . The biggest gripe most men have is that their wives are spending them into penury."

Hunsaker's advice hints at the dark side of the marital bargain. Superficially, the clock had been turned back a hundred years and the wife was once more the angel in the house. But she was missing something essential, that moral authority that Victorian culture conferred on her. The home was no longer the seat of all goodness and woman its curator. Rather, the home had become, in the intervening years, a temple to consumption, and women had nothing left to curate but appliances and children.

Marriage meant very different things to men and to women in the postwar era. A 1947 ad for a New York City bridal shop called "The Tailored Woman" pictured two gleeful girls in white gowns with a headline reading, "Tra-La-Tra-La . . . we've got our men!" Charles Lewis, in his Ph.D. thesis on Minnesota photography, describes standard "comic" poses from the 1950s like grooms being "dragged" through the church door by groomsmen, or women hugging their grooms while pointing, for the camera alone, to the marriage certificate—and winking. Marriage was something women wanted more than men. A candid snapshot in a 1952 issue of *Bride's* spells out the male point of view with a placard on a getaway car reading, "Married at last / Carefree days are past."

For men, it must have felt like that. They were under enormous cultural pressure to be "mature" and "well adjusted." In the late 1950s the average age at which a man married was only twenty-three—to delay marriage meant dodging responsibility. Conformity was applauded, so the rebel who avoided matrimony was a threat to everyone—possibly even a "deviant." But the responsibility of marriage was immense for a young man, especially once he had children. Even if his wife had worked after they were married, society on the whole disapproved of her doing so. In some circles, having a wife who worked meant you were an inadequate earner.

Life in the suburbs was competitive, too—it was easy to see who had a new car every five years and who was driving a patched-up jalopy. American industry kept coming up with ways to improve housewives' lives, with cake mixes and dishwashers and electric coffeepots—a husband could be forgiven for wondering just what his wife did all day, if all of these machines were doing the housework. To some, the corporation assumed the role of refuge, while others took solace in the bar car of their commuter trains. It was no accident that *Playboy* was founded in 1953. Hugh Hefner's brilliant notion was to indulge men's escapist fantasies; he provided a vision of delicious sex and a rebellious lifestyle, with no apron strings in sight.

And although a 1962 Gallup poll found 60 percent of American women happy with their lives, other statistics weren't looking so cheerful. In 1946, the divorce rate reached one in four marriages, a new high. Over time, as many as a third of the American marriages of the 1950s ended in divorce. The roles of breadwinner and domestic goddess, assumed with such energy by postwar newlyweds, turned out to be unsustainable for many couples. The breadwinner turned anxious, resentful, and prone to heart disease while his wife drove carpool and wondered why she was bored literally to tears. Betty Friedan's *The Feminine Mystique,* published in 1963, provided some answers. In the culture of the 1950s and early '60s, the approved role for women simply did not allow them to *matter.* "It is my thesis," Friedan proclaimed, "that . . . our culture does not permit women to accept or gratify their basic need to grow and fulfill their potentialities as human beings." She pointed out the difference between the heroines of women's magazine fiction published in 1939—career women whom men appreciated "as much for their spirit as for their looks"— and the superhousewives idolized ten years later. She cited statistics about women's college educations, women's penetration of the professions, the paltry number of fictional heroines of the 1950s who held jobs. "Fulfilment as a woman," she said, "had only one definition for American women after 1949— the housewife-mother."

The Feminine Mystique sold more than a million copies. Friedan's clarion call turned out to be just one of a series of groundbreaking events of the 1960s whose significance emerged only gradually. In 1960, the Food and Drug Administration approved oral contraceptives for the general market. In 1963, Martin Luther King led civil rights marches in Birmingham and in 1964, the Civil Rights Act passed. Fifteen thousand students marched to protest U.S. involvement in Vietnam in

1965. The cultural upheaval of the late 1960s and 1970s grew out of this series of fundamental alterations to the status quo.

The status quo, however, did not crumble all at once. Where weddings—conservative by their very nature—are concerned, the status quo maintained its shape remarkably well. In fact, by the late 1960s the traditional white wedding was looking so well preserved that it simply had to attract the restless eye of rebellious youth and come in for some tweaking. Until that point, though, the wedding surged along on the path set for it a hundred years earlier. The biggest change at midcentury was simply that the grand formal ritual, once the province of America's upper class, then the aspiration of the upwardly mobile, became the standard for every bride.

In 1948, Edward Streeter, a successful New York banker who moonlighted as a writer, published an entertaining little novel about an unassuming suburban lawyer whose daughter gets married. Told almost entirely from the point of view of Stanley Banks, *Father of the Bride* is a delicious tale of the average man swept up in the domestic and financial cataclysm of staging a wedding. With its artful blend of irony and occasional sentiment, the novel struck a chord. It went on to be a bestseller and, in 1950, a movie. Spencer Tracy, America's Everyman, was cast as Stanley Banks, the embattled paterfamilias helpless in the face of the Wedding Imperative. Joan Bennett played the indomitable wife and mother, Ellie Banks, and the Bride herself, Kay, was played by the dewy, gorgeous, and irresistible Elizabeth Taylor. What man in America could have held out against that pair?

The showdown comes early. Poor Stanley (in a performance that netted Tracy an Academy Award nomination), all unwitting, drives home from his commuter train to what he anticipates as a pleasant evening with the family. At the dinner table, Kay casually announces that she's planning on marrying her boyfriend, Buckley Dunstan. Her father is horrified: "You're not talking about a church wedding!" He turns to his wife: "You were married in the front parlor in a blue suit!"

Turns out that was exactly the wrong thing to say. A little later, discussing the wedding, Ellie says, "Stan, there's only one time in a girl's life that she can be married in a bridal dress, just once! I don't want Kay to miss it the way I did."

Banks remonstrates—he can't believe such a thing really mattered to his practical wife. She has to elaborate: "Stanley, I don't know how to explain, but a wedding, a church wedding—it's what every girl dreams of. A bridal dress, orange blossoms, music—it's something lovely for her to remember all her life."

And that, in a nutshell, was the wedding doctrine of the postwar era. Once in a lifetime. Your special day. Every girl's dream. Just as a wedding had been a kind of apotheosis in the Victorian era, so it was again in postwar America—only this time around, there were no Mollie Dorseys left out of the fun, cobbling together their nuptials out of calico and wildflowers and home-baked cake. Every girl could be a bride in white.

The media promoted this prospect relentlessly. In 1949, *Modern Bride* published its first issue and was sold on the newsstands. *Bride's,* until then strictly a subscription-based magazine, followed suit, entering into a duel that continues to this day, apparently to neither magazine's detriment. *Bride's* got thicker with ads, going from 188 pages in the spring issue of 1945 to 304 pages in the spring issue of 1960. The addition of color in the magazine in the late 1940s persuaded the cosmetics companies to join the mixture of silver, china, wedding attire, and travel ads. Linens and furniture soon followed as

For Carol Gardner's informal afternoon wedding in 1953, groom William Wallace wore a sporty white jacket rather than a stuffy morning coat. Despite the modernity of the carnation and palm-frond bouquet, the bride wears the sentimental standby, orange blossom, in her hair.

ad sales reps persuaded media buyers that there was very little brides *weren't* buying in the months preceding their weddings. In 1959, Condé Nast bought *Bride's,* pushing publication from four yearly issues to six in 1964 and to eight in 1969. (It has since gone back to six.)

Clever cross-marketing with other corporate entities was a regular feature of *Bride's* in the 1950s and '60s. In the summer of 1955, a "Most Beautiful Bride" contest was launched with the participation of *The Bob Hope Show.* Engaged girls could obtain entry blanks at the housewares departments of certain stores. They would fill out the forms, attach a photograph, and leave their entries at the stores. The judges included Helen Murphy, the editor-in-chief of *Bride's*; John Robert Powers of the Powers modeling agency; Bob Hope himself; and a vice president of General Electric, which was contributing a range of appliances as part of the grand prize. Although that contest was not repeated, in 1957 *Bride's* hooked up with the famous Pillsbury Bake-Off contest. The baking mix company had held the baking contest since 1949, with junior and senior divisions: 1957 was the first year it had a competition especially for brides. The summer 1957 issue of *Bride's* featured three winners' recipes and a paragraph about that year's guest of honor. Usually this was a celebrity, but this time she was a young Hungarian newlywed who had escaped her native country (recently overrun by the USSR) with nothing but the clothes on her back. *Bride's,* hewing as ever to its readers' interests, pointed out that the young lady had been married wearing a borrowed wedding gown, and that this was a common practice in Hungary. American girls, it was implied, should consider themselves fortunate that in their great free country they didn't have to wear other girls' dresses.

This was an unusual intrusion of politics into the bridal reverie. Current events rarely influenced a girl's wedding planning, though the movies or television might. For instance, Scarlett O'Hara's wedding gown from the film version of *Gone With the Wind,* rendered for the public in "Flirtation" rayon satin, was made available for eighty-five dollars from Best and Company. In 1949, *Life* ran an entertaining series of photographs of women in the dressing rooms at Macy's, trying on copies of Rita Hayworth's wedding dress. Versions of gowns from vehicles as famous as Grace Kelly's *High Society* and as obscure as Lucille Ball's *Forever, Darling* (both 1956) were adapted and offered to a delighted public. Sometimes a movie had a broader effect on fashion—*Sabrina* from 1954 popularized a shallow scooped neckline called the "Sabrina neck" that was popular on wedding gowns throughout the mid-1950s. (Flattering though the look was, it still wouldn't turn you into Audrey Hepburn.) In a similar but more generalized borrowing, wedding fashion in the early 1950s was influenced by the ballet, with full tulle skirts and snug silk bodices abounding at various price points. The Sadler's Wells Theatre Ballet had toured the United States in 1954 and apparently reminded one designer after another how attractive all the girls in those Degas paintings looked.

The wedding industry may have borrowed enthusiastically from popular (and high) culture in the postwar era, but the reverse was also true. Staging a wedding became a standard ploy to add some oomph to the fading popularity of a TV show. The live sitcom *Mr. Peepers,* which starred Wally Cox as a slightly dorky high school science teacher, married off its hero to the school nurse when its ratings started to drop. Much was made of the wedding on the show: a month elapsed between the engagement episode and the wedding it-self, allowing curiosity to build. Advance publicity appeared in *TV Guide* as well as newspapers nationwide. NBC even ran a promotion that invited fifty couples honeymooning in New York City to be part of the live audience. The ratings were en-tirely satisfying as anything-but-glamorous "Nancy Reming-ton" (played by Pat Benoit) made her trip up the aisle in a white lace dress with a single modest string of pearls, an elbow-length tulle veil, and a carnation bouquet. Needless to say, most of the weddings shown on television were the traditional, formal kind. Inger Stevens, playing *The Farmer's Daughter* in 1965, got her trained white dress and her three attendants—though she was a Swedish housekeeper, marrying her congressman employer. Even Jeannie the genie was married in white harem pants, with a white fez and veil, when she finally reeled in Ma-jor Nelson in 1969.

In fact, weddings permeated pop culture in the 1950s and 1960s. CBS ran a daytime show called *Bride and Groom* from 1951 to 1953, when it moved to NBC for another year. Real-life engaged couples wrote to the network, telling their courtship stories. If they were chosen, they went to New York to be wed on the show. The host interviewed them, then they were married by a minister (brides often wearing gowns loaned to them by the network) on the air. CBS picked up the cost of the honeymoon and gave each couple substantial gifts like furniture, silverware, and appliances. The whole show lasted for fifteen minutes and was sponsored by companies like Betty Crocker and Pontiac.

There was a bridal board game in the 1960s that pur-ported to simulate the experience of getting ready for a wed-ding: players went around the board accumulating various necessities: the gown, the bouquet, the cake, the ring. The first player to amass them all won by reaching the "Ceremony" space. (The groom was assumed—he never appeared in the game.) There were bridal paper dolls, bride costumes for little girls, and, once Barbie appeared in 1959, bridal Barbies.

Barbie's remarkable characteristic was her figure, which made her the ideal fashion plate. In her debut year, twenty-two costumes were introduced with her, one of which was a wedding dress. Much has been made of the notion that Barbie was the original career girl, suiting up to head into space in 1965, but the vast majority of her clothes through the 1960s suggested that she was a gal far more interested in her social life than in any nine-to-five grind. The culmination of dating was, naturally, marriage, and Barbie has never been without a wedding dress. The models succeeded each other through the 1960s, gently updated but always entirely appropriate. In fact, the conservatism of Barbie's wedding gowns reflected the conservatism of bridal fashion. In 1966, garments for Barbie and her friends included innovations like panty hose, vinyl raincoats, and bell bottoms. When the time came for Barbie to head up the aisle in 1967, though, she did so in a satin number with a full petal-shaped skirt opening over a point d'esprit petticoat. Needless to say all of Barbie's wedding dresses were white or ivory and the sets always included a bouquet, white shoes, and a headpiece with tulle veil—the standard equipment of the postwar bride.

Oh—she had a groom, too. Barbie's consort, Ken, joined her on toy store shelves in 1961, with nine outfits including a tuxedo so that he could squire Barbie to the many parties on her calendar. His costumes kept pace with hers in hipness (the

Ken looks unwontedly dashing here with his ascot, but he's a little underdressed for Barbie, in her "Bride's Dream" wedding gown (available 1963 to 1965). It came packaged with an orchid bouquet, elbow-length gloves, a tulle veil, and pearls, but maybe she dressed down to keep Ken company.

1966 "Ken a Go-Go" featured a furry black wig to cover his molded plastic crew cut when he played a set on his guitar at the hootenanny) but lagged on the matrimonial front. Until 1966, when Mattel issued a morning-coat outfit for Ken, he had to meet Barbie at the altar in his regular tuxedo. His buddy Alan, the best man, never did get upgraded to the gray tailcoat and top hat.

It hardly seems fair, since the poor best man had a demanding role to play in the formal wedding. He was to deliver a clean, sober, and perfectly dressed groom to the church on time. He had custody of the wedding ring and the check to pay the officiant. If limousines weren't rented it was his job to drive the bride and groom to the reception. And, most onerous of all, he was usually expected to make a toast to the bride and groom at the reception. It was all a far cry from the historical origin of the role, in which he merely stood ready to help when his buddy rode into the next valley to carry off a young maiden. The ushers, in contrast, had a pretty easy time of it. American social life has historically let men off lightly— they tend to be regarded as all but dispensable at events that are planned by women since males work so hard to earn a living. If an usher danced with a few of the plainer bridesmaids in addition to his escort duties in the church, he had done his job.

Even the groom, it must be admitted, is almost faceless in most of the writing and scholarship about American weddings. It can be argued that historically, it is the woman whose life changes most drastically when she marries, and that she should therefore play a bigger part in the ritual. It can also be argued, probably more successfully, that women are the chief consumers in American society, and that as the wedding became more explicitly a consumer rite, it became more female-dominated. In this connection it's worth noting that movie grooms tend to be secondary characters at best. In *It Happened One Night,* Ellie Andrews flees King Westley, while in *Father of the Bride,* Buckley Dunstan is little more than a name. In *The Philadelphia Story,* Tracy Lord (played by Katharine Hepburn) prepares for her wedding to George Kittredge, a self-made man who ultimately betrays his unworthiness of her. Meanwhile suave ex-husband C. K. Dexter Haven (Cary Grant) and poetic reporter Macaulay Connor (James Stewart) both make more plausible love interests. It's only at the end that Grant steps in to nab the bride, a last-minute but satisfying substitution for the intended groom.

CHAPTER 7

All Eyes Are on Her

THE PRINCESS BRIDE • THE TIARA CONNECTION •
MISS AMERICA • BRIDAL COSTUME •
"I STILL BELIEVED THAT MOST BRIDESMAIDS WERE VIRGINS" •
PLAGUE OF EVERY POPULAR GIRL

Although Barbie was perpetually ready to marry Ken, her narrative stopped there. While bridal magazines and marketing pointed to a conjugal future of furniture, first homes, and newlywed entertaining, none of the many accessories and costumes created for Barbie and her friends so much as hinted at an existence beyond her wedding reception. Even her "Dream House," an extravaganza of hot pink plastic, suggested the sorority house more than the honeymoon cottage. The spell Barbie cast was always that of potential, never of fulfillment (and its attendant disappointments). She was courted and won, but never took up the responsibilities of womanhood. This made her life span an ideal playing field for fantasy.

The figure of a princess offered a similar opportunity. Courted, feted, beautifully dressed, she led a life of perpetual festivity. Laying foundation stones for civic centers and producing heirs to the throne were reserved for the future. In that sense, an engaged girl entered into a similar state in the weeks before her wedding. The focus was on her ritual walk down the aisle, the moment when she would be the center of attention, in the grandest dress of her lifetime, complete with those anachronistic features, the train and the veil. This was as glamorous as her life was going to get, as close as Everygirl would come to being royal.

It was a similarity the media could hardly overlook, especially once the young Princess Elizabeth of England became engaged to gorgeous Prince Philip of Greece. Through the summer of 1947 royal rhetoric permeated the American bridal magazines. Readers were invited to imagine themselves a bit more regal in ads like one for the department store Bon Marché, which showed a crowned bride surrounded by turbaned pageboys. "We are the servants of the queen . . ." read the copy. "We bring rich gifts of service to every bride who crosses our threshold." They meant wedding planning and bridal registry, which wasn't quite the same as having a prime minister kiss your hand.

Once launched, the royal imagery stayed afloat. In 1949, *Bride's* proclaimed, "You are the queen of the day, surrounded by your ladies-in-waiting." And Edward Streeter momentarily dropped the ironic tone in *Father of the Bride* to describe Kay when her father first glimpses her in her white gown. She is "no longer a brown-haired girl of five feet four, but a princess from some medieval court. Her head was thrown back slightly and she watched the effect upon her courtiers with the calm assurance of one born to the cloth of gold."

By the 1950s, Cinderella had somehow become conflated into the metaphor. *Bride's* ran a promotion in the spring 1955 issue illustrating a gown copied from Leslie Caron's costume for the MGM musical *The Glass Slipper*. The impossibly ornate dress was composed of pale pink tulle and "imported Chantilly-type lace" with drapery and nosegays and a deeply pleated flounce. This "fantasy-come-true" was available for $160. Its manufacturer, a company called Arden, adapted another film wedding dress a year later: this was the gown Grace Kelly wore as Tracy Lord in *High Society* (the musical verson of *The Philadelphia Story*). Tracy is marrying for the second time, so she can't claim the full virginal splendor of, say, Cinderella. The costume, not quite full length, is made of blush pink organdy embroidered with fetching white flowers. Of course it's not a patch on the dress that Kelly wore in real life to marry her real prince and come as close to Cinderella as any beautiful blonde from Philadelphia's Main Line could hope.

Whatever machinations went on behind the scenes of the Monaco marriage—Did Aristotle Onassis really engineer the match? Had Grace really been around the block once too often?—the bare outlines of the story were very satisfying. The beautiful movie star met handsome Prince Rainier while performing ceremonial duties at the Cannes Film Festival. They corresponded while she went off to shoot another movie, *The Swan*, in which she played a commoner courted by a prince. (Imagine!) He visited her family for Christmas, and they got engaged. She made one more film, *High Society*, before embarking on the SS *Constitution* for her own royal wedding.

It was a press extravaganza of astounding proportions. Kelly's studio, MGM, played a part in the wedding planning but nobody could have anticipated the level of interest from both print and television outlets around the world. TV news was in its infancy, so the Monegasque failure to accommodate hundreds of soundmen and cameramen and reporters was perhaps understandable. The press representatives outnumbered the Monegasque army eight to one. MGM's PR man had to beg the palace to issue daily briefings, simply to pro-

Princess Grace at prayer during her wedding. Behind her stand her child attendants and her seven bridesmaids in yellow organdy, lined up in the strict symmetry of a royal ceremony.

vide the newsmen with something to file. Grace's every move was tracked by the cameras, and MGM later released a documentary called *The Wedding in Monaco.*

Despite the initial missteps, it was very satisfying. As the economist and journalist Walter Bagehot wrote in the nineteenth century, "A princely marriage is the brilliant edition of a universal fact, and as such, it rivets mankind." Every matron could watch Grace glide down the long aisle of Monaco's cathedral and remember her own walk toward her groom. Every girl could admire Grace's astounding beauty and trust that marriage would make her, too, lovely. There were bridesmaids in lemon organdy and unmanageable hats. There were difficult in-laws. There was a massive six-tier cake that Rainier and Grace cut with his sword. And if the children of Monaco were out of school and the businesses were closed so the populace could cheer the newlyweds, wasn't that just the way it should be for every bride?

The American bridal industry, in the midst of processing the postwar wedding boom, clasped Princess Grace to its heart. Her gown had been designed by MGM costume supervisor Helen Rose and constructed in the MGM shop. It used twenty-five yards of peau de soie, twenty-five yards of taffeta, one hundred yards of silk net, and three hundred yards of Valenciennes lace. High-necked, long-sleeved, with a snug bodice and a full skirt, it was both regal and immensely pretty. Knockoffs were available in American stores shortly afterward, but there was no reproducing the delicacy of the antique rose point lace of the bodice, which Helen Rose claimed to have bought from a French museum. In the summer 1956 issue of *Bride's,* ads and editorial copy were studded with phrases like "Your Serene Highness" and "regal romance" and "fairy-tale princess."

When Princess Margaret married in 1960, Americans were less closely involved, but the editors of *Bride's* took the opportunity to use royalty as the theme of their fall issue. The headline on the lead editorial page read, "By Appointment to Her Majesty, the Bride," and went on, "Your Royal Highness, every page of this issue is dedicated to you. Whether or not you choose to wear a crown on your wedding day, you will be Queen of all you survey! Arrayed in a dazzling dress, with ladies-in-waiting to attend you and loyal subjects to do you honor, you'll hold court in a golden kingdom of your own. . . . The following pages are filled with wedding fashions—all worthy of your coronation."

The average American bride was no more going to be crowned than Princess Margaret, but the editors of *Bride's* were onto something. The royal imagery had appeared steadily in the magazine through the fifties and would persist well into the sixties. As late as 1967, a caption called wearing a train "a privilege long accorded to royalty and brides" (this at a time when minidresses and go-go boots were everyday wear). The point was that getting married was like being crowned in those days. It was the culmination of a girl's life and her assumption of a new role. If the real (nonbridal) world was beginning to reconsider the traditional relationship between the sexes in the late sixties, that only intensified the escapist appeal of the royal metaphor. In the face of disconcerting rumbles about gender roles, the conservatism of a monarchy cast an alluring spell.

It's hardly any wonder, then, that one of the preferred bridal headpieces of the day was the tiara. Tiaras have been associated with brides since the classical era, and by the early 1300s a jeweled crown for a bride was a symbol of the marital state. In nineteenth-century England, brides of high rank were often given a tiara, either by their families or by their grooms. It was not until a woman was married that she could correctly wear one: tiaras were reserved for matrons. (Royal-watchers will remember that Sarah Ferguson processed up the aisle wearing a wreath of white flowers, and came back from the altar in a diamond tiara as the Duchess of York.)

Americans with social pretensions have hardly been immune to the appeal of the bridal coronet. Earlier in this century a tiara would be reserved for a bride like Estelle Manville, daughter of the asbestos millionaire, who married Count Folke Bernadotte in 1923. His uncle was King Gustav V of Sweden, so when the count gave his bride a pretty little nine-pointed diamond coronet to wear instead of the conventional wreath of orange blossoms, that made some sense. As *The New York Times* solemnly pointed out, "the coronet will be worn by the bride when she is presented at the Swedish court in January." There was an entirely different aesthetic and social agenda operating when Jeanne Duquette married George Newman in Los Angeles during World War II. Jeanne's wedding was designed by her brother Tony, a decorative artist whose work was characterized by a kind of fey excess. The bride's dress was an exact copy of an 1874 Worth, the house was swathed in pink and green tulle, and the cake's decorations—prancing white unicorns—were made of plaster "to solve the sugar shortage problem," as *Bride's* explained. Only Jeanne's headpiece was modern: Tony had a spiky coronet crafted from Lucite and, naturally, the traditional orange blossoms.

Irony probably had nothing to do with the rash of coronets and tiaras used to secure veils in the late 1950s and early 1960s. They were just one option among many at the time:

pillboxes, flat bows, stiff little halos of lace and beading all served equally well to secure the bouffant tulle veils that were in fashion. In 1958 *Bride's* intoned, "Once in a lifetime it's your privilege to wear a wedding dress with a train and a crown with a veil. . . ." Of course, the crown was supposed to refer obliquely to the transition to womanhood, the culmination of sexual attraction, the loss of virginity—which certainly didn't describe Priscilla Beaulieu's situation when she married Elvis Presley in 1967, the moment she was eighteen and legally permitted to wed. She'd been living with him for five years and the Vegas ceremony merely made official an accepted fact. But she may just have liked the way her crown looked.

Increasingly, it seems, that's why tiaras are worn at weddings. When Diana Ross married Swedish shipping magnate Arne Naess in 1986, she went whole hog: white satin dress, tulle veil, diamond tiara—despite the presence at the wedding of her children by two other men. Well, why not? By then, the standards they were a-changing. Less and less at a wedding did the trappings actually stand for anything: more and more were they merely a fashion statement. This may explain why, after Diana Spencer's wedding in 1981 administered CPR to the wedding industry, tiaras didn't catch on as well. Big sleeves, full skirts, beading and seed pearls and lace and mammoth bouquets, yes to all these things. But the headpieces of the era tended to sit lower on the head, which in any event was covered with pneumatic curls since big hair was also in fashion. Tiaras would simply get lost.

Now, though—today if you go to a bridal salon and ask to see headpieces, you'll be shown a shelf of tiaras. They aren't stiffened lace crowns or beaded headbands or even haloes studded with seed pearls: these are metal crowns studded

Priscilla Beaulieu Presley's "skimmer" wedding dress was all the rage in 1967.
The loose outline of the gown does not hide a pregnancy; Lisa Marie Presley
was born nine months after her parents' wedding.

with crystals. The better ones are imported and prices start at three hundred dollars. (Movie stars tend to borrow the real thing from estate jewelers.) They look splendid on the smooth updo of today's soignée bride, with her clean-cut strapless gown and her simple tulle veil. Nobody's calling her royal at this point; the rhetoric has died down. Or maybe we've just absorbed it; it need not be mentioned any more. Every bride knows she's queen for the day.

Of course, America has its own royalty, in the form of Miss America. The roots of the beauty contest probably go back to medieval Catholic May Day ceremonies, in which ceremonial queens were selected for their virtue. In the late nineteenth century, a number of midwestern cities created annual civic festivals that celebrated the features of their towns. The Denver Festival of Mountain and Plain was typical, and included a representation of the mythological contest in which Paris chose the fairest of three goddesses. (Aphrodite won, but only because she promised Paris the love of the world's most beautiful mortal, Helen of Troy.) Pasadena's Tournament of Roses is the most famous of these events now, and like so many others, it features a queen and her attendants. They are all single, unlike the original queens of Mardi Gras in New Orleans, who were upper-crust matrons, chosen by luck. The everyday version of the tradition is enacted in every high school that chooses a prom queen or a homecoming queen.

In fact, for much of the nineteenth century, contests to judge women purely on the basis of their looks were considered improper. A woman publicly displaying her physical charms came too close to prostitution. P. T. Barnum tried to mount a commercial pageant in 1854, well before most civic festivals came into being. He was willing to dower the winner if she was single, or give her a tiara if married, but no respectable women could be persuaded to enter the competition. Carnivals and dime museums ran beauty contests in the following years, but they were hardly considered family entertainment. The resort of Rehoboth Beach, Delaware, held a "Miss United States" contest in 1880. The entrants had to be single and under twenty-five, and were judged on their poise and grace as well as their looks and their outfits. The girls were referred to as "vestals," which suggests they were all honest spinsters. One of the three judges was Thomas Alva Edison, better known for his expertise in other fields.

Rehoboth Beach's contest was not repeated, but a group of businessmen came up with a similar notion in Atlantic City in 1921. A "Fall Frolic" mounted in 1920 was sufficiently successful to persuade the group to expand it for 1921. A series of beauty contests, for entrants in different categories, was added to parades and balls. Miss Margaret Gorman, age sixteen, of Washington, D.C., won the contest among the seven "civic beauties," i.e., amateurs (as opposed to "actresses, motion picture players, or professional swimmers" who were presumably accustomed to unveiling their limbs in public). In a runoff against the professional Miss Virginia Lee, the judges preferred Miss Gorman's juvenile charms. The next year, 1922, fifty-eight girls came to Atlantic City after having won local contests in their cities like Philadelphia, Los Angeles, and Toronto. Though the pageant went on hiatus from 1928 to 1933, it was back in force by the mid-thirties and in 1938, the coronation of Marilyn Meseke as Miss America was shown on newsreels in movie houses all over America.

The Miss America Pageant was first televised in 1954, entering into the complex network of media and commercial relationships that still sustains it. The wedding industry naturally participated. In 1961, Miss America Nancy Fleming modeled a Priscilla of Boston gown in the pages of *Modern Bride*. The pageant switched its allegiance to *Bride's* the following year when former Rockette Maria Beale Fletcher wore "another kind of crown—a beautiful coronet—authentically inspired by the official Miss America symbol and fashioned from lovely 'Ban Lon' Bridalace. Although she cannot marry during her reign, she, like young girls the world over, clearly envisions the day when she will be a radiantly happy bride. In her dream she is wearing the lovely wedding gown of 'Ban Lon' Bridalace shown on the opposite page." The gown, manufactured by midprice company Alfred Angelo, appeared both in a two-page advertising spread and a two-page editorial feature. The promotion was successful enough to be repeated the following year with the same players—Alfred Angelo, Miss America, and the manufacturer of synthetic Ban Lon fabrics—and expanded to include, in the subsequent issue of the magazine, Misses Texas, Wisconsin, South Carolina, and Hawaii, each modeling an Angelo gown available in bridal shops in her state. A similar configuration appeared in 1964 as well.

The coronation of Miss America was thus made equivalent to the coronation of each girl in her role as bride. And though by the 1960s America's beauty queen was selected in part for her talent and poise, there was no obscuring the subtext behind that and most other contests among women since Hera squared off against Aphrodite and Athena. It was all about the way she looked. The term "Miss America" had been used by illustrators to describe a certain kind of fresh young loveliness long before anybody proposed a pageant in Atlantic City. As the newly crowned beauty queen makes her weeping way down the catwalk in Atlantic City, and as the bride paces toward the altar on her father's arm, each is profoundly aware of one fact: everyone is looking at *her*. For most women, their walk up the aisle as a bride is the only time they will know that heady assurance. It is the moment she will come closest to being America's sweetheart, the popular girl, the chosen. Kitty Hanson, in an unusually skeptical view of the wedding industry published in 1967 called *For Richer, For Poorer,* writes that, "For today's brides, the wedding is the big production number just before the end of the movie, the scene where all the attention is focused on the star. For this day, this moment, all eyes are on her, her hair, her gown; everyone is concentrating on how she looks, moves, and speaks. This wedding production provides each girl with a chance to stand out on her own."

In an era of conformity like the early 1960s, standing out wasn't easy to achieve. *Bride's* Miss America features reassured its readers by pointing out that, however gorgeous and celebrated the beauty queen might be, what she *really* wanted was to be in their shoes: to be getting married. A tiara might mark you as royal or special, but at the end of her reign, Miss America would happily swap it for the regalia of a bride. "Mrs.," after all, was the lasting title, and the one that really counted.

It stands to reason that the Miss America contestants' participation in *Bride's* consisted of modeling wedding gowns. Naturally, as beautiful women, that was what they would do. Just as Miss America's crown was her trademark, the white gown was the trademark of the bride. And the postwar years in America comprised the era in which the wedding gown became totemic.

Miss America of 1954 flanked by her runners-up looks more like a Valkyrie than
a bride. The title of "Mrs." would have to wait until she
relinquished her Miss America crown.

The process may have begun during World War II.
There's no way to estimate whether American servicemen
really cared about white wedding gowns the way the media
claimed they did. If asked, they probably would not have vol-
unteered that they were fighting for the right to a grand formal wedding. Yet the white dress seems to have picked up
some emotional freight during the war. It may have symbol-

ized normalcy to eager brides and grooms. It may have been a status symbol that brides' families could only afford because they were flush with wartime savings. It may simply have been forbidden—or at least hard to obtain, with wartime fabric limitations—fruit, and thus more desirable. It is certainly during this period that the white wedding dress emphatically took leave of everyday fashion and became a costume.

No development like this is ever sudden, of course. Through the 1930s many bridal gowns had been constructed with removable jackets or trains so that a woman was left with a stunning white evening gown for her married social life. After the war, though, bridal fashions didn't keep up with the normal cycles of style. Sweetheart necklines, for instance, disappeared from street clothes in the 1940s but kept appearing in wedding gowns, a "romantic" motif that wouldn't go away. Satin, too—that emblematic bridal fabric—hung on long after civilian clothes had followed fashion's inevitable cycle and gradually gone matte. Formal photographs and stills from movie weddings through the 1940s show over and over the combination of satin-clad bride surrounded by bridesmaids in voile, marquisette, or other lusterless fabrics. In 1945 and '46, the separation of bridal from nonbridal style became more explicit with a rash of quotations from earlier eras. Hoopskirted wedding gowns appeared, sometimes paired with pantalettes. Full skirts were inflated further with bustles or panniers. Ordinary evening clothes were still mostly vertical and broad-shouldered, but brides suddenly looked like extras from *Gone With the Wind*. By 1952, *Bride's* had taken notice: "Your wedding dress is the only costume that can borrow from any flattering fashion in history." There—it was officially a costume.

For a while in the 1950s the bridal silhouette paralleled the New Look–influenced lines of fashionable clothes, with a snug bodice and a full skirt. It is irresistible to point out the parallel between postwar neo-Victorian attitudes toward gender roles and the neo-Victorian look of the era's clothes. The tight, breast-emphasizing tops and full, fertility-suggesting skirts invoked a man-pleasing style of femininity. Even cosmetics followed suit for a while as strong Joan Crawford red lips and nails were replaced by demure pinks and corals, at least for the wedding. In the spring of 1948, *Bride's* urged its readers to aim for a "decorous emphasis on fragile pink makeup, pearl pink nails . . . blush pink lips." None of that assertive "Fire and Ice" for the virginal girls in white!

The nature of fashion is to change, so the suggestive New Look relaxed into a more modern, minimal style as the 1950s went on. Not in bridal gowns, though. By the spring 1954 issue of *Bride's* all the clothes advertised for the trousseau are vertical in line: the skirts of the wedding dresses stay full. In 1956, an editorial description in *Bride's* says a gown "must adhere to a beloved tradition—one that is forever loyal to a snug little fitted bodice, a huge skirt. . . ." In 1959, it's "tiny-waisted bodices and an exaggeration of whispering skirts." (Satin, finally, had given way to matte fabrics, with lace and nylon tulle in the ascendant.) In 1960, skirts might be as full as four yards around. This was, by then, the bridal look, all but frozen in time. Not style, but tradition. As Eric Hobsbawm points out in *The Invention of Tradition,* it's when an object loses its real-life utility that it's free to take on traditional meaning. The less a wedding dress resembles current fashion, the more emphatic its bridal significance.

Needless to say, these dresses were not intended to be reworn. Manufacturers sometimes paid lip service to the notion of a practical wedding gown for more than one use. As in the 1930s, these notions involved uncovering the upper body and removing the train to leave a "dinner dress" or "dance dress." These were usually less formal gowns, made of lighter fabrics like organdy rather than the telegraphically bridal delustered satin or heavy, matte peau de soie (which, combined with alençon lace, shrieks "bridal" to this day). However, there was a tremendous amount of "dream come true" rhetoric to counter practicality. "Your wedding is your once-in-a-lifetime opportunity to bring your dearest dream to life," *Bride's* announced. "Only a bride," a 1962 ad pointed out, could wear a trained white dress with a veil. The wedding gown was "the only ensemble that is designed for one occasion alone, for one purpose and one day." Well, of course. You sold more dresses if each and every bride had to have one. Obviously millions of girls did fall for the bridal industry's eloquence, so it's a relief to hear of one group of practical brides Kitty Hanson mentions in *For Richer, For Poorer.* The Le Boeuf Company of East Orange, New Jersey, offered in the 1960s a wedding-gown restoration service. It cleaned, preserved, and stored your gown after wearing. An official with the company told Hanson of their growing bewilderment when the same very simple white dress passed through their hands nine times. On each occasion, it had been worn by a different girl in a different part of the country. Finally, the puzzle was solved: the girls were all "hostesses" with American Airlines, handing down a wedding dress from bride to bride until it literally fell apart. Not the fate of most wedding gowns, falling apart. Even less is it the fate of the dread bridesmaids' dress, which suffered a similar divorce from normal styles at around the same time as its white cousin.

If in the 1920s brides were just beginning to consider

their weddings as pageantry, by the postwar era that consideration was taken for granted. Marjorie Binford Woods's 1942 manual *Your Wedding: How to Plan and Enjoy It* is very blunt about the maids' role. Though she felt eight girls was enough (more looked like the Rockettes), they had better be decorative. "Bridesmaids, like ladies in waiting, furnish the colorful backdrop to your wedding pictures, so the prettier the girls, the lovelier the wedding." So much for the original purposes of bridesmaids: confusing evil spirits or expressing virgin solidarity.

The virginal imperative was fading anyway. When Nellie Wilson married in 1914, her sister Jessie served as matron of honor, a rather novel idea. In studio-run Hollywood, a movie star's attendants were often chosen from the studio's ranks of girls who needed a little exposure. Constance Talmadge and Bebe Daniels stood up for Vilma Banky in 1928, while Marion Davies served as bridesmaid for both Norma Shearer and Edith Mayer (daughter of Louis Mayer, MGM's irascible boss). Edith and her sister Irene were bridesmaids for Norma, too—it was all very cozy. Cecil Beaton was thrilled to be an onlooker at the marriage of movie star Bessie Love in 1930. "Rather naively," he confided to his diary, "I still believed that most bridesmaids were virgins. But perhaps they realised they couldn't find enough; so the retinue had been culled from the bride's friends, both married women and divorcées. Norma Shearer crept toward the altar, looking chiselled from alabaster. Her unseeing eyes stared out of a flawlessly complexioned face. Bebe Daniels, once a Mack Sennett bathing beauty and now a big star, walked behind Blanche Sweet, the maid of honour." The word *maid* was obviously being used quite loosely at that point. John Wayne and Josephine Saenz (the daughter of the Panamanian consul in Los Angeles) wed in 1933 in Loretta Young's garden. Young was maid of honor, though she had been married three years earlier. Apparently her short-lived elopement to actor Grant Withers (annulled) didn't count.

By the postwar era, no one cared whether or not brides-maids were virgins, married, younger, or older than the bride. (The sole remaining taboo was that they not be visibly preg-nant: this was apparently too explicit a reference to the pro-ceedings of the wedding night.) Serving as bridesmaid for your female friends became a standard social rite of passage, to the extent that by 1961, only two years after her introduc-tion, Barbie was equipped with a bridesmaid's dress. A yellow strapless sheath worn with a lacy full-skirted overdress, it was quite a bit more chic and imaginative than what the average attendant got stuck with. Of course Barbie's costume design-ers generally did very well by their client—the same could not be said of the folks who made bridesmaids' dresses.

The maids' portion of the bridal apparel industry didn't take shape until after well after World War II. Before the mid-fifties, the closest thing to an ad for a bridesmaids' dress showed a simple informal wedding gown that was also avail-able in a few pastel colors. Gradually, more variety was of-fered. *Bride's* began featuring a few maids' gowns in each issue. Until this point, bridesmaids had often worn custom-made outfits, but the spread of synthetic fabrics and factory-made dresses brought a new ease to the process of getting those girls kitted out in their uniforms. Instead of riffling through patterns and purchasing fabric and requiring maids to submit to fittings (especially difficult if they lived in differ-ent towns), a bride could just select a dress from her bridal salon and order six or eight of them in the appropriate sizes. Best of all, the offerings were not terribly expensive. Emily Kimbrough, the novelist famous for writing *Our Hearts Were Young and Gay,* contributed to the fall 1954 issue of *Bride's* an article comparing her daughters' weddings and her own in 1927. She regards as a "blessing" the improvement in options for the maids. "My wedding dress was made to order, and hideously expensive. Ditto the veil and bridesmaids' dresses. A famous Chicago store prided itself on a service bureau where wedding gowns and maids' dresses could be ordered from sketches and sample materials. A bridesmaids' dress I wore at a wedding in which I participated cost $125, the hat $50. It was made to order and did not fit." Her daughters' maids wore off-the-rack dresses that cost only thirty-five dollars and coronets of roses in their hair.

Of course, this was also the dawning era of the hideous bridesmaids' dress, plague of every popular girl. Manufacturers and the bridal magazines always claimed, and *still* claim, that these garments can find meaningful existence beyond the reception. Attempts are constantly made to create bridesmaids' frocks that somehow convert to normal dresses. In the late 1950s, for instance, as skirts deflated and stylish women appeared in sheath dresses, the slow-moving bridal world offered bridesmaids sheath dresses with removable full overskirts. The idea was that maids with their no-longer-stylish full skirts would resemble the bouffant-skirted bride for the duration of the wedding, and whip off the overskirt to reveal the sheath dress for cocktail parties at a later date. (In an especially gruesome example, the overskirt was also recommended for use as a cape.)

The problem was partly the fabrics. Traditionally, a maid

Outfitting bridesmaids became an important part of the wedding industry after the war, when brides like this one got their eight best friends to accompany them up the aisle. For this wedding of the early 1950s, though, the maids' gowns were probably made to order.

pays for her own outfit, which includes matching shoes and, well into the 1970s, some kind of vestigial headgear. In order to keep the prices of these gowns reasonable, manufacturers are limited to less-expensive materials. The colors and textures may not be especially subtle. What's more, uniformity is the essence of the exercise. A good-hearted bride must select a dress that will be equally flattering to all of her attendants, who may differ considerably in size and shape. And the attendants are, after all, not much more than background for the bride. The individuality that each woman ordinarily expresses in her own clothes must be foregone. The bridesmaids' dress is a costume just as much as the wedding gown, which is why maids had to have *something* on their heads for so long after women stopped wearing hats in houses of worship. A wedding is not real life, it's a ritual event, and the participants need to look different from the witnesses. How do you pick the maids out of the crowd on the dance floor at the reception? They're the ones in salmon pink taffeta with baby's breath in their hair. Attendants in near-normal clothes at a formal wedding tend to look strikingly underdressed.

Not that the bridal industry hasn't tried, over the years, to respond to attendants' complaints about their outfits. Year in and year out, their ads hopefully proclaim that they've licked the "wear-again" problem. In the late 1960s, they tried to achieve this by responding to the new freedom in fashion. In the August/September 1967 issue of *Bride's,* the attendants' options included dresses in knee-length pleated crepe, full-length brocade—and one tangerine chiffon number that was actually culottes. By the 1970s manufacturers were offering numerous alternatives to the conservative dignity of the loose A-line bridesmaids' gown in a yummy color. Unfortunately, the "fashionable" options looked worse than the stuffy ones. The Victorian revival (think granny gown) brought weskits, pinafores, eyelet, and taffeta to bridal salons. Quilting was in fashion, briefly, and appeared in bulky dirndl skirts. Then there were the informal selections: Lurex turtlenecks paired with long velveteen skirts, or plaid skirts with velveteen blazers. The struggle to be groovy got feverish, resulting in ventures like denim gowns trimmed with lace, or T-shirt dresses in boldly colored Qiana. The nadir, however, was reached in 1975 with a full-length, long-sleeved blue chambray number sashed, collared, and cuffed in red and white. The bodice and sleeves were embroidered all over with a pattern incorporating the letters M and S—"Ms," "Ms," "Ms." It was enough to make turquoise chiffon look good.

CHAPTER 8

An Immense and Highly Organized Industry

"A WEDDING WITH ALL THE TRIMMINGS" • THE PROFESSIONALS
TAKE OVER • "BASIC BUYS" • "FROM A GARMENT INTO A
SYMBOL" • MANUFACTURING DREAMS • "FOR SHEER MAGNIFI-
CENCE . . ." • GOOD TASTE, BAD TASTE • PICTURING IT ALL

The basic theme of Edward Streeter's novel *Father of the Bride,* faithfully repeated in the film version, is that Kay Banks's insistence on a formal white wedding tosses her family into a whirlwind of unprecedented spending—which, in the end, is justified by the emotional catharsis of the wedding itself. (This made both book and film the perfect apologia for the still-developing wedding industry.) Much of the humor derives from the perfect masculine naïveté Mr. Banks exhibits at every turn, and from the artless ease with which his womenfolk manipulate him. Kay, offered fifteen hundred dollars to elope, protests, "Why, you *know* Mom would *die* if I didn't have a wedding with all the trimmings. I guess I would too. Not have any *friends* to see me get married—and all the people I've grown *up* with. Why, it wouldn't be getting married, Pops." Ellie, in turn, reminisces wistfully about the simplicity of her own wedding. Banks never stands a chance. Even less can he hope to control the commercial forces unleashed by Kay's nuptial plans. "[H]e suddenly appeared to be the sole customer of an immense and highly organized industry. He reminded himself of the Government during the war. 'Keep those production lines moving for Banks. Get the finished goods to him. . . . We're all behind you, Banks; behind you with caterers, photographers, policemen, dressmakers, tent pitchers—behind you with champagne and salads and clothes and candid cameras and potted palms and orchestras and everything it takes to win a wedding.'"

Ellie Banks handles all of these entities with aplomb, confirming her husband's long-held suspicion that she is "a natural-born purchasing agent." In 1948, she didn't have much choice. For an upper-middle-class woman, the option of sewing her daughter's gown or arranging the flowers for the church had long since vanished. This left the mother of the bride coping with vendors of all those goods and services cited by Banks. Some department stores, it's true, offered a kind of consulting service in their bridal departments. In addition to helping a bride choose her china, crystal, silver, linens, and trousseau from among the store's offerings, the consultant might recommend a caterer or a photographer, or answer questions of protocol. Mary E. Lewis, author of *The Marriage of Diamonds and Dolls,* advised the readers of her 1947 book on "How a Bridal Secretary Can Help You." She claimed that there were about five hundred bridal consultants in the country, working out of the "best retail stores in America." Their services, she said, extended to dressing the bride at the church and sending the wedding announcement to the newspapers. But five hundred consultants could make scarcely a dent on the nearly two million weddings of 1947. It's also worth noting that the comically intimidating Franck, the bridal consultant in the 1991 remake of *Father of the Bride,* was merely a snooty caterer in the book and the first movie. Wedding planners were just not that common yet.

By 1954, when Emily Kimbrough had married off her daughters and written about it for *Bride's,* the existence of "the lady who will take over the whole business" was better established. "Her services include the securing and arranging for all the other services." Kimbrough acknowledges that it is stubbornness alone that put her in charge of "the florist, the caterer, the man in charge of parking cars, [and] Omar the tent-maker, who set up in my modest garden a marquee under which a circus only a little smaller than Mr. Ringling's might have performed. . . ." *Bride's,* in 1965, acknowledged that "so bewildering can be the labyrinth of details surrounding a wedding and reception" that a family would do well to avail itself of professional planning help.

This development marked two changes in the nature of the wedding industry. The first, relatively minor, is that the customer's point of contact with the industry had shifted since the 1930s. Before World War II, jewelers and fine gift stores purveyed expertise about weddings—which was often limited to the protocol governing the invitations and a kind of rudimentary gift registry. It was not until the expansive days of the 1950s and '60s that putting on a wedding became a logistical feat involving a set of vendors like caterers and florists and custom dressmakers who were new to the middle-class family. This was the other great change in weddings, a change that had come about gradually since the 1920s—the professionalization of an event that had begun as a homegrown effort. Where once the refreshments at the reception had consisted of the proudest culinary efforts of family and friends, caterers now produced the elaborate cake and the trays of tea sandwiches or canapés that were passed among the throng by hired waiters. In the 1930s, the bride had been driven to the church in the family car; in 1948, the Banks family rides in two gleaming black limousines. The modest at-home wedding for the upper middle class gave way to the tent-in-the-backyard model, in which hundreds of people were entertained with champagne and dancing. Of course, consumers needed help sorting out florists and orchestras and photographers. And it was only natural for the consultants in department stores and bridal salons to step in, whether formally or informally. Their expertise in all matters bridal was what made them authorities, and it was their authority that made them effective salespeople. Needless to say, they never lost sight of the fact that a wedding was first and foremost a sales opportunity.

The concept of a registry for wedding gifts was apparently still a difficult one for the American bride to accept, despite the prewar efforts to promote the notion. As more and more guests came to give gifts to the bride, the burden of furnishing the newlyweds' first home was lifted somewhat from the bride's family. No longer did a new wife come to her husband with a lifetime's worth of hand-hemmed sheets, and no longer were wedding gifts limited to the decorative. By the 1950s a couple expected that some of their more everyday requirements, like china or glassware, would be provided as presents from friends and family. But registering for these items flew in the face of traditional etiquette. For one thing, it smacked of asking for a gift—always taboo. A wedding registry also broke the seal of secrecy about the value of gifts. If a girl registered for a pair of crystal elephant-shaped bookends, she knew that they cost twenty dollars. If her fiancé's aunt and uncle gave them to her, she knew that they'd spent twenty dollars on a gift (no mean sum in the late 1940s). It took years of concerted effort and advertising by department stores to bring brides to an understanding and acceptance of the registry. Throughout the 1940s (with less emphasis, to be sure, during the war), *Bride's* was full of ads that laboriously explained the merits of the system. In 1942, Carson, Pirie Scott of Chicago devoted a full page to the problem, with a facsimile of the form a bride should fill out and a headline reading, "Carson's Sees That You Get What You Want." The copy ran, "Etiquette still bars a bride from shouting preferences such as 'Give me Wishmaker's Modern Dinnerware,' but grandmother's bridal dilemma of staying silent and receiving 'seven coffee pots' is not for you. Just confide your hopes on anything from a silver pattern to a lamp motif in a trained Consultant from Carson's Gift Service." The training was important—increasing professionalization of the industry was a theme throughout these years.

So was education, especially consumer education. A wife's primary job, in the 1950s and '60s, was to keep house, raise children, and spend money correctly. The Depression was over, the economy was roaring, and buying what you wanted was the patriotic duty of every citizen. As a *Bride's* editorial trumpeted in 1945, "The only way that we can pay our tremendous war debt and the only way we can put our returning soldiers to work is to produce more and sell more . . . With a steady demand the wheels of production keep turning; men and women keep working. What you buy and *how* you buy it is very vital in your new life . . . and to our whole American way of living."

The immense power of the advertising industry was fully deployed in creating those desires. Throughout the 1950s and 1960s, advertising in the bridal magazines purported to be educational. Dense paragraphs of copy explaining workmanship and materials blanketed ad pages. Lenox china, Drexel furniture, and DuPont carpets all set out to enlighten the bride and secure her home-furnishing dollars. A mattress ad of 1961 preyed on the newlywed's anxiety, asking the reader to rate whether or not she was a "good wife." Did she balance her husband's nutrition? Encourage him to exercise? A good wife "doesn't talk about wanting a swimming pool until her husband has at least finished paying for the new second car." Instead, she "makes her money go further by informing herself on the products she buys . . ," including, naturally, a Koylon foam rubber mattress.

So there was the bride-to-be, new diamond gleaming from her finger, wedding six months in the future, with a major project before her. As *Bride's* said in 1953, "We know that you must select a wedding costume, bridesmaids' dresses, a wardrobe, lingerie, and furnishings for a brand new home. We know that you have never had to buy so much before, nor ever will again, within such a short space of time. . . ." The cover of a 1961 issue shouted "YOUR NEW HOME Basic buys in SILVER CHINA GLASS LINENS FURNITURE CARPETS GIFTS SHOWERS." It was no wonder Mr. Banks began to feel queasy. His apprehension of the "immense and highly organized industry" was faintly prescient but accurate—up to a point.

In some respects, the wedding industry (strictly speaking, the businesses that provide the goods and services for the wedding itself) can never really be highly organized because too many of its components are by definition local. Caterers cannot travel very far or their chicken roulades will spoil. Nor can florists, limousine companies, or tent and rental outfits, all of whom have to transport bulky (and, in the case of flowers, highly perishable) items. At the very top end of the market, photographers like Bradford Bachrach and bandleaders like Lester Lanin have been able to establish enough of a reputation so that brides' families will pay their travel expenses. Martha Stewart started her career as a caterer and was hired for weddings as far afield from her Connecticut headquarters as Quebec and Texas. Most brides, though, will still choose from local vendors except in the matter of their gowns. Even there, though manufacturers are national, the small, local retailer still holds a significant place in the bridal market. The national discount chain David's Bridal is a relatively new entry in the field.

Despite the fragmentation of the industry and its dominance by very small businesses, there is still a distinct bridal industry that identifies itself as such, and it reached this level of identity in the postwar era. To be sure, the Bridal and Bridesmaids Apparel Association had been in existence for years—this body successfully lobbied the War Production Board to permit relaxation of fabric rationing on wedding gowns during the war. By 1948, Brides House, Inc., the publishers of *Bride's* magazine, had diversified a little and offered ancillary products, *The Bride's Reference Book* and *The Bride's Notebook*. (Though bookstores are crammed with wedding planners today, this was a new notion in 1948.) The company's slogan was now "Publishers to the Brides of America."

General awareness of brides as a special consumer group was emphatically signaled by a survey performed in 1958 entitled *The Bridal Market*. The publishers of the study, National Analysts, Inc., pointed out to potential advertisers how much money brides and their families had, how much education, how they typically spent their money. They made the point that readers of *Bride's* magazine tended to plan longer engagements than other brides, which gave them, presumably, more time to spend money on products advertised in the magazine. The most startling information gleaned from this survey of some twelve hundred brides was that National Analysts predicted $235 million worth of potential honeymoon sales per year for all American brides, and another $1.5 billion in home furnishings and household products—in 1958 dollars. By 1967, Kitty Hanson claimed that the nationwide wedding industry produced an annual $7.2 billion dollars worth of revenue, $3 billion of which was "directly related to the wedding day itself."

National Analysts wanted to show how lucrative the bridal market was, while Hanson thought this level of expenditure was ridiculous. A survey produced by the Bridal and Bridesmaids Apparel Association (BBAA) in 1966 was unintentionally comical in its attempt to demonstrate that formal weddings had an effect on divorce rate. The study was commissioned in 1965 and claimed that of two thousand first-time brides over eighteen years of age who were married in long dresses, a mere 5.9 percent had divorced. Of those first-time brides who wore short or street-length dresses, 12.3 percent had divorced—proof, the BBAA proposed, that the investment in a big formal wedding was symptomatic of a "deep psychological commitment" to the married state.

Well, maybe—and maybe not. But it's undeniable that the single emblematic object of a wedding, the item that shouts "Bride!" is the long white dress. Various cultures have their white-dress ceremonies for women: fifteen-year-old Latin girls celebrate their *quinceañero,* which often prefigures the wedding, while upper-middle-class girls appear to "society" as debutantes. Both ceremonies are coming-of-age rituals. Catholic girls traditionally make their first communion wearing white. For graduations from certain schools, white dresses are de rigueur for girls instead of academic gowns. We have seen how Queen Victoria's example brought the white dress to prominence as the desirable costume for a bride and how it was adopted by the upper classes in the late nineteenth century. Upward mobility, media celebration of lavish weddings both real and fictional, and a rising standard of living for the middle class—as well as a refreshing simplification of the dresses themselves—brought the white dress into reach for more women in the 1920s and 1930s. It is the postwar era, though, that made the long white wedding dress the icon it is. With a snug bodice and a full skirt, a veil, and perhaps a train, the classic gown no longer represents virginity or fragility or purity or any of those once-desirable feminine attributes. The long white dress now simply signifies the bride. It was the developments of the 1950s and '60s that turned the gown from a garment into a symbol, by making it available at any price point to every girl who wanted to have her princess moment.

Much is made in the bridal literature of the transformative power of a wedding gown. Brides are urged to fall in love with their gowns, to choose a dress that expresses their inner character, to live out their childhood dreams. Wedding dresses, we are frequently told, release some inner quality of fantasy in the most pragmatic and unromantic of women. Hard-driving professionals enter a salon looking for a tailored gown and leave having chosen a bouffant number with a tulle skirt. Women gripped by doubts about the merits of a formal wedding reconsider once they slip into some white satin. Most convincingly, men and women who work in the bridal industry, more skeptical than the average bride-to-be, tend to confirm the cliché, saying over and over again, "When the girl puts on the right dress, she *knows*." (Brides are always "girls" in bridal salons.) Even the feminist writer Naomi Wolf, in an essay called "Brideland," confirms the unreasonable grip on the psyche that this white gown possesses.

Part of its power comes from simple tradition—even if that tradition is more recently formed than the industry would have us believe. It is not true that generation after generation of women have stood at altars in white dresses to make their vows. Still, for most of the women marrying today, it *is* true that their mothers did. Some brides wear a gown or a veil that has adorned another family member. Some brides borrow a dress from a friend. So personal is this connection that each of the women who worked on Princess Elizabeth of England's wedding gown embroidered a strand of her own hair into the gown, as a way of embodying her good wishes for the princess bride. Wedding dresses link us to other women who have done as we are doing. Edward Streeter, in *Father of the Bride,* takes his tongue out of his cheek for a moment as Stanley Banks prepares to walk his daughter up the aisle toward her groom. "A thousand generations of women were standing behind Kay now. For a mystic instant she was a generic part of that selfless, intuitive race. . . ."

Kay Banks was, in the thinking of her era, fulfilling a woman's destiny as she became a bride. Elizabeth Taylor as the film's Kay Banks, in the very flower of her spectacular beauty, was splendid. The white satin bodice of her Helen Rose–designed gown, with deep tucks from her shoulders to her waist and the dramatically deep neckline filled in with exquisite lace, looked virginal and regal, untouchable and sexual, the epitome of 1950s womanhood. Two weeks before the film's release, marrying hotel heir Nicky Hilton, she had worn another Helen Rose gown of white satin, this time with pearl-beaded white organza to veil her lush décolletage. It was nothing short of an apotheosis, as the movie star took the only step that could add to her luster, and became a wife. This was also the only step that most American girls could take that would approach anything Elizabeth Taylor ever did. And if Helen Rose had nothing whatever to do with their dresses, they would still look, on the whole, like Liz Taylor's.

The first step in the definitive democratization of the white wedding gown was the development and, more important, refinement of synthetic fabrics. Rayon had been invented in 1920, and became immediately popular: production of the fabric in U.S. mills increased from eight million pounds to fifty-three million pounds in only five years. The invention of nylon in 1938 had a profound effect on wedding gear since it was used not only for stockings (by 1940) but also, after the war, for the crinolines that kept skirts full, for imitation silk tulle veiling, and for endless varieties of machine-made lace that successfully mimicked the priceless handmade silk stuff.

It was the war, of course, that brought synthetic fabrics to greater prominence because silk simply couldn't be had. Rayon satin was the mainstay fabric during the early '40s, often woven in a special, heavy "bridal" weight. By 1947, silk was again available, but only for the most expensive gowns. Why would a girl bother, when the synthetics were so appealing? Further technical advances brought the introduction of (and the advertising campaigns for) a series of new options. A company called Skinner made the benchmark heavy rayon satin, but other mills produced satins with names like "Step Forward" (from Burlington) and "Bridal March" (Celanese)

Elizabeth Taylor in *Father of the Bride* was the model bride of the postwar era. In fact, her actual wedding to Nicky Hilton preceded the film's premiere by just two weeks and the gowns for both events were designed by MGM costumier Helen Rose.

as well as "Reprise" taffeta, "Paris" faille, and "Parliament" brocade. The price differentials were significant: a Saks ad in 1950 featured a long-sleeved, trained satin gown that cost $250 in silk and $185 in rayon. By 1960, gowns might be available in a whole range of fabrics, from silk gros de londres (a heavy ribbed material with a lustrous finish) at $290 to Skinner's "Bouquet" taffeta for only $165.

Fabric, though, represents only part of the cost of a wedding gown. Manufacturing is the other significant element. And like the range of materials available, it changed significantly after the Second World War. Until 1945, there were only twelve or fifteen companies manufacturing wedding dresses in the United States. More common by far was the custom dressmaking arrangement, whether carried out at a department store or at a bridal salon. The mass manufacture of wedding gowns did not take off until the late 1940s and early 1950s, when the swelling numbers of women marrying made the enterprise worthwhile.

Even so, buying a wedding dress is not like buying any other dress. The discount chains that have sprung up in the late twentieth century replicate the everyday retail experience, when you leave the store with a garment in your hand. Traditionally, choosing a bridal gown is a special process, reminiscent of the custom dressmaking model from which it's descended. Bridal salons within department stores began developing in the 1930s and 1940s. Instead of choosing fabric and pattern in the custom sewing department, a bride would pick from a number of available models of gowns. Her selection would be made to order following her measurements. Soon enough, accessories and bridesmaids' gowns were also available in the bridal departments. Stand-alone stores began

White satin was the trademark of the bride for decades. This photograph of Peggy Buttress (married in 1948) emphasizes the light-catching sheen of her long train. The sweetheart neckline was popular for brides long after it had faded from everyday use.

to appear at around the same time; one of the first was the Minissale Trousseau Salon in Philadelphia, which advertised in *Bride's* in 1940. It offered gowns, costumes for attendants and mothers, formal dresses for other occasions, as well as the services of a consultant who could order invitations, line up a photographer, recommend a caterer. Ready-to-wear gowns cost between thirty and seventy dollars: custom from forty to three hundred.

By the mid-'40s, department stores' bridal boutiques often carried a similar mix of custom designs and ready-to-wear. The atmosphere, however, was and remains very different from the rest of the store. Bridal departments are furnished with chairs, tables, and large, comfortable dressing rooms. The inventory is not usually hanging on racks for anyone to see—a few gowns may hint at the selection, but most are carefully hidden away, bagged in plastic. The intervention of the saleswoman is essential to the process. She sizes up the bride, literally and figuratively, then brings sample gowns to try.

The sample gowns, though, are not the actual dresses the brides wear. They are what their name says: samples. Each retail outlet, whether a department within a larger store or a small business, purchases samples from various manufacturers. A bride tries on a variety of gowns and her selection is cut and stitched for her. Depending on the price level of the dress she chooses, it may be one of a group of size eight ivory strapless sheaths that, say, Alfred Angelo is cutting on a given day—or it may indeed be made for her alone. At the highest prices, brides can order changes like sleeves added or subtracted, necklines or hems raised or lowered, trims switched or eliminated. Each factory alteration, of course, costs more.

The dresses are cut by machine and sewed by machine, sometimes in sizable batches. But even at the most modest price points, a wedding gown is closer to a custom-made garment than most other outfits a woman will wear. Some manufacturers manage to have most of their ornamentation applied by hand; the higher-end houses will actually cut gowns to a bride's individual measurements rather than to a standard size; and almost every bride undergoes the process of alterations that gives a dress an individual fit. This anomalous process of ordering, manufacturing, and alterations explains why bridal salons today require six months' lead time or longer—though in 1950, according to *Bride's* calendar feature, a girl needed only two months to select her gown and have it fitted.

This is the system that came into being in the postwar era. Lower prices were not the only advantages to this method—as *Bride's* pointed out in a 1956 article on a designer, the "luckless" prewar bride who bought a custom gown "had to spend long and tiresome hours at her dressmaker's." Nevertheless, price points were important. In the early 1950s a chain of stores called "Emily Fifth Avenue" advertised regularly in *Bride's*. Its slogan was "The Career Girls Store" and its prosaic locations (Hackensack, New Jersey; White Plains, New York) indicated that it served working girls shopping on their lunch hours. The gowns it advertised tended to be less grandiose than the regal white satin numbers, but they were unmistakably bridal. In 1951, for instance, one offering was a gown of nylon tulle and nylon Chantilly lace, with a full ballerina-length skirt and a shoulder-length veil. It cost only forty-five dollars, at a time when the middle range for formal gowns hovered around one hundred dollars. For a while in the late 1950s, *Bride's* ran a feature called "Dream-at-a-Price" that bundled together all the elements of a bride's outfit, from headpiece to shoes (and including the essential net petticoats, stockings, sometimes even gloves or imitation pearls) at a strikingly low price, usually under a hundred dollars.

For some girls, even that hundred dollars was beyond reach, but the white dress and all it stood for could still be theirs if they were willing to give it back when the weekend was over. New York's Lower East Side was home to several wedding gown rental shops that would purchase dresses from manufacturers in a few sizes. For twenty-five dollars, a girl could have the gown of her choice altered to fit her, and it would be in her possession from Friday until Monday. The bridal industry never acknowledged such arrangements, any more than they encouraged brides to wear their mother's gowns or slip off to a justice of the peace. (Legend has it that designer Priscilla Kidder, aka Priscilla of Boston, had a sign on her desk that read "Don't elope.")

Bride's did recognize, though, that there was still considerable difference in wedding standards between one locale or social group and another. It ran intermittent articles detailing the costs of various kinds of weddings: a small at-home ceremony, an intimate restaurant wedding in a big city, and the classic suburban tent-in-the-backyard model. One of the reasons the wedding as it is currently formulated (religious ceremony plus feast) has lasted for so long is that the tradition is infinitely flexible. As long as the form of each element generally corresponds to what the families and guests expect, they will be satisfied.

One big shift that reached most of the country in the postwar years was in the nature of the refreshments served at the wedding. Fashions in gowns may not have been monolithic in the postwar period but they were certainly consistent. Food, however, varied very widely among social groups. The least assimilated of immigrant families look to the old country for feasting standards both in the quantity of food and drink served and in its nature. Middle-class ideals in the 1950s and '60s were marked by such decorum and restraint that trays of tea sandwiches and cups of spiked punch, along with slices of wedding cake, were deemed a perfectly satisfying menu. (This is what the Banks family chooses in the novel *Father of the Bride,* even though the caterer sniffs, "Of course you can have what you wish, madam, but that is usually what we serve at children's parties.") For groups with closer ethnic ties, tea sandwiches would have seemed unbearably cheap—generosity and inclusion were far more important, and expressed via lavish portions of expensive dishes as well as sentimental favorites from the home country.

Before World War II, a catered event was primarily an upper-class phenomenon. In small towns or less prosperous groups, food for weddings tended to be contributed by family and friends of the bride, a kind of gala potluck. The wedding of Jean Winkelmann and Bob Hardy in small-town Nebraska, as recounted by Katherine Jellison in Ohio University's publication *Forum,* illustrates a kind of intermediate step. Jean Winkelmann was the daughter of Ella Bischoff, who had been married in Culbertson, Nebraska, in 1930. Jean grew up in a bigger town than Culbertson and her 1959 wedding was a far cry from her aunt Sophie's German farm wedding. As Jellison points out, "Do-it-yourself wedding receptions and dances were now a thing of the past." The reception for the Hardys consisted of a brunch held in the parish hall of the Lutheran church where the wedding took place, and the food was provided by a farm woman who had started a small catering business.

At this level, catering is a relatively easy business to enter, since the capital costs are quite low. Jean Winklemann's caterer was probably one of many who used her culinary skills to make a little money on the side. In 1948, the Department of Commerce reported that catering was a $66 million annual business, mostly industrial. By late 1964, *Catering* magazine described a $1.2 billion business employing 120,000 employees in 5,000 to 6,000 individual companies. A common pattern occurred when a GI came home from the war and married, often in the meeting hall of a fraternal order like the Elks or the Veterans of Foreign Wars. Frequently food for such weddings was provided by the group's Ladies' Auxiliary, if not by a church group—sometimes the local baker had diversified beyond wedding cakes into wedding feasts. It was apparently a logical step from customer to owner of such a business, as so-called "function halls" began to spring up across the country. They served a real need. John Modell's analysis of wedding habits in Minnesota shows that, while postwar urban brides and grooms could avail themselves of hotels or restaurants for their receptions, those in smaller towns frequently turned to their church reception rooms or a local catering hall.

The latter certainly offered more to the eager couple. It was hard to make a church room look like anything besides what it was—sometimes a big shoebox with a linoleum floor, acoustic tile ceiling, and an institutional paint color. The catering halls, especially by the mid-'60s and especially in the New York City area, provided fantasy. It was primarily a dream of grandeur, made inexpensive by economies of scale. These wedding palaces were vast, sometimes cycling as many as a dozen weddings through successive rooms with split-second timing. Moments before Wedding A moved from the chapel to the Venetian Room for cocktails, Wedding B left the Venetian Room for dinner in the Fountain Court. A common kitchen produced endless quantities of elaborate fare while discreet staff kept each event moving along at the requisite pace. Ideally, the illusion was maintained that each group was the only one holding a wedding that day. Some catering businesses assumed the mantle of the department store bridal secretaries and supplied every element of the wedding short of the gown. They could order invitations, secure an officiant, hire a photographer, even buy the rings and gifts for the attendants. Of course they could also arrange for flowers, but the decor at some of these establishments put nature to the blush. The Huntington Town House, in Huntington, Long Island, was one of *Bride's* magazine's faithful advertisers beginning in 1964. Its ad crowed, "This is the age of luxurious catering establishments . . . but for sheer magnificence, there just has never been anything like the new Huntington Town House. . . ." The ad went on to praise the "lovely country estate setting," the "custom designed crystal chandeliers, elegant wood paneling, palatial lobbies, French and Italian Provincial furnishings, cascading water displays, stone fireplaces and gradually ascending oval staircase." That staircase was to facilitate the climactic entry of the bride, unless she chose one of the even more dramatic methods of materializing, like the "Silhouette Walk," which made use of scrims, colored lights, and a revolving platform to produce an entrance worthy of Broadway, if not Las Vegas.

The "Silhouette Walk" was a startling effect, but the stakes were high. Larger venues allowed brides to invite more guests; more guests meant that people, quite simply, went to more weddings; and going to more weddings led inevitably to comparisons. Somehow the specialness and individuality leached out of the proceedings when you had spent every June weekend at Leonard's of Great Neck, enjoying the "Complete Reception with Champagne Toast." This is the kind of situation that prompts American commerce to ingenuity, and the extras (or excesses) of the late 1960s catering palaces boggle the mind. The halls had to redecorate constantly, of course, and purchase ever-new sets of "heavy gold encrusted china." In addition to the set menus at various prices (ranging from "chicken dinner" to "prime rib"), extras like a Vienna table of desserts or a breakfast service of eggs, crepes, and bagels could be served. Ice sculptures and champagne fountains were fairly predictable: to really wow guests you had to provide an orchid tree, with an orchid corsage for each female guest. At the very least, you could send every couple home with a copy of the next day's newspaper.

One way to look at these grand weddings of the 1960s is to say that they brought an element of fantasy to the weddings of girls from modest backgrounds. It was not at all uncommon for a bride's father to save for years in order to give her a grand send-off. It is notable, looking at the bridal fashions for 1960 and onward, that the simplest dresses cost the most. At the lower prices, brides insisted on a more elaborate and imposing fashion statement. While a rich girl would probably have plenty of chances to wear an evening dress again, this truly was a once-in-a-lifetime moment for a working-class bride and she wanted to make the most of it.

This temporary adoption of a more elaborate lifestyle made some bridal observers nervous. There had always been a strong current of disapproval in the bridal media of women who were considered to overreach their social station on their wedding day. In the 1960s, though, those censorious voices gained volume and the taste police grew very loud in their condemnation of the "Status Wedding." Kitty Hanson, author of *For Richer, For Poorer,* griped that "the sumptuous wedding has joined the mink coat, the mortgage, and the power boat as that visible 'proof' of financial and/or social superiority that is the chief preoccupation of the American middle-income class." She is particularly horrified by families who use the wedding as a business or professional event, though the nineteenth-century rhetoric about the sacredness and "delicacy" of the wedding ritual had long since been silenced.

Still, Hanson's ire can perhaps be forgiven when we remember what a throwback the formal wedding still was. Though no longer expressing the values of the Victorians, it clung to their forms, which was a source of confusion to the many families who were newly able to afford this kind of celebration. The upper class in America retained some of the formalities of the previous centuries, and did so nowhere more than at a wedding. A Park Avenue bride whose mother went to charity balls knew all about receiving lines and the exact difference between black tie and white tie for men. A bride whose father worked on the line at Ford Motors needed help with these irrational rituals and distinctions. Bridal consultants filled in some of the gaps, as did etiquette books, and *Bride's* did its level best to maintain the standards of yesteryear, but they were all just damming a dike with their thumbs. "Good taste" often made no sense. If your sister was pregnant, why *shouldn't* she be your matron of honor? Why should your wedding announcement not mention how you met your fiancé? What the heck was *wrong* with throwing the garter? In *Bride's* magazine's "Etiquette Question and Answer" feature (which appeared regularly from the early 1960s), the question of response cards enclosed with invitations came up at least annually. Brides wanted to use them, *Bride's* forbade it: "Although frequently done, the use of reply cards is in very poor taste: It is an insult to your guests, implying that they are incapable of composing a correct reply to a formal invitation." Since the correct reply to a formal invitation is written in the third person, centered and spaced so as to reflect the wording of the invitation, only people brought up to the usage knew how to do it. The magazine is actually comical in its horror of tacky decor: "The only word of caution concerns the over-cute gimmick-napkins scrolled with lovey nicknames (save 'kitten' for your hours alone together) or—in the decorative line—an oppressive swelling of pink hearts." This was a 1960 diktat, but as early as 1958, "Joan Cook, Bluebook for Brides" was advertising bridal merchandise like honeycomb tissue paper wedding bells with place cards affixed, plastic cake toppers, satin ring pillows lavishly encrusted with lace and ribbons, and discreet aluminum cases for douching equipment. *Bride's* might not sanction such tackiness but, clearly, there was a market for it anyway.

It seems obvious that on the etiquette front, the magazine was behind the times, so it is all the more surprising that, during the 1960s, it entered a halcyon phase of editorial service. Some of the coy locutions left over from the 1930s were axed: brides were referred to as "women" rather than "girls" and the B-word was no longer capitalized, as it had been since 1934. Useful advice on renting apartments, health insurance, birth control, sexual fulfillment, balancing a career and marriage, and the changing roles of women shared the pages of the magazine with the ever-present photographs of long peau de soie gowns trimmed with alençon lace. But still, the view on manners was far more conservative even than the gowns. By the mid-1960s, the magazine was showing eye-popping options like lace-ruffled bridal jumpsuits and hot pants modeled with clear go-go boots, while still ranting about engraved invitations: "the only correct colors are white, ivory or cream, with absolutely no decorations such as borders, flower sprays and so on. . . . It is not permissible to use semi-prepared forms or colored inks."

Permissible is a pretty strong word for what was, after all, a matter of taste. But the fuss over etiquette issues and "status weddings" reveals some real discomfort at the class confusion of the postwar era. A wedding is a time to stake your claim to social position, and Old Money was aghast at the flood of New Money mimicking patrician weddings in factory-like catering halls or cheerless hotel ballrooms. Hence the insistence on arcana, especially prominent in the fixation on the engraved invitation. If New Money spent freely and obviously, Old Money spent inscrutably, insisting that invitations be engraved by hand, no substitutes accepted. Although a process like thermoplating produced the distinctive raised script of hand engraving, it cost a fraction of the real thing. The giveaway was the slight indentation on the back of the invitation, and canny matrons knew to turn cards over in a raking light to check their authenticity. The important thing was, the right people could tell the difference.

The mark of the Old Money wedding, in fact, tended to be what it *didn't* have. No master of ceremonies welcoming "for the first time, Mr. and Mrs. George Rose!" No chafing dishes full of ziti. No children ("seen but not heard," remember?). No folk dances, no gifts of money to the bride. Wedding presents, in fact, were likely to be on the stingy side among the upper middle class. Overall, their attitude toward wedding planning was a casual sense that this was just another big party, not much out of the normal, and that making a fuss was déclassé. Of course Dad owns his tuxedo—in fact, it's a little battered from wear. Yes, Frances is wearing her mother's dress, doesn't it look lovely? Even though her great-grandmother's veil *is* terribly fragile. . . . Oh, we'll put the tent in the orchard, where it always goes.

A wedding is not just a routine party, though, as the role of photography in the proceedings demonstrates. The maturing wedding industry had made formal white weddings available to an ever-broader social spectrum, and the media had played a part in demonstrating what all these weddings looked like. Wedding stories were a staple of *Life* during the 1950s and 1960s, running the gamut from thorough coverage of White House weddings to a feature on a sixth-grade teacher from Gary, Indiana, whose students were honored guests at her ceremony. Candid wedding photographs also had a lasting effect, though, on the structure of the wedding day itself.

Before the 1930s, the enduring photographic records of a wedding were formal portraits. At their most elaborate, they'd include the entire wedding party, but the only activity of a wedding day to be recorded on film was "posing for pictures." Candid photography expanded that repertoire: soon mini-events like "leaving the church" and "getting into the limousine" and "cutting the cake" became part of the story. Instead of being displayed in frames, wedding pictures were bound into albums that formed a chronological narrative.

The use of small, light cameras allowed photographers to capture charming unscripted moments like this one at a 1950 wedding on Long Island.

Wedding photographers began to shoot from a list of expected situations—the bride dressing, the first dance, the bridesmaids catching the bouquet. After World War II, as candid photography flourished, it became clear that these were the shots that customers wanted in their albums. As Charles Wesley Lewis puts it, "The story of the wedding day did not develop individually with each new wedding event— the story was mostly that created by the photographer, not experienced by the couple. Routines were followed at each wedding; certain pictures were always taken so the story could unfold."

This innovation made it possible for brides and grooms to preserve the event with an unprecedented completeness. Not only the solemnity of the occasion, but also its festive highlights could now be made permanent. Favorite guests could be pointed out to photographers, still lifes taken of the wedding feast, unscripted moments of intimacy captured. Yet at the same time, in unexpected ways, the conventions of wedding photography have outsized influence on the rhythm of the wedding day. Since many houses of worship do not allow flash photography during a ceremony (and the presence of the photographer in the midst of the proceedings can only be a distraction), families must schedule extra time between service and reception to take the expected pictures of bride and groom with the officiant, lighting the unity candle, or kissing. Many couples like to have photographs taken at an outdoor location. These are experiences that are not, in themselves, significant and have nothing to do with two people vowing to spend their lives together. They take place only to ensure that the right pictures are in the album. This phenomenon is taken to an extreme in Japanese wedding parlors. Ofra Goldstein-Gidoni, author of *Packaged Japaneseness,* points out that many Japanese couples opt to include a "cake-cutting" at their wedding celebration although the "cake" is made of wax and the Japanese do not in any event eat cake. It's a photo opportunity and nothing more.

In the 1950s and '60s the exhaustive photographic recording of the wedding lay in the future, but the standardization of the American wedding was well under way. The growth of the wedding industry was partially responsible. In the days when wedding gowns were stitched by a local seamstress and cakes baked by a favorite aunt, there was little chance that one wedding would duplicate another. But if two girls from the same town both ordered their gowns from Josie's Bridal and had the deluxe reception at the Wedding Palace, who could tell the two events apart? The photographer-driven scripting of the wedding day actually nudged nuptials into a predictable sequence of events. As Charles Wesley Lewis points out, young couples often relied on the photographer to instruct them on the proceedings. The result was a degree of similarity, even predictability, in American weddings that hadn't been seen since the traditions began to form a hundred years earlier. In the conformist atmosphere of the earlier 1960s, this might have been seen as a virtue. But with a speed that left many Americans gasping, the cultural discourse changed directions. By the early 1970s the calm assurance guaranteed by following tradition gave way to a reflexive suspicion of the Establishment—headpiece, pearls, and all.

CHAPTER 9

Do Your Own Thing

SEX, DRUGS, AND WEDDINGS • WHY, THEN, MARRY AT ALL? •
THE SQUARE WEDDING • BRIDAL GOWNS GET GROOVY •
CARROT CAKE AND DAISIES • THE PEACOCK REVOLUTION
IN MENSWEAR • "AMERICA'S HAPPY COLOR!"

Fashion, that frivolous craft, has a way of signaling society's
preoccupations before we can begin to articulate them
ourselves, and observers who cringe at rising hemlines or
baggy pants may be responding as much to the significance as
to the aesthetics of new fashions. Headmistresses of the 1960s
who took rulers to schoolgirls' knees were not wrong to insist
their pupils roll their uniform kilts down—those bare thighs
were a sexual come-on, even if the fifteen-year-olds didn't know
it. Sex *was* in the air. And though we may think of "hippie"
fashion as expressing the social ferment of the late 1960s and
the '70s, the ferment had really begun in the early 1960s with
civil rights marches, antiwar protests, and the gradual erosion
of authority. While serious young men were marching in Birmingham wearing narrow ties and Superman glasses, women's
fashion was producing its own revolution. Rising hems were
the least of it. The invention of panty hose, eliminating stocking
tops and garters, permitted skirts to shrink, while a sleek silhouette brought to mind the flapper dresses of the 1920s. Ag-
gressively "modern" effects like Yves St. Laurent's Mondrian-
inspired shifts made a clean break from the ladylike fashions

of the late 1950s. In fact, as in the 1920s, the fashions and indeed the attitudes of the mid- to late 1960s suggested a repudiation of the previous era. If the years after World War II were neo-Victorian, the late '60s were neo–Jazz Age. War shadowed the period and created a sharp divide between generations, with the powerful demographic of the baby boomers wakening to its cultural power.

The youthquake left the elders feeling like stuffy squares, just like the dowagers marooned by the Roaring Twenties. The young wore outfits that were indecent or slovenly—hair, of all things, was a major flash point—and listened to loud, primitive music. Their dances looked like sex standing up. Kids in the twenties got drunk; kids in the sixties got stoned. Not all of society's changes were superficial, needless to say. It was a new era of activism and optimism. Major gains in civil rights were accompanied by concerted efforts to address another one of society's remaining inequities: the status of women. But while the first-wave feminists of the 1920s had won for women the right to vote, the second won the right to work.

Of course, women had worked all through the twentieth century, in substantial percentages. In 1960, close to a third of wives held jobs. They did not usually have *careers,* though. What made this wave of feminist rhetoric different was that the fundamental bargain at the heart of marriage came under examination. For the past hundred years, men had gone out to work while women raised children and maintained the home. For the first time, women in large numbers asked themselves whether this arrangement really suited them. Would they prefer to be doctors? Engineers? Truck drivers? And if so, what was stopping them, beyond the status quo? Clusters of housewives read *The Feminine Mystique* and joined consciousness-raising groups and remembered that they had always been fascinated by the law. Driving carpool, by 1968 or so, began to look like drudgery.

This iteration of women's quest for equality drew strength from a contemporary development in the field of mental health, which had not loomed large in the average American's awareness until then. But in the late 1960s the theories of psychologists like Abraham Maslow and Fritz Perls were popularized and widely embraced in forms like self-help books and encounter sessions and iconoclastic new therapies. The point was that anyone could feel better emotionally and fulfill his or her potential with some help from these new schools of thought. Betty Friedan had defined "the problem that has no name" as the widespread frustration of housewives who found no scope for satisfaction in their socially mandated role. But the thinking of the late 1960s urged all Americans to new growth—emotional, professional, sexual.

Especially sexual. This was another way in which the social upheavals of the 1960s differed from their predecessors in the 1920s. Flappers might drive around with boyfriends their parents disapproved of, drink bathtub gin, and neck enthusiastically, but they generally remained virgins until marriage. The sexual revolution of the late twentieth century, though, did away with that expectation. The mass-marketing of the birth control pill in 1960 is often credited with sparking the broad change in attitudes about sex by definitively severing the link between sexual activity and reproduction. But other factors came into play as well. The teachings of the human potential movement could be construed as encouragement to casual sex: "If it feels good, do it." Emotional and ethical consequences seemed to have been released from the sexual act along with the reproductive ones. At the same time, as attitudes about women's careers gradually changed, the basic financial bargain of marriage—man works to support woman—lost much of its logic. By the 1970s, social prospects for America's young women offered unprecedented freedom. They didn't need marriage to earn their keep: they'd support themselves. They didn't need marriage to legitimize the infant products of sexual activity: they could prevent conception.

The institution of matrimony was not exactly discredited in the 1970s but it was certainly deposed from its privileged position. A landmark Supreme Court case in 1971 struck down a Massachusetts law prohibiting the sales of contraceptives to unmarried couples. As Nancy Cott points out in *Public Vows*, the decision indicated that the government thus "moved toward displacing marriage from the seat of official morality." The opinion even defined a married couple as "an association of two individuals each with a separate emotional and intellectual makeup." And as steeply rising divorce figures began to demonstrate in the mid-1960s, those individuals joined in matrimony could be sundered without too much difficulty.

Why, then, marry at all? The incentives of the postwar years were gone. Young people didn't rush toward adulthood, longing to claim maturity with a job and a wedding band and a baby. They didn't need to marry to have sex. They didn't even need to marry to get out of their parents' house, since in the 1970s young single people began to live on their own in massive new numbers. There was no social pressure at all to wed. In 1957, a poll showed that 51 percent of respondents considered unmarried adults "immoral" or "sick." By 1976, two-thirds of the respondents saw single people with neutral or approving eyes. The stigma that had clung to divorcés into the late 1960s vanished and in the 1970s, the whole "singles" industry—bars, restaurants, resorts—made the unattached, unfettered life look glamorous. Nevertheless, marriage rates did not evaporate. There were around 1.5 million marriages in the United States in 1960, but by 1970 the annual number had soared to nearly 2.2 million, where it has hovered for the last thirty-odd years.

The spirit of the 1970s wedding was different, though. The bride of 1965, with her pillbox headpiece and bouffant veil, experienced the apotheosis of the marriageable. Her younger sister, barefoot in a meadow, married to fulfill her individual destiny. She and her groom could hardly *help* getting married, it was their souls' requirement. And they wanted their wedding to reflect this fact. Marriage, for most young couples in the counterculture era, wasn't the next step in a predictable sequence. It was a highly individual choice. So their wedding, if possible, should reflect this.

The first sign of change in the wedding culture appeared in the gowns themselves. For nearly twenty-five years, since World War II, a wedding dress had been a costume bearing little relation to daily fashion. As the silhouettes for street clothes inflated and deflated, the wedding gown remained staunchly neo-Victorian, with its snug bodice and full skirt. Finally, in the mid-1960s, the skirt narrowed and the waist rose to hover somewhere below the bust, though bouffant models could still be bought at lower price points.

That was not the only change of the mid-sixties, though. Suddenly, after all those years of fashion-free limbo, bridal gowns got stylish. The first evidence of this was a series of babyish dresses that appeared in *Bride's* in 1966. Organdy,

Bridal fashion gone mod: Sharon Tate's wedding dress features a Victorian high collar and leg-of-mutton sleeves with an extremely short skirt. Few brides would have had her courage.

dotted Swiss, and narrow ruffles of Valenciennes lace appeared on gowns decorated with smocking or little puffed sleeves. The "skimmer" silhouette, a straight-cut garment that hung loosely from the shoulders, was made up in organza. Instead of demure pillboxes, models wore white eyelet kerchiefs. White lace minidresses were shown with point d'esprit panty hose. The word *kicky* was applied to bridal wear.

Then the floodgates opened, producing a jumpsuit and cape of tiered Val lace, pantaloons in silver brocade, a caftan gown with a jeweled neck. In 1967, *Bride's* suggested "How to swing without being way-way-out: a mini-pant dress makes the scene at a semiformal home or garden wedding! Dress your attendants in minis, too . . . it's what the action is!" By 1969, patchwork, macramé, Nehru collars, and the gypsy look invaded bridal territory.

Which is not to say that a girl couldn't still get peau de soie and alençon. Most bridesmaids did not actually wear minis or even synthetic green braids. But these options were available. John Burbidge, who designed for Priscilla of Boston during this period, points out that the most outlandish outfits were basically publicity stunts, intended to be photographed rather than worn. The striking fact is that the hermetic world of bridal design began responding to fashion in a way that it hadn't for a generation. And the question is: why?

The answer must lie in society's changing attitude toward marriage itself. If we look back at the late 1940s, the era when wedding dresses first became costumes rather than garments, that change came in response to a new view of marriage. After the stress of the war, marriage represented the best hope for a normal, productive life. Twenty years later, though, there were some cracks in the edifice and rumblings of discontent from the carpool brigade. The institution of marriage was beginning to lose some of its luster; maybe it wasn't the answer to everything. As marriage became less monolithic, so did the dress that had become its primary symbol.

The trend only intensified as the 1960s turned into the 1970s. It was almost as if the fashion editors of *Bride's* were tuned into two competing radio frequencies. One set of editorial pages was devoted to the old standbys, sober gowns with their high necklines and long sleeves, while in another section models were wearing—almost anything. Tunics and pants with rope belts. More caftans. Shirtdresses with patch pockets. Colorful brocade gowns like something out of Zeffirelli's film *Romeo and Juliet* (1968). Once synthetic knits like Qiana became fashionable, bridal designers used them with abandon, creating frankly slinky outfits that were shown (as fashion demanded) with turbans and ropes of pearls. By the late 1970s, some brides were ready for the disco floor, in jersey or lamé, with dark-shadowed eyes and glossy red lips. As *Bride's* said in 1977, "Sophistication for a bride is just about the newest look."

Well, yes. Sophistication for a bride was not just a new look, it was a new concept. Look how far the whole idea of brides had come in a hundred years: from innocent to demimondaine. The entire notion of the virginal bride, of nuptial decorum and modesty, had vanished. And even if a late-seventies bride avoided the Studio 54 aesthetic, it was hard to ignore the fact that many of the most fashionable options in wedding apparel were frankly antibridal. What is a bride going to do with patch pockets? What does it say when she weds in square-necked rose-colored brocade? How about that turtleneck gown with the dirndl skirt? Women who wed in dresses like these seemed almost embarrassed to be walking up an aisle at all. If the white lace-trimmed gown was the symbol of a Bride, they wanted nothing to do with it.

In fact, the traditional formal wedding was facing a low point in prestige—at least in the popular rhetoric. As the two Johnson daughters married at the White House with all the formality and pomp of the grand Victorian wedding (Luci had twelve bridesmaids in raspberry pink), hostility toward the Establishment was growing. Heaven knows that if there was an Establishment ritual, it had to be the white wedding, a holdover from the past that trafficked in feminine subjugation and meaningless social display. The growing rift in values between youth and the older generation seemed to run right through the wedding itself, in fact. To parents, a formal wedding represented tradition, continuity, and an enjoyable social opportunity. To their children, it was irrelevant, if not outright hypocritical.

The Graduate, released in 1967, is often hailed as a movie that captured the spirit of its era. Dustin Hoffman's affectless Benjamin embodied a mood of alienation that was apparently widespread. His affair with Mrs. Robinson remains the memorable feature of the film but in fact, he is in love with her daughter, Elaine. Their relationship, however tentative and undefined, is the only genuine one in the film. Only with Elaine can Benjamin speak his mind, and only with Elaine does he break out of his passivity. He doesn't realize her importance to him until Mrs. Robinson has whisked her off to be married, so Benjamin has to seek her out at her wedding.

It's the film's view of the wedding itself that is so telling. Elaine is conventionally dressed in a long-sleeved gown of organza and lace, with a bouffant tulle veil. The ceremony takes place in a stark modern church, with an old woman playing

Luci Johnson's 1966 wedding made no concession to the whims of late-sixties fashion. Her gown and those of her dozen attendants were extremely conservative, but they made a striking picture on the steps of the National Cathedral.

the traditional bridal recessional—out of tune. As Elaine and her husband, Carl—for she is married by the time Benjamin appears—turn to walk out of the church, Benjamin calls out and Elaine moves toward him. In the resulting melee, and in her following mad dash with Benjamin, Elaine's behavior is antibridal. She is not demure, modest, compliant, or pleasant. She picks up her train and runs to catch a passing city bus, to escape with the man she really loves. In the final moments of the movie, we see Benjamin and Elaine sitting side by side in the back of the bus, breathing hard, glancing at each other. Elaine seems perfectly unconscious of her new gold ring, her wedding dress and veil, which all the other passengers stare at. She has found love and forgotten that she is a bride.

In *The Graduate,* marriage is bundled together with the rest of the sanctimonious, destructive adult behavior attributed to Benjamin's parents and their friends. The wedding, with its empty formality, is obviously Mrs. Robinson's futile ploy to control her daughter. It is a damning view of the ceremonial, but worse was yet to come. *The Graduate* negated the significance of marriage but it at least took the ceremony seriously. The institution might have lost its power but the forms were acknowledged. John Lennon and Yoko Ono's marriage in Gibraltar in 1969, followed by a two-week "bed-in" in Amsterdam, seemed to be poking fun at the tradition. When the two musicians produced *Wedding Album,* boxed with an ersatz marriage certificate, the irony was underlined. The nadir (of taste, if not of respect for the wedding process) was reached, though, with Tiny Tim's marriage to Miss Vicki on *The Tonight Show Starring Johnny Carson.*

Tiny Tim was a strange entertainer of the era, a long-haired musician who sang old ballads in a falsetto voice, accompanying himself on a ukulele—his big hit was "Tiptoe through the Tulips." Was he pathetic? Was the audience mocking the musical pretension of an outright weirdo? Or was he in on the joke? It was never clear. Equally, it was never clear whether his marriage to seventeen-year-old Victoria May Budinger was a publicity stunt or a genuine love match.

Nevertheless, on December 17, 1969, announcer Ed McMahon opened the Carson show by saying, "We cordially request the pleasure of your company at the marriage of Tiny Tim and Miss Vicki right here on *The Tonight Show*. But right now, here are some words of wisdom from Pepto-Bismol. . . ." That was pretty much the way it went, a jarring pastiche of commerce and convention. The set was painted to resemble a chapel and decorated with banks of tulips, a nod to the groom's musical fame. The hosts, crew, and guests (Phyllis Diller, Florence Henderson) were all dressed formally. Tim had on a Victorian-look frock coat and a ruffled shirt, while his bride wore a high-necked, lace-frilled wedding gown and a lace veil. The groom had written the vows, which had to be squeezed in between commercial breaks. After the show, the newlyweds held a press conference, then made their appearance at the reception.

It was Tom Thumb all over again—a brilliant promoter using the public taste for weddings to his own end. The real difference, though, was in the spirit of the enterprise. P. T. Barnum played to the sentimental as well as the prurient tastes of his audience. He wanted the world to believe that Tom Thumb and Lavinia Warren had found true love. Lavinia was leaving his employ to be a housewife, and the two little people would enjoy *all* the benefits (wink, nudge) of married life.

As for Tiny Tim and Miss Vicki—who knows? The marriage didn't last, but nobody expected it would. Tiny Tim's career flamed out, like that of any other entertainment oddity. Did the pair really ever love each other? Did they believe in marriage at all? Or was it all a charade? And finally—did anyone believe in marriage in 1969?

Well, the Nixon girls did, thank you very much. Surely if there was an antithesis to the Tiny Tim/Miss Vicki coupling it was the match between Julie Nixon and Dwight David Eisen-

When Tiny Tim and Miss Vicki were married on *The Tonight Show*, the hosts obligingly dressed in tuxedos, to befit the formality of the occasion.

hower, which took place just ten days later. The pair had first met when David's grandfather (the president) and Julie's father (the vice president) were sworn in. In 1969 they were both young, clean-cut students, he at Amherst and she at Smith. The pair chose to be married not at the White House, but in New York by Norman Vincent Peale, author of *The Power of Positive Thinking.* Julie wore a Priscilla of Boston dress with puffed sleeves and a scoop neck, while David wore a morning coat. There were eight white-gloved bridesmaids and sister Tricia as maid of honor.

Julie's wedding was relatively private for the daughter of a president, but Tricia, marrying eighteen months later, submitted to the full-scale barrage of the world's press. (Perhaps her beleaguered father's advisors thought the perky bride could temporarily distract his critics.) The week before her June 1971 ceremony, *Life* magazine featured the bride on its cover, beaming in her Priscilla of Boston V-necked lace gown. A ten-page spread shared with *Life*'s readers the homey little details of a White House wedding: Tricia showing off her china and crystal patterns, Tricia writing thank-you notes beneath a massive crystal chandelier, a White House flunky pushing a shopping cart full of shower gifts along a corridor. The recipe for the lemon sponge wedding cake was released by the White House press office in scaled-down proportions—and, embarrassingly, produced failure after failure when the nation's food writers tested it. Reporter Marcia Seligson, sent by *Life* to cover the wedding itself, reckoned that the press outnumbered the guests by about a third.

Seligson, a magazine writer who was at that point researching a book on weddings entitled *The Eternal Bliss Machine*, noted in her article that Tricia and Eddie Cox's wedding, while inflated in scale, differed little from any other formal wedding taking place on that June Saturday anywhere in America. Her book leaves readers in no doubt that the formal wedding, despite rumors to the contrary, was still alive and well. On page one of *The Eternal Bliss Machine* (1973) she marshals statistics to show that the marriage rate had held steady over the previous ten years, that nearly 90 percent of couples marrying for the first time did so in a house of worship, that 80 percent of weddings were formal, that 96 percent of couples celebrated their marriage with a reception, and that 84.5 percent of new brides wore a "formal bridal gown"—lace jumpsuits notwithstanding. The formal wedding might have been discredited by the culture and reflexively considered "square" by the young, but when the time came to tie the knot, apparently most of them still did so in traditional style.

Anecdotal evidence reinforces Seligson's statistics. Historian John Modell's *Into One's Own* examined the wedding announcements of Minnesota newspapers in rural areas, small towns, and cities. Although his sample was very small, he found no evidence that weddings got simpler in the 1960s and '70s—on the contrary. Modell actually concluded that during the twentieth century the celebration of a wedding became steadily more elaborate. Elements like receptions and showers, which occurred sporadically before World War II (especially in the rural areas), gradually became normal, then obligatory. Receptions moved from homes to church buildings to—in the cities—banquet halls and hotels. Guest lists became larger, and the number of individuals mentioned in wedding announcements as attendants, readers of Scripture, keepers of the guest book, or "coffee pourers" became more numerous.

The pages of *Bride's* tend to confirm Modell's analysis, especially in the etiquette column that appeared in each issue. In 1970, the magazine mentions "the large and costly dinner receptions" that had become popular, and the increasing practice of the groom's family offering to contribute to escalating nuptial expenses. Limousine rental (1971), wedding favors (1971), color schemes (1971), and rehearsal dinners (1973) are among the topics addressed in the column. In fact, considerable elaboration seems to have occurred during the swinging seventies; in 1971, *Bride's* listed monogrammed matchbooks and Jordan almonds as potential favors but made it clear that "the only favor you are required to give your guests is the memory of a warm wedding and a happy reception." In 1979, though, the magazine had graduated to "small picture frames, silk flowers, Christmas tree ornaments, a small plant, a split of Champagne" as suggested favors. Perhaps most telling of all is the question of planning time. Since the 1930s, *Bride's* had published a calendar suggesting deadlines for specific tasks related to the wedding. As late as the 1960s, the lead time could be as little as three months, though six months was preferable; by 1973, the magazine instructed its readers that it took as long as a year to plan a big formal reception. Seligson concurs, noting that in 1972 the average length of engagement was eleven months; it had doubled in ten years. It took that much longer to get every detail organized.

On the one hand, then, the late 1960s and the '70s were marked by a general skepticism about marriage and the rituals of an older generation. On the other hand, the marriage rate remained steady and weddings actually became more elaborate. How can both of these things be possible? The fact is that the entire bridal culture was affected by the spirit of the era, and while some brides married in the style of the 1950s, far more of them embraced some part of the era's characteristic informality.

It showed up first, as we have seen, in the clothes. The innovative mood expressed by shift dresses and miniskirts and Marimekko prints took women's wardrobes in a playful, youthful direction. The wilder alternative bridal wear—the pantaloons and mink-bodiced minidresses—may have been publicity stunts but even at the very highest levels of fashion, a new breeze was blowing. Why, in 1969 Yves St. Laurent created a magnificent wedding gown for the Duchess of Orléans—in an artful patchwork of velvet and silk.

Perhaps no garment expressed the yearning for informality better than the Mexican wedding dress. It first appeared in a dressed-up version, copied for the carriage trade in organza and crochet lace, with a hefty price tag. Soon enough entrepreneurs were bringing back the authentic cotton versions from south of the border, and selling them at a startling markup. They were still much less expensive than traditional wedding gowns and made excellent graduation dresses, too. The most conservative mother could find nothing to object to in the modest, full-length garments with their rows of tucking and bands of lace (especially if they were rendered in silk). The most rebellious daughter could agree that such a dress was pretty and be appeased by its folkloric appeal. The ethnic trend inspired satisfying alternatives to the bridal industry's pristine white columns, and it was widespread—a store called "The Barefoot Bride" opened in New York in 1972 and carried caftans and Indian muslins, in addition to the inevitable Mexican wedding dresses.

The fashionable tendency of the late '60s to cut dresses away from the body, resulting in loose "trapeze" and "cage" silhouettes, drew bridal design in an informal direction. So did the fad for "Flower Power," resulting in daisy-patterned lace, ribbons, stockings, prints, even daisy-trimmed shoes. It was probably the revival of Victoriana, though, that had the widest influence. Ironically, as women were claiming new roles in society, they were embracing motifs in fashion that looked back to a period of feminine limitation. But unlike the Victorian revival of the New Look or the wedding gowns of the 1950s and early '60s, this wave of adaptation focused on the details rather than on the silhouettes of the earlier era. The hyperfeminine, tight-waisted, and full-skirted outline of the mid-nineteenth century was ignored. Instead, through the early to mid-1970s, the calico and lace, full sleeves and ruffles that reached their apogee in the granny gown made a strong impact on wedding wear. Even Barbie's wedding dresses followed suit, with their high waists, bibs and yokes, aprons and jabots, and leg-of-mutton sleeves. Finally, color leavened the formality of the all-white gown, and color was everywhere in the early '70s. Sheer fabrics like voile veiled colored slips, pastel embroidery brightened white fabrics, and ribbons of every color and description threaded through lace or sashed waists.

Naturally bridesmaids' costumes showed similar influences. While Luci Johnson's attendants in 1966 preceded her up the aisle in plain pink silk with a padded "wedding ring" neck and deeper pink tulle veils, Tricia Nixon's maids in 1971 looked neo-Victorian. The dresses were made of layered silk organza (lavender over mint for the three maids, mint over lavender for matron of honor Julie) but the ruffles over the shoulder, the narrow bow tying the waist, and the floral trim on the skirt made them much less formal than the nearly ecclesiastical simplicity of Luci's pink. And finally, attendants lost their headpieces. Through the 1960s and into the early '70s, designers had to concoct some kind of vestigial "hat" for the bridal parties since many churches and synagogues required women to cover their heads. (*Cover* was defined quite loosely.) Hats shrank and shrank, from stiffened fabric caps in the early '60s to bits of veiling to headbands or flat bows or silk flowers on a barrette. As late as 1975, *Bride's* showed maids with braided cord that matched the trim on their

gowns twined into their hair. The vogue for retro, costumey
hats—bowlers or big floppy sun hats—took care of the issue
for a few more years and then vanished, leaving nothing behind but a comb trimmed with baby's breath or, at most, a
wreath of rosebuds. Even some informally dressed brides left
off their veils during this period; the Mexican wedding dress
proved difficult to accessorize.

Wedding gear, however casual, was only following the
crumbling of formality in civilian fashion. Most controver-
sially, women got it into their heads to wear pants, even out of
the house. (Some formal restaurants refused to serve them.)
The new high-collared Nehru jacket appeared for men and in
some cases seemed an adequate substitute for a conventional
jacket and tie. In an etiquette column in 1971 a reader asked
Bride's how to instruct her guests that her wedding was black
tie, and the magazine simply tossed the ball back at her: "You
don't. . . . [N]o matter what your guests turn up wearing (and
in these informal days, it's as apt to be embroidered jeans as
dinner jackets), you should make them welcome."

And as fashion went, so went weddings in general. It
wasn't that the average wedding turned into a "be-in"—
merely that the level of ceremony was generally reduced. Even
the church ritual in many cases lost some stiffness. In October
1971, *Life* covered the wedding of four California sisters—
Judy, Janice, Joanie, and Jeannette Hund. The article outlines
the logistics of marrying off four daughters at once, and reveals that the brides overruled their parents and insisted on a
folk Mass accompanied by guitars instead of the more traditional Catholic Mass with organ music. Some brides carried
daisies rather than orchids and asked their little sisters to play
the recorder during the ceremony. Even that traditional bone

of contention, the invitation, underwent some changes. The response card, so recently taboo, was tolerated by *Bride's* in 1977 and endorsed in 1979. The stuffy black engraving on an ivory card could now—properly, according to the experts—be replaced by options as exciting as colored ink. Borders were deemed "tasteful" and the paper could be metallic, parchment, or even the same stock as a brown paper bag (such fun!). The ritual wording could be altered and in 1976 the magazine even urged its readers to include "a line of poetry."

The informality that marked the era was largely fueled by its rebellious spirit. To the younger generation that had somehow hijacked the cultural spotlight, formality, their parents' social style, seemed stuffy at best. It smacked of authority, and authority was at an all-time low ebb in public opinion. If you were an engaged couple in the early 1970s and you shared the generational mistrust of Richard Nixon, you probably didn't want to get married the way Tricia Nixon did. Her wedding seemed like an event run by and for the old fogies, to whom Tricia seemed, prematurely, to belong. You'd want instead an event that spoke to your own generation. Hence the insistence on rock music at receptions and vows written by the participants. Brides wanted carrot cakes under the statutory white icing because carrot cake was a trendy new healthy-sounding treat that people actually ate because they liked it, not because it was expected. The cookie-cutter weddings of the postwar years satisfied a generation whose watchword was conformity, but their children wanted none of it. What they sought was authenticity and a ritual that somehow reflected their individual tastes.

So the weddings of the late '60s and the 1970s were marked by this drive for couples to differentiate themselves from other couples as well as from their parents. The majestic predictability of tradition, which had been a selling point only a generation earlier, was now seen as tainted. An ad for Worcester Crystal (is there anything more "traditional" than crystal tableware?) in the 1970s showed a woman with a finger on a wine glass. The copy read, "Listen. The only traditional thing about Worcester Crystal is its ring. Everything else about your fine hand-blown crystal from famous Worcester is clearly new."

Newness was not what the wedding industry had, until then, produced. Formal dresses and magnificent cakes and busy catering halls had long evoked visions of late-nineteenth-century grandeur. Above all, the industry had brought a level of standardization to the celebration of weddings. It was precisely this similarity that the brides and grooms of the 1970s wanted to avoid. They were marrying not because they were eager to embrace marriage, but because they were eager to embrace each other. The cultural rhetoric of the early '70s harped constantly on romance. The ringleted hairdos for women, the Yardley perfumes and guitar-playing minstrels and love poetry all spoke of that mystical connection between men and women—which alone, it seemed, persuaded them to head down to the county clerk's office for a marriage license. This bond seemed at once too fragile and too remarkable to be expressed in the predictable product of a mass-market wedding.

So trend-setting couples began to take back some of the responsibility for producing their own weddings. Why have a florist make up a stiff bouquet when Queen Anne's lace in a loose bunch would look just as pretty with a muslin gown? Why should the bride process up the aisle to Mendelssohn's "Wedding March" when "Here Comes the Sun" would sound so great? Why pay the price for a "real" wedding dress when you can combine two patterns and stitch up something unique? Kitty Hanson's *For Richer, For Poorer* was published in 1967. After her scathing commentary on the bridal industry, she described, with approbation, the wedding planned by a pair of students at Antioch College in Ohio. It took place on the banks of a river with the guests encircling the bride and groom. Everyone participated in the ceremony, singing or playing instruments and reading "a favorite literary passage of the bride and groom—from Winnie the Pooh to Shakespeare." After cutting the cake, the newlyweds changed out of their formal duds (the bride did wear white) into jeans for the celebratory picnic, and they rode off to their honeymoon on horseback.

That was a truly radical approach for the 1960s, but within a few years the impulse to individualize the standard ceremony injected personal touches into most weddings, even the ones that were largely the productions of the commercial wedding industry. After all, the traditional vows, spoken between bride and groom, are the very heart of the wedding. The words of the Episcopal Prayer Book, often adapted for other Protestant Christian weddings, establish a tone of great intimacy, starting with the officiant's greeting to the assembled group, "Dearly beloved." If intimacy was appropriate, couples reasoned, why not go all the way and use their very *own* private words? Or use poetry? Or the text of an especially meaningful song? In fact, why not have that song performed during the ceremony? Excesses, of course, were committed: in its etiquette column, *Bride's* sanctioned a bride's crooning "I Love You Truly" to her husband. But an earnest desire to make the wedding ceremony more meaningful can hardly be faulted. By the mid-seventies *Bride's* ran a regular feature called "Creating a Ceremony," which led readers step by step through the process and recommended sources like Khalil Gibran's *The Prophet* and the poetry of Rod McKuen.

Vows and readings weren't the only part of the ceremony that could reflect a couple's inmost souls, of course. The predictable choices of venue (home, hotel, reception hall at the house of worship) gave way to far more inventive sites. *Bride's* ran a recurrent feature on planning an outdoor wedding, full of important considerations like park permits, catering difficulties, and the necessity for temporary sanitation arrangements. The magazine encouraged its readers to plan weddings that expressed their unique qualities: "Your wedding tells everyone how you like to celebrate. But it can say much more. Maybe that you and he intend to fight pollution vigorously— like the couple who pedaled to church on a tandem bike. Or that a woman's place is not necessarily in the home, as [with] the pair who vowed that she would continue to go by her maiden name." Extremely quirky weddings got publicity, like the couples who married on skis or underwater or stark naked in Times Square. The merely unusual became commonplace.

Wedding garments became pretty unusual, too. The hippie era was in full flower, and for some people, every day was Halloween. Ethnic looks from all over the world jostled with period details, sometimes in the same garment. While even the most conventional wedding gowns often had a Victorian flavor, true individualists were rarely content to stop with something they bought at a bridal boutique. Style was in the details, like a piano shawl or Grandma's cameo or lace-up kid boots. Even Priscilla of Boston, purveyor of stodgy lace gowns to presidential daughters, caught the fever. A big 1973

The pregnant bride, the ethnic garments, the bearded officiant, the outdoor setting—this photograph of a 1970s wedding captures everything emblematic of that era. We can almost hear the guitar playing in the background.

advertising spread in *Bride's* urged readers to "Do your own thing—unforgettably! in designs by Priscilla."

Another unforgettable aspect of the era's wedding outfits is its menswear. It was the time of the Peacock Revolution, when (some) men shook off their Brooks Brothers straitjackets and experimented with color, pattern, bell-bottoms, and facial hair. Few of these exciting new possibilities were appropriate for even the least formal wedding ceremony, but they inspired some startling innovations in masculine dress. For nearly a hundred years, the wardrobe options for the well-dressed groom had been as limited as the options for the correct formal invitation. To a formal evening wedding men wore "black tie," i.e., a black tuxedo and black bow tie. An ultra-formal wedding might require "white tie," that is to say a long-tailed coat with a stiff-fronted, wing-collared shirt, white piqué vest, and white tie. For informal ceremonies men could get away with dark suits or combinations of navy blazer and flannels. Formal daytime weddings, though, required an archaism: a "morning coat," or "cutaway," which was a long-tailed gray coat worn with striped trousers, a vest, and a black-and-white-striped ascot.

The morning coat is one of the casualties of the twentieth century; few men own them anymore. In the 1930s, *Bride's* gently dissuaded a bride from planning a formal morning wedding on the grounds that her fiancé might not be able to afford the purchase of a morning coat that he would seldom wear. Companies that rented formalwear solved this problem. They began to form in the postwar period, when the formal wedding came into the financial reach of most middle-class Americans. In *Father of the Bride,* Mr. Banks is very proud of the fact that he owns his own cutaway, "a splendid thing—a badge of old-world aristocracy." (The fact that it no longer fits provides considerable comedy.) The July 25, 1949, issue of *Life* included a photo-story on a real-life father of the bride. The article followed a steel tank manufacturer in Northern California, Peter Saracco, through the arduous process of marrying off his daughter Joanne. He is photographed being fitted for a cutaway, which he rents for ten dollars: the caption reads "Clerk says he keeps lights dim to hide the fact that coats and pants do not always match." Saracco, though he can afford a reception for five hundred guests, is obviously not from the same kind of established Old Money background as Stanley Banks, but the wedding industry ensures that this no longer matters. Joanne Saracco can have a correct formal wedding, too.

"Correct" meant that men didn't wear evening clothes before six o'clock. This was another one of those rules that etiquette authorities stressed and that, increasingly, average citizens ignored. Strictly speaking, a man dressed in a tuxedo before nightfall was likely to be a waiter or member of a symphony orchestra. (Strictly speaking also, children should never wear black tie—because they should never be present at an occasion where a tuxedo is required!) But for many a bride of the 1960s, a wedding was the only occasion to lay claim to the glamorous formal social life of the upper crust. In the face of that opportunity, who cared what was correct?

Soon enough, de rigueur yielded to groovy anyway. The traditional boxy cut of the tuxedo jacket got a little more exciting, with a higher armhole and a nipped waist. Lapels, narrow through the mid-'60s, began to creep wider. The staid black broadcloth of the jacket began to yield to more thrilling choices like crushed velvet. In 1971, the *Bride's* etiquette column fielded a query from a woman who wanted her groom and his ushers to wear green tuxedos to match her bridesmaids' gowns. The magazine replied that black and white looked best for a formal wedding. Green shirts were permissible, but you probably couldn't rent green dinner jackets anyway.

That was about to change. In 1972, the formalwear company After Six ran an ad showing brocade jackets with velvet lapels, shirtfronts exploding into ruffles, and a weird hybrid style of jacket with a deep Western-style yoke of velvet and pointed, buttoned pocket flaps. It was, said the company, "as different as you hope your gown will be." The bridal magazines throughout the early 1970s are full of advertising from Lord West, Gingiss, Palm Beach Formals, and After Six, showing page after page of men with puffy hair modeling outfits that drifted ever farther from the austere look of traditional black tie. The jackets themselves morphed into new forms including the hybrid "tail-tux" and the deliciously titled "Hotspur" from Lord West, which featured inch-wide black velvet ribbon outlining the notched lapels and slash pockets. (Each outfit had a name, and most were Waspily pretentious, like "Claremont," "Kensington," "Peale," and "Chaucer.") Once lapels could no longer widen without flapping in the wind, they rounded and took on the "clover leaf" silhouette. Fabrics got even more startling than crushed velvet as technology presented America with the opportunity to wear double-knit polyester in textures that could resemble dermatological disorders.

It is the colors, though, that look most astonishing in retrospect. In 1973, an After Six ad in *Bride's* proudly announced, "Until now you couldn't really color-coordinate a wedding" because men were required to wear black. After

Six, however, came to the rescue with tuxedos in blue, lavender, and pink (the most likely colors for bridesmaids' gowns?)
all with black lapel piping and buttons. Somewhat defensively
the ad copy concluded, "If America's most respected maker
of fine men's formals shows color, color is correct." Apparently the market was ready for it, because what followed was
a positive rainbow. Patterns like plaid and paisley, textures
like mohair, denim, brocade, and Dacron waffle-weave, decorative trim like grosgrain ribbon and gold lamé made men's
formalwear more exciting than it had ever been. Champagne,
ginger, pale yellow, salmon pink, dusty rose, pale green, and
lilac nestled on racks next to cowardly options like beige and
pearl gray. Some of the combinations of color and trim look
today like something you'd find on a marching band. An ad
for Gingiss formalwear proclaimed, "we're finding more and
more men are expressing their individuality in the formalwear
they wear. Outdoor weddings are now commonplace, white is
being worn all year round, men are wearing morning suits in
the evening and full evening dress in the morning."

It was almost time for fashions to cycle back to conservatism. By the mid-'70s, innovative wedding gowns were less
common. Satin and lace were coming back, with the occasional big sleeve to hint at the future. Somewhat more slowly,
menswear also relapsed back into convention. In 1975, *Bride's*
registered its disapproval of the peacock look, opining that
men's outfits should never actually *match* the bridesmaids'
gowns. Instead, the magazine urged "handsomely traditional
or subtly modern quiet-toned menswear." So much for the
lilac tail-tux.

The telling word here is *traditional*. After a dozen
years in the discard pile, tradition was about to come roaring

The late 1970s was the golden age for dandies. Here Jake Hooker, in his pale suit with the wide satin lapels, almost outshines bride Lorna Luft despite her satin-striped trouser outfit.

back into favor. In the 1980s, weddings would begin to take on the grandeur, even grandiosity they exhibit today. The disdain for convention that animated the seventies practically vanished.

It did, however, leave behind a few substantial alterations in wedding traditions. As we have seen, much of the pageantry of the wedding ceremony originally celebrated the bride's virgin state. Even her attendants were originally fellow-virgins. The twentieth century's growing indifference to the bride's sexual experience and that of her cohort wrought a few changes. First came the married bridesmaid, or "matron," often the married sister of the bride. Well into the 1960s it was still considered taboo, though, for a bridesmaid to be visibly pregnant. However, by 1976 *Bride's* had changed its tune. Asked about the propriety of inviting a pregnant woman to be matron of honor, the magazine suggested that she herself should decide whether or not to join the wedding party. The bride needn't worry about "embarrassing your guests." (Because the pregnant bridesmaid reminded everyone of sex?)

The "do your own thing" years had left their mark on the strictures relating to second weddings, as well. White, of course, was the perquisite of the virgin bride and well into the 1960s a woman marrying for the second time would not have considered herself entitled to wear a white gown. Gradually that taboo eroded as the divorce rate (and thus the incidence of second marriages) increased. In 1971, a bride-to-be queried the *Bride's* etiquette column about the propriety of her wearing white to marry even though she had a three-year-old son by a man she had never wed. The magazine's reply was equivocal. On the one hand, tradition reserved white for first-time brides. On the other hand, pillar of the wedding establishment Priscilla Kidder (Priscilla of Boston) felt every bride should wear white because "It's America's happy color!" (Mrs. Kidder apparently apprehended the profit potential in second weddings.) By 1980, *Bride's* approved white for a second wedding, forbidding only the wearing of a veil.

Once again the magazine was attempting to maintain standards that were becoming obsolete. Robert Altman's 1978 film, *A Wedding,* shows how very far from old-fashioned tradition wedding behavior had drifted. The director's satire, of course, exaggerates wildly. But anyone who regularly attended late-'70s weddings can attest to the real sense of dislocation between the ostensible proceedings—the pairing of a virginal girl and a man who will support her, before the approving eyes of the community—and the actual event. Everyone knew the bride and groom had gotten out of bed together that morning. Bridesmaids and ushers were intently scoping each other out with a view to later illicit activity. Underage guests got into the champagne and there may well have been a joint or two consumed behind the barn. The forms and rituals of the traditional wedding were something that the young people often moved through, tolerantly, for their parents' sake, while a looser, parallel event took place just out of sight of the grown-ups.

In *A Wedding,* Geraldine Chaplin, as the wedding planner Rita Billingsley, represents the dead hand of the past. She keeps interrupting the (admittedly) unruly proceedings with speeches that remind the participants what they are supposed to be doing, and why. "Ladies and gentlemen, we will follow tradition," she proclaims, outlining the order for the bride and groom's first dance together. "Then the FOB will cut in and dance with his daughter while the FOG will cut in on his son and dance with the MOB. . . ." As we learn more and more about the relationships among the bride and the groom and their respective families, it becomes apparent that the lavish preparations and formality of the wedding mask a misalliance. By the time the cake is cut we know that most of the characters' marriages are foundering if not defunct, yet Miss Billingsley declares brightly, "Ladies and gentlemen: Marriage is the single most important event of a lifetime. The interests of the community, and of nature, fuse at this moment though they so often conflict during the rest of man's life. Now, there are certain accepted customs which one must observe." Director Robert Altman's comedy, throughout the film, lies in the discrepancy between the "accepted customs" and the untraditional behavior indulged in by the characters. Hypocrisy exposed is always good for a laugh.

Ten years earlier, in *The Graduate,* Mike Nichols had used Elaine Robinson's wedding to highlight her mother's insincerity. Elaine's wedding was a charade, but she managed, the film suggests, to find an honest relationship with Benjamin. At the end of *A Wedding,* the bride has just caught her new husband in a shower with another man. The groom's father has run away from his drug-addicted wife. The bride's sister, who prefers not to speak, has mutely revealed that she is pregnant by the groom—or by one of a dozen other men. The members of the wedding party who aren't high are having sex in doorways with other people's spouses, and only the uniformed security staff is left to sit down to the formal dinner. Society itself is in chaos, and the formally choreographed rituals of the wedding provide nothing but comic relief.

CHAPTER 10

The Bride Is a Symbol

ROYAL WEDDING 1981 ·
THE GOLDEN AGE OF THE GRANDIOSE BRIDAL ·
THE NEWEST KIND OF MARRIAGE · WEDDING GOWN AS HIGH
FASHION · THE CELEBRITY BRIDE · THE BRIDE AS CELEBRITY ·
"THE WHOLE WEDDING FANTASY"

Altman's corrosive humor made the formal wedding look like a superannuated irrelevance, but a mere three years later, a far more positive nuptial vision was presented to a far larger audience. When Lady Diana Spencer married the Prince of Wales on July 29, 1981, 750 million people around the globe witnessed the televised ceremony. The studied informality of society in the 1970s often made brides and grooms uncomfortable with the old-fashioned ritual they enacted as they married—hence the uneasy attempts to update the ritual with amendments like personalized vows. Charles and Diana, though, paced through their archaic ceremony with both gravity and grace, as if they believed in the importance of every gesture.

The glamour of that wedding was irresistible. Like a character in a fairy tale, the heir to the throne had chosen a young, beautiful wife. She was arrayed in a glorious confection of a dress, all cream-colored taffeta and heirloom lace and yards of floating tulle—the kind of dress that made brides-to-be wake from their haunted dream of slinky Qiana columns or muslin and bare feet. Women who grew up in the 1960s saw the rav-

The iconic bride of the 1980s, Lady Diana Spencer had it all: beauty, grandeur, a diamond tiara, a horse-drawn carriage, a massive bouquet, a veil dozens of yards long—and the Prince of Wales as groom.

ishing young princess in her tight bodice and full skirt and realized that they really could dress like their Barbie dolls. The immense bouquet, the sprinkling of sequins, the balloon sleeves—not to mention the groom's full-dress naval uniform—launched a vision of grandeur that ordinary brides the world over took very seriously. Of course they wouldn't fill a church with two thousand heads of state in remarkable hats. Of course a famous opera star wouldn't serenade them, and they wouldn't ride to the reception in an open horse-drawn carriage, waving to hundreds of thousands of spectators. But it became apparent very quickly that the slightly shamefaced posture of many brides of the 1970s had been replaced. If the wedding dress of 1973 said, "I'm really not your typical bride," the 1983 version said, "Look at me—I'm getting married!"

None of this would have happened without one of those shifts in the zeitgeist that appear sudden at the time but predictable in retrospect. By 1981, the vagaries of the late 1960s and the '70s were fading into painful memory. A pair of bell-bottom blue jeans in the closet evoked a tiny shudder and barbers were once more clipping men's hair so their ears showed. *The Official Preppy Handbook* was a bestseller. Wealth now prompted admiration rather than suspicion. The president was not only Republican but jubilantly conservative and for much of the country, this was cause for relief. Rebellion is tiring for everyone; Americans wanted to return to earlier norms and see what, in the end, had changed.

Although it's always hard to judge the recent past, many of the social shifts brought about in that period are obvious. Some civil rights inequities were addressed, though hardly resolved. On the domestic front, sexual emancipation was apparently permanent, as were women's rights to work. Most of

America's all-male universities admitted women. Girls graduated from college expecting to support themselves. In the early 1980s, they wore suits with floppy bow ties as they navigated the corporate hierarchy. There was still a great deal of confusion about women's rightful role in the world, but it was certainly a more generous and prominent place than had been conceived of before.

These changes, like any widespread social shift, had their effect on the way Americans marry. The resumption of grandeur prompted by the Wales's wedding in 1981 has simply never let up. In fact, the story of American weddings for the last few decades has been one of ever-escalating expense and elaboration. The brides of the early 1980s were inspired to embrace in their weddings a formality that seemed exotic and appealing after the "let-it-all-hang-out" 1970s. Very little has happened since then to change this. Predominantly expansive economic times through the 1990s and a culture that profoundly approved of the acquisition of wealth have combined to turn the American wedding into an all-out extravaganza. The difference between the weddings of the 1980s and the weddings of the 2000s is generally one of degree. The brides of today, like their predecessors of twenty years earlier, are still electing to marry as formally and grandly as they can. The difference is that today's weddings scale levels of complexity and detailed planning that make earlier events look like Sunday-school picnics.

And yet the miracles of event planning that unite today's brides and grooms are not the coronations of the 1960s. A young woman marrying today does not walk up the aisle toward her husband as toward her fulfillment or her fate in life. In fact, bewilderment persists concerning the relative roles of men and women in the workplace and the family. Anatomy pushes in one direction, visions of equality in another. Nevertheless, in the early years of the twenty-first century, women survey a dominion whose horizons are immeasurably wider than they have ever been. A mere 150 years ago, a girl could look forward to marriage, child rearing, and house-keeping as her crowning achievements. Society celebrated these roles, but little else.

Now, though, domestic issues are only part of a woman's bailiwick. Seventy-five percent of married women work, and over 60 percent of married women with children under the age of six work outside the home. The widely discussed re-search of sociologist Arlie Hochschild suggests that for those women with jobs outside the home, family life comes at a con-siderable cost of time and effort. In fact, it can be argued that marriage offers women very little at all. While their great-great-grandmothers needed the support of a man's labor sim-ply to live, no woman requires that anymore. Ask the harried mother, swooping down the supermarket aisles on her way home from the office, what benefits she gleans from marriage and on a bad day you'll get a glazed look and a shrug. Becom-ing a wife confers infinitely less prestige now than it did fifty years ago.

Yet marriage statistics appear quite stable. Provisional figures from the U.S. government for 2000 tally some 2,344,000 marriages. That's down from the 1990 figure of 2,448,000, but that year represented at all-time high. What are all these people thinking? Financial stability is an issue: though the majority of women are self-supporting when they marry, two incomes certainly provide a more pleasant lifestyle than one. People marry for companionship. They marry for a fulfilling, safe sex life. And they marry to have children, though the link between marriage and parenthood is dissolving.

In fact, while the raw number of marriages has been steady recently, different statistics present a different picture. Of those 2.34 million marriages, nearly half join a bride or groom for the second (if not third or more) time. The *rate* of marriage, at 8.5 per 1,000 people, is at an all-time low in the United States. Nearly a quarter of adults in this country never marry; single-parent households total nearly a quarter of those in the United States; little more than half of the adults in the country are currently married; and the number of heterosexual unmarried couple households multiplied by ten times from 1960 to 1998. Then, of course, there are the divorce statistics. According to the government, around 45 percent of marriages currently end in divorce. Nancy Cott, in *Public Vows,* points out that, "In the Pacific states, which have tended to lead the nation, the rate between divorces and marriages in the mid-1990s was closer to seven to ten."

These numbers are no secret. The National Center for Health Statistics makes them public, but a casual look at one's friends and acquaintances is likely to confirm them. The institution of marriage, once taken for granted as the natural social unit in this country, is immensely diminished in significance. Yet couples make the trip to the altar in steady numbers— many of them doing so several times. The eighteenth-century wit Samuel Johnson famously characterized an acquaintance's second marriage as "the triumph of hope over experience," and the same dynamic seems to animate many weddings today. After all, we live in an optimistic culture. A survey published in *The New York Times Magazine* in March 2000 found that 86 percent of respondents, if married that very day, would expect to be married to the same person for the rest of their lives. In 2002, Pamela Paul, an editor at *American Demographics* magazine, published a book entitled *The Starter Marriage,* an investigation of the high incidence of short-lived marriages among her age group (Generation X, born between 1965 and 1978). She suggests that the expectations for marriage today are simply unrealistic: "We want marriage to make us feel intellectually stimulated, emotionally fulfilled, socially enhanced, financially free, and psychologically complete."

The situation is reminiscent of the 1920s. We have seen how authors Phyllis Blanchard and Carlyn Manasses, in *New Girls for Old,* related that the young women of 1930 sought "a new kind of marriage . . . a perfect consummation of both personalities that will involve every phase of mutual living." Divorce rates leapt in the 1920s with the change in expectations for marriage, just as they have done in recent years. Brides and grooms of the twenty-first century face an additional barrier to conjugal felicity, though. Eighty-odd years ago, it was still likely that a young man and young woman facing each other before the altar came from similar backgrounds. Social mobility was still quite limited in this country and people didn't often meet counterparts from a different class, race, nationality, or religion. That circumstance has changed dramatically. Young people leave home for college, travel for work, even "meet" on the Internet. They set out to spend their lives together but may approach this task with very different values, assumptions, and habits. Hope, exhilaration, and love bring them together, but often preserving their unions requires a level of effort and diplomacy beyond the reach of most mortals. In this instance the Prince and

Princess of Wales's marriage, like their wedding, was what Walter Bagehot called a "brilliant edition of a universal fact," marked by infidelity, gossip, warring friends, and wounded children.

Still, when it comes time to plan a wedding, nobody remembers the odds. If weddings do represent "the triumph of hope over experience," the participants see the operative word as "triumph." Elaboration is the watchword of the day, a state of affairs that has been the rule since the 1980s. Although the all-out grandeur of the Wales's wedding in 1981 can't be replicated by mere American citizens, today's brides and grooms aspire to unprecedented levels of formality and lavishness to mark their unions. Nowhere is this more visible than in that primary symbol of a wedding, The Dress. Fashion is cyclical, of course, so the reaction to the informal ruffles-and-pinafore look of the late 1970s might have been predicted. Of *course* we have arrived at the strict minimalist formality of a duchesse satin sheath. The intermediate steps are interesting, though.

One hallmark of wedding gowns in the late 1960s and the '70s was matte fabric. From Tricia Nixon's chaste organza down to an unbleached muslin smock dress, the fabrics did not shine. If they were trimmed with lace, it was often made from coarser fibers like cotton. Macramé was not unknown. Silhouettes were generally vertical, with the waist quite high. When the design team of David and Elizabeth Emanuel sketched Lady Diana Spencer's gown, they both followed and departed from the fashions of the day. They chose a cream-colored silk taffeta, crisp but very light, with a subtle gleam rather than an overt satiny shine. The sleeves were enormous, foreshadowing the big-shoulder look of the mid-eighties when the silhouette for women's wear was an inverted triangle. Equally enormous, though, was the skirt, which billowed over several layers of net, giving the princess the traditional bridal look that harked all the way back to Queen Victoria.

The public loved it. Though the fashion press sniped somewhat at the excess fabric (the dress was often compared to a meringue), Diana's dress was not only copied on an unprecedented scale, it also pushed bridal fashion in a new direction. Many of the nineteenth-century motifs of the previous ten years were retained; high collars, leg-of-mutton sleeves, and piecrust ruffles were simply translated into finer fabrics. The sequins that were sprinkled lightly onto the panels of heirloom lace on Diana's gown were tossed onto less expensive dresses with less restraint. Ditto beading and pearls. In November 1981, America was once again transfixed by a wedding on TV, but this time it was the soap opera matrimonial of *General Hospital*'s Luke Spencer and Laura Webber. It was no doubt the outlandish plot that drew fourteen million spectators for a show that aired at 2 P.M., right in the middle of a work or school day. (The raffish Luke had actually raped Laura on a dance floor months earlier, though she was at the time married to . . . oh, never mind.) The producers hired Elizabeth Taylor to appear as a guest star and media hysteria ensued, perhaps primed by the Charles/Diana spectacle. It was another grandiose event, set at a Los Angeles mansion with an "Indian summer" theme for the decor. Laura's gown followed the high-waisted silhouette of the late 1970s, but the sleeves were gathered to fullness and the bodice was overlaid with beaded lace—details that looked forward to the more ostentatious gowns of the 1980s. The imposing headpiece, though, epitomized the style of an era. Actress Genie Francis's face was framed from ear to ear by a wide band of orange blossom and beading, while billows of tulle framed her long wavy hair. More was definitely more.

It is worth remembering that many of the brides who married in the 1980s were baby boom children. Their own mothers' wedding dresses would have conformed to the silhouette that the Princess of Wales wore, with a tight bodice and a full skirt. To that archetypally feminine outline were added decorations in every conceivable medium. Restraint, in the late 1980s, was not a regular feature of bridal design. Nancy Savoca's film *True Love,* released in 1989, tells the story of two young Italian Americans, Donna and Michael, who are marrying in the neighborhood where they grew up. Donna's dress is a poufy arrangement of satin with liberal applications of beading. Its huge shoulders and ruffled neckline are explicitly reminiscent of the iconic Lady Diana Spencer dress, while her heavily trimmed headpiece belongs to the same family as that of *General Hospital*'s Laura Webber. In *The Wedding Singer,* released in 1998 but set in 1985, the fussiness of the era's bridal fashions becomes a comic point, with beaded lace, shirred sleeves, and elaborate headpieces overwhelming bride after bride. We know Drew Barrymore is the heroine because *her* wedding dress is simple, cleanly cut white shantung.

It is only in the past dozen years that unadorned lines have become the hallmarks of bridal fashion, and it is a change that worked its way from the top down. Vera Wang is frequently given credit for bringing a high-fashion sensibility to bridal design. The often-told story is that in 1990, when Wang married at the age of forty, she had worked at *Vogue* and at Ralph Lauren, and had a sophisticated aesthetic. She

As Donna in the 1989 film *True Love*, Annabella Sciorra wears a gown that
shows the Diana influence. Her busily beaded headpiece, though,
was a late-'80s fashion.

could not find a dress that she liked; bridal salons offered only ornate confections studded with satin roses or puffs of lace, in silhouettes that made her look like a bundle of laundry. As Wang's wedding plans became ever more elaborate, she ended up buying three gowns, though she ultimately wore a pink Scaasi evening dress for the ultraformal reception. Her frustration prompted her to start a business that same year to bring real fashion to brides. She used exquisite fabrics and relied on a simple, elegant silhouette that was sparingly ornamented. A signature Wang look in those early years was a gown with a low-cut bodice or back, veiled in "illusion," a sheer, stretchy fabric. The gowns, while discreet, thus hinted at the sexual nature of the bride.

It was a watershed moment, anyway. Couturiers have always made wedding gowns for their best customers, and have traditionally ended their fashion shows with a wedding dress as a kind of climax of finery. Some have occasionally lent their names to bridal manufacturers for a handful of high-end gowns. This practice continued during the 1980s as Carolina Herrera and Oscar de la Renta, designers known for their felicitous evening wear, waded deeper into the wedding market. At the same time, new entrants to the bridal field, like Amsale Aberra, were closing the gap between bridal and mainstream design. By the mid-1990s, Giorgio Armani had a wedding collection and the design duo of Mark Badgley and James Mischka were turning out sleek, sexy gowns for brides.

We have seen how wedding gowns follow fashion in a parallel current. Wedding dresses are special; their color and formality set them apart from even the most elegant evening wear. (It must be said that designers do tend to steer clear of white evening gowns lest they look too bridal.) In certain eras, though, bridal design comes closer to mainstream fashion than in others. During the twentieth century, wedding apparel has been at its most totemic at the times when becoming a wife carried the most prestige. The brides of the 1950s and '60s embraced marriage as their destinies, and they went to the altar proudly in their neo-Victorian regalia. As the social unrest of the later 1960s and the '70s prompted the next generation of brides to regard marriage with some misgiving, wedding dresses deflated, became less formal, and admitted a certain streetwear influence. Of course there were still proudly conservative brides like Tricia Nixon who opted for the traditionally costumelike white lace. To many other brides, though, the triumphal assurance conveyed by the conventional wedding gown felt a little uncomfortable.

The 1980s were a more conservative period, and bridal fashion took a correspondingly conservative turn, away from punk-influenced streetwear. Headbands and rumpled linen and leggings, or power suits worn with sneakers, were the clothes of every day. Brides, though, turned out in full-sleeved, bead-crusted lace with immense tulle skirts. A woman, when she elected to marry, assumed the bridal identity. Critic Holly Brubach, writing in *The New Yorker* in 1989, ruminated on this disjunction. "A bride is supposed to be young, demure, graceful, happy, and serene. But what a bride is *not* supposed to be is in some ways more telling. She is not sexy. . . . She is not skeptical or ironic, since these are qualities come by through experience. Nor is she funny. . . . She is not worldly wise. The bride is a symbol, and in symbolic terms she is blank."

By the mid-1990s, though, brides were no longer willing to be blank. Average age at marriage was rising. Women came to matrimony with college degrees, jobs, history. Sometimes they came with stock portfolios, sometimes with children from a previous union. They were not willing to erase themselves to assume the identity of Bride. Some found the pressure toward girlishness to be an affront. Some were embarrassed at the vestigial references to virginity implicit in the white dress. "Demure" may never again be an accurate description of a woman about to wed. American women are neither sheltered, nor self-effacing, nor helpless. Least of all are they inexperienced.

The biggest difference between today's wedding gowns and those of the previous 150 years is sex. Throughout the twentieth century it was considered imperative for a bride to cover her back and shoulders in a house of worship, so even the lowest-cut dresses had straps or removable boleros or shrugs. As recently as the mid-1990s, the plunging necklines and backs of fashionable dresses were veiled with illusion. This is no longer the case. Sleeveless, backless, strapless brides march up the aisle with their skin gleaming, leaving little to anyone's imagination. Furthermore, though full-skirted ball gowns held on well into the '90s (witness Mariah Carey's duchesse satin Vera Wang, worn in 1993), the strapless sheath silhouette and its close relative, the slip dress, have had a spell of dominance since then.

As any designer will tell you, both styles are hard to wear; their snug vertical cuts don't flatter women with roundness or curves, and in fact many brides opt for a fuller, more forgiving skirt. By the same token a strapless gown, with its straight line across the top of the bodice, is merciless to women who might bulge a little bit. But in our culture, a slender physique is the ultimate status symbol. The woman who is thin enough to

Not a bride but a model, captured at a wedding photographers' convention in Las Vegas in 2002. Her strapless gown and tiara, so typical of current bridal fashion, are far from the virginal styles of a hundred years ago.

wear a figure-hugging gown up the aisle either is genetically fortunate or has invested hours (and probably many dollars) in exercise or surgery to achieve the fashionable figure. Women who work hard at their figures want to show them off, even at the moment when, traditionally, they are removing themselves from the sexual marketplace. In fact, this phenomenon is established enough to have spawned books of exercise and diet regimes aimed specifically at the bride. That walk up the aisle with hundreds of eyes on you is as daunting as it is exciting. If a wedding isn't the ultimate chance to show off, what exactly is it?

In today's thinking, it is also a chance to define yourself. And the wedding gown, in addition to trumpeting a woman's attractions to all observers, is required to encapsulate her personality—"It's me!" In an interview with *InStyle Weddings,* designer Reem Acra provides the following advice for brides choosing a gown. "You have to think, What do I want to say at my wedding? 'I'm sexy?' 'I'm elegant?' Do you want to say, 'I'm pure and innocent?' I always ask my brides, 'Who are you and what do you want to tell everybody?'"

No wonder brides are willing to spend enormous sums on this garment. In Laura Wolf's 2001 novel *Diary of a Mad Bride,* the narrator calls her dress "the most important, most photographed, most expensive item of clothing I will ever wear once in my life." Charles Wesley Lewis, in his Ph.D. thesis, refers to the gown as "the central ritualized object of most weddings and . . . one of the most expensive objects displayed in ceremonies." Observers can't help harping on the cost. A thousand-dollar dress is a relative bargain, and there is no upper limit at all. When Catherine Zeta-Jones married Michael Douglas in 2000, her custom-made Christian Lacroix gown of ivory duchesse satin trimmed with eighteenth-century Chan-tilly lace was rumored to cost $160,000. Few brides can dream of spending that much, but the options hovering between five thousand and ten thousand dollars certainly are numerous, appealing, and widely advertised. An "inexpensive" wedding gown is much harder to track down.

In fact, Catherine Zeta-Jones and her ilk are part of the problem. The dynamic of wedding planning in America has always involved some yearning glances toward a higher social stratum. In 1863, Tom Thumb's wedding was an imitation of a New York patrician wedding. The popular press and, later, movies and television have told the masses how the upper class married and the masses, to the extent possible, followed suit. After World War II, when the wedding industry really swung into gear, the financial qualifications for mounting a grand formal wedding dropped further down the socioeco-nomic scale until working-class families could afford to marry off their daughters with wedding parties in black tie, white limousines, and multicourse dinners served to hundreds of friends and relatives. Just like Newport or Palm Beach.

In recent years, though, celebrities have usurped much of the nation's attention. The huge success of *People* magazine after its 1974 launch exposed an insatiable public appetite for the mundane details of the lives of the famous—usually actors and actresses. *People* tracked their marriages and divorces, their arrests and vacations and trips to the rehab clinic. It wasn't long before other publications and media outlets caught on. Decorating glossies ran features on the celebrity homes. The women's magazines put stars on their covers. In 1994, Time Inc. launched *InStyle,* a fashion monthly that fo-cused on what celebrities wore and bought. It, too, was an enormous success. Readers apparently longed to wear the same lipstick as Michelle Pfeiffer and burn the same scented candles as Sandra Bullock.

Weddings, naturally, were a staple feature of these celebrity-driven publications. Weddings have always been fascinating, providing as they do an intimate glimpse of a stranger's emotional and sexual life in an event that the average person has also experienced. They are visually thrilling and require very little verbal explanation (one reason they were so often featured in silent motion pictures). And they are almost always photographed professionally, so that clear, usable images of each step of the ritual abound. It didn't take long for the press agents of actors and actresses to grasp the delightful opportunity offered by *People* and, later, *InStyle*. All they had to do was provide a publication's photographers with access, make sure the reporter had accurate information (the bridesmaids' dresses were melon, not shrimp), and they were assured uncritical coverage for their clients. Even weddings with apparently minimal chance for success were covered breathlessly. When Jennifer Lopez married Cris Judd, a dancer on one of her videos, *People* quoted guests gushing about the simplicity and sincerity of the proceedings. (The marriage lasted mere months.)

At the same time, the opportunities for the average bride and groom to take on star status had multiplied. The upper-class attitude toward publicity, as we have seen, has been reversed since America's wedding practices took form. The solicitude for the privacy of the virginal bride that animated mid-nineteenth-century families had evaporated by the turn of the century. Every newspaper's social pages were filled with news of the teas and dances and engagements and weddings

The ubiquitous coverage of celebrity weddings sets a high standard for the average couple to match. Here, Adam Sandler's elegant bride, Jackie Tritone, helps him create a moment of intimacy for the photographer.

of the community's worthies. They were a roughly accurate indication of the social status of the bride and groom; the higher the parents' standing, the more ink was expended on details like flowers, dresses, and wedding presents.

The standards were fairly stable right through World War II. David and Mary Hatch presented a paper at the Eastern Sociological Society in May 1946 (it was later published in the *American Sociological Review*) that spelled out what they called the "Criteria of Social Status" manifested by the marriage announcements of *The New York Times*. This is one of those studies whose merit consists of stating the obvious: the *Times* featured the weddings of young people whose parents or grandparents were rich and distinguished, frequently in business. A third of them had second homes and "there were no addresses in the Bronx or in Greenwich Village." Most of them went to private schools, and the boys frequently attended Ivy League colleges while the girls' histories alluded to debuts and membership in the Junior League. Although many of the grooms were in business, it is clearly the family backgrounds of the couples that render them worthy of inclusion in the *Times*'s pages. About 16 percent of the couples mentioned ancestors who had been prominent in early American history, signers of the Declaration of Independence or the like. Not one of the ceremonies mentioned had been Jewish.

The New York Times was a more local paper back in the 1940s, but even as its reach became national, the social pages remained quite parochial. By the 1980s they were referred to flippantly by their constituency as the "Women's Sports" pages and the competition for inclusion was intense. Exclusion of minorities had long since gone by the board and mentions of the Society of Mayflower Descendants were more scarce, but Hotchkiss and IBM and the American Yacht Club still predominated. Gradually the newspaper shifted its emphasis to couples who had managed to rack up their own achievements before deciding to wed. Foreign names started to creep in amid distinctions like fellowships in orthopedics (for the bride) or clerkships for Circuit Court judges.

The big change, though, came in 1992 when a writer named Lois Smith Brady was dispatched to provide more complete coverage of one wedding per week, which ran in a separate boxed item entitled "Vows." Brady spent several hours interviewing her subjects as well as attending their wedding, and larded her columns with quotations from bride, groom, friends, and family. The photographs illustrating the "Vows" weddings were more varied than the age-old studio head shot of the bride in her white regalia; the photographer, Edward Keating, captured unscripted moments from unconventional angles. What's more, Brady covered weddings like the peripatetic Manhattan celebration of Melissa Richard and Frank Oteri (who, with their thirty-odd guests, traveled from a Hell's Kitchen coffee shop to Bryant Park to the Dia Center for the Arts, getting officially hitched on the No. 1 subway train), as well as the formal Greenwich nuptials of Ariane Noel and Marco Sodi, whose four hundred guests had dinner at the Round Hill Country Club.

The "Vows" innovation was very popular, and as if in response, the rest of the *Times* announcements loosened up. Photographs began to include both bride and groom, and were more likely to be informal shots of the pair grinning on a mountaintop than the couple in their finery. (Newspapers must have photographs in hand well before the wedding day, and rare is the groom who will don his nuptial togs just for the sake of a visit to a photographer's studio.) The copy began to include details like how the bride and groom met and what they saw in each other. Engagement announcements were discreetly dropped. Finally, in September 2002, "the newspaper of record" took an unprecedented step and ran the news of a Vermont civil union ceremony between Daniel Gross and Steven Goldstein. Since then, homosexual couples, both men and women, have been scattered casually into the mix.

The changes at *The New York Times* and the social pages of newspapers all over the country, in addition to broadening the pool of candidates for coverage, brought a new potential for notoriety to brides and grooms. Your wedding announcement, if the paper ran it, could be studded with personal details of a nature that would have made a nineteenth-century bride faint. The lucky few brides were thus doubly feted: first, in an age of anxiety about the mere possibility of ever finding a spouse, they were among the fortunate chosen. Then they really hit the jackpot by being celebrated in the press. Getting married brought not only public affirmation of your lovability: it also brought that greatest of all millennial goodies, fame.

There's another kind of fame, though, even more thrilling than having your story told in black and white for thousands to read. We have become, in the last quarter century, a society of the image rather than of the word. So, gratifying though it may be to have your new husband's special nickname for you tossed onto thousands of doormats on a Sunday morning, it might be even better to have *pictures* of your wedding published. The "Vows" column is only partially satisfying, since newspaper reproduction is grainy at best. But if your wedding of the early 1980s was photographed for Martha Stewart's 1987 *Weddings,* that was a whole new kind of celebrity. The book sold immensely well, not merely because it was a practical help in wedding planning, but because it offered a glimpse into the hugely attractive celebrations of dozens of attractive people. Some of the weddings were as modest as the potluck Martha's Vineyard ceremony of Mimi Dabrowski and Tom Thomas, which took place in a sunny September meadow. More were like the high-society Long Island event that joined Hilary Cushing and John Block. All of them, photographed by Christopher Baker, look intensely glamorous.

The wedding magazines had always acknowledged actual brides and grooms. Through the 1930s and '40s, for instance, *Bride's* ran formal portraits of brides from around the country, usually submitted to the magazine by the big photo studios like Bachrach. By the mid-'90s, the practice of including real weddings in the editorial mix was firmly established. For magazines, the benefits were clear. Though the editorial effort involved in scouting acceptably photogenic celebrations was considerable, nothing gave a publication as much credibility with its readers as the inclusion of real people amid the posed pages of gowns and fussy cakes. Bridal magazines present themselves as friendly, trustworthy guides for brides-to-be: the inclusion of genuine brides and grooms in their pages guarantees that they know what they're talking about.

One curious result, though, is that being a bride looks more and more like being a celebrity. Of course not every bride is going to appear in the pages of *Modern Bride* or even the *Bride's Guide for Northern Indiana and the Chicago Suburbs*. But some everyday women do turn up on those glossy pages—and the effect is honestly not that different from the pictures of, say, Sarah Michelle Gellar's wedding in *People*. The lines are blurring: celebrities' private lives are exposed to public view, while private people are elevated to the rank of celebrity for the period of their wedding.

We see this not only in print, but in the immensely powerful medium of television as well. TV has traditionally made
use of weddings to boost ratings or to end a season with a
bang. *Runaway Bride* director Garry Marshall, who also di-
rected and produced years of television comedies, told Amy
Spindler in a *New York Times* article, "That was the tradition
in TV. When your ratings went down, you turned it into a
wedding. We got Fonzie married, we got Richie married, we
got Mork married. We almost got Laverne married. We got
Shirley married. Brides and sweeps weeks go together in TV.
When you leave it out, they ask you about it." Weddings look
good, they provide an excuse to bring all the characters together, they are a familiar situation that viewers grasp instantly
so they require little time-consuming exposition—yet they
provide a real alteration in the characters' relationships that
promises interesting new dynamics.

Of course, what can be done with sets and costumes and
highly paid actors can also be done—infinitely less expensively—with real people. This is the premise of the Learning
Channel's *A Wedding Story*. Each half-hour segment follows
one couple through their wedding preparations to the reception, one wedding per episode. Interviews with both fiancés at
the beginning of the show establish their back story: how they
met, how they began dating, when they knew "it was serious,"
and how the proposal came about. Cameras accompany the
couples through visits to the reception site, to the florist's, to
the wedding rehearsal. We meet the in-laws and see them
meeting each other, often a moment of real tension. We watch
the bride's transformation at the beauty parlor on the morning of the wedding. We walk up the aisle with her and witness
the vows. At the reception—in the backyard, on a yacht, in

the church meeting hall—we hear the toasts and watch the cutting of the cake. The Learning Channel runs two segments of these shows back to back as often as five times a week, but it's not the only cable television channel sending cameramen to follow brides up the aisle. Lifetime produces a special entitled *Weddings in America* that spends an hour on four real-life weddings all over the country. Then there's the notorious Fox show entitled *Who Wants to Marry a Millionaire?* that aired in February 2000. Fifty would-be brides were chosen from among one thousand women who contacted Fox. Each of them was willing to marry, on-screen, a man chosen for her by a TV producer. The groom, a plausible rogue named Rick Rockwell, selected the perky blonde Darva Conger, and the two were wed on the spot with all the pomp a girl could dream of. Twenty-three million viewers shared the spectacle, which was about all it amounted to. Darva came back from the Barbados honeymoon asking for an annulment. News of the restraining order that a former fiancée had filed against Rockwell in 1991 didn't help.

A somewhat more dignified tack is taken by the morning shows, which have a rather more conservative audience to please. Both *Good Morning America* and *Today* marry couples on-camera. In the kind of dizzying corporate arrangement that media companies refer to as "synergy," the shows' producers link with established wedding authorities and vendors who provide their goods or services and reap the incredible publicity afforded by the show. There's even an element of audience participation. In May 2002, *Good Morning America* spun out the planning process for Sandy Bass and Junius Chambers's wedding over more than a week. Ten days before the wedding, the bride's dress was chosen (with online voters' help) from among five that Sandy had approved. Each gown was modeled and its price noted: the audience chose for the bride a fresh-looking layered tulle ball gown with multicolored embroidered flowers and a peach tulle underskirt, listed at three thousand dollars. The bridesmaids' gowns, settled on the next day, were orange and coral chiffon, to pick up the warm tones of the gown. Then the flowers could be selected, with a photogenic trip to New York City's flower market: Sandy and the floral designer liked peonies, sweet peas, and roses in the same warm palette. The cake, a version of which had appeared in *InStyle Weddings,* was a model called "Pleats and Pearls." When the wedding finally took place at 8 A.M. on a cool, rain-spattered morning in Times Square, it was an extremely stylish celebration.

One of the benefits to Sandy Bass in getting married on television was that she looked magnificent. She was a very pretty woman to begin with, but under the ministrations of TV makeup artists, with the perfect hairdo and a dream of a gown, she reached the groomed-and-styled apogee of looks that passes for beauty today. This is one of the striking features that sets apart today's brides from those of even twenty years ago. It's comical to read beauty articles from *Bride's* in the 1960s or '70s: what the magazine recommends as a routine to maximize bridal gorgeousness is pitifully sketchy. Where are the waxing, the exfoliation, the sleeping in gloves to soften the hands, and hot oil packs to condition hair, starting four months in advance? Where are the facials for your back, the almond milk pedicures, the trial professional makeup applications at $150 a shot? In those innocent old days, brides were expected to pluck their eyebrows, file their nails, and apply rosy pink lipstick, but a more polished presentation would have looked outlandish. Nowadays, though, the beauty culture is so highly developed that not only the bride's primping, but that of her groom and his ushers, comes under scrutiny. It's not uncommon for bridesmaids to wear matching nail polish (one bride took things a step further and insisted that they all have their hair highlighted the same shade of blonde). Another woman required all the groomsmen to have pedicures for her beach wedding. Yet another couple's nuptials were so meticulously styled that the guests were instructed to come outfitted in white linen. Party coordinator Colin Cowie told *InStyle* that "it was a stunning visual effect," but it sure makes a celebration resemble a photo shoot.

This is the unfortunate corollary of blurring the lines between celebrities and real people: the standards get impossibly high. We avidly watch famous actresses doing something we intend to do. The brides are always slender, their gowns are always from Vera Wang, their engagement rings are never smaller than three carats, and the cake never has fewer than three tiers. How can we live up to this? How can everyday brides make themselves as attractive as twenty-six-year-old TV stars? How can the average working couple put on a wedding that measures up to Madonna's? The older service-oriented magazines like *Modern Bride* present a corrective of sorts with their articles on "$20,000 Weddings That Wow," but it's hard to counteract grandiosity like *InStyle Weddings'* airy statement (Spring 2002) that "Many brides are presented with family jewels to wear at their wedding. . . ." And honestly, what is more interesting? An intimate dinner for fifty-five guests in Tiburon, California? Or Keely Shaye Smith's marriage to Pierce Brosnan in a castle in Ireland? To which she wore a Richard Tyler silk dress covered with a long-sleeved, pearl-beaded lace coat, and an antique pearl and diamond tiara? Who wouldn't prefer to read about the Brosnan/Smith flowers that required fifteen florists and their own tent for storage? Or the five-tier carrot cake inspired by Jacqueline Bouvier Kennedy's? Then there's Toni Braxton's wedding to musician Keri Lewis, which was Tiffany-themed. Yes, Tiffany & Co. is Braxton's favorite store, so the flower girls carried, instead of bouquets, boxes in that telltale shade of robin's egg blue. The linens and chairs at the reception, even the carpet, echoed the color scheme. The rose centerpieces cascaded out of . . . blue boxes. The wedding favors came from a certain fine jeweler, and even the cake was a stack of trompe l'oeil boxes with blue icing. Only the bride's tiara broke ranks, since it was a 116-carat antique on loan from Los Angeles jeweler Stephen Russell.

Some observers interpret this kind of grandiosity as social climbing, whether it's enacted by celebrities or civilians. As Amy Spindler pointed out in a *New York Times* article in 1998, "It's the only formal party some people are ever invited to. It's the only couture dress many women will ever own. It's the only catered event many people ever attend." All of which is true. The existence of a wedding industry has made this social event available to many people whose wedding announcements are never going to be in *The New York Times.* Back in the 1960s, when a remnant of the traditional WASP oligarchy still held positions of power in government, business, and the media, the social practices of that class still held sway. In some circles, it seemed uppity for, say, a postman's daughter to aspire to a black-tie wedding.

Those days are long gone. You can still find an etiquette expert to tell you that men should not wear tuxedos before 6 P.M., but who is going to care? And who wants to be a WASP anymore, anyway? To the extent that the average person has an idea of how the wealthy live, it's not in the discreet, private comfort celebrated in Philip Barry's *The Philadelphia Story.* (In the film, Tracy Lord's reluctance to expose her wedding preparations to the public is a major plot point.) Instead, it's a vision of luxury gleaned from movies and television shows, like *Dallas* or *Lifestyles of the Rich and Famous.* The traditional hallmarks of good taste ("we don't wear diamonds at breakfast," for instance) have long since given way to a more obvious idea of splendor and expense, which naturally animates the ordinary bride's desires when it comes to wedding planning.

But the social climbing notion may hold more water if you look at celebrities as today's upper class. This is the point behind *InStyle* magazine and it is perfectly logical in our consumer culture. You are what you buy. If Nicole Kidman furnished her living room with a certain chair, your possession of the chair endows you with some of Nicole Kidman's qualities. If Toni Braxton and Keely Shaye Smith wore tiaras up the aisle, by doing so you may share some of their nuptial glamour.

In fact, for many women, being a bride provides the sole taste of celebrity status they'll ever know. They get an enormous amount of attention. They are admired, photographed, applauded. In Charles Wesley Lewis's Ph.D. thesis, he quotes a Minnesota bride as saying, "It was like for one day I was going to be the star of the show. It's not too often you get to do that. . . . Everyone looks at the bride. Everyone was waiting on you for once—I felt pampered." The elaborate preparations for the wedding day contribute to the feeling. How many brides routinely have their hair arranged in intricate curled "updos"? How many have ever had another person ap-

The photographer twitches the bride's train into place before getting his "bride, groom, and groomsmen" shot. The flower beds and lush grass provide the perfect setting for wedding pictures.

ply their makeup? How many have undergone the sublime tedium of having a dress fitted by a skilled seamstress to their own inimitable bodies? How many women have ever stood at the end of a large room and heard the rustle of everyone turning around to gaze at them?

Movie stars, that's who. Royalty. Recording artists. Models. As Gwyneth Paltrow put it in an interview with *W* magazine, many women "have the whole wedding fantasy. It's their day at the Oscars: to have hair and makeup and wear the big dress." And, of course, to be followed everywhere by a photographer or two, a videographer, and their guests, equipped with disposable cameras provided at the reception. Many wedding days are now planned to include an interlude for formal photography, whether at the church or synagogue, at the reception site, or at a third, picturesque location. On summer weekends, the prettiest city parks are often lined with limousines as wedding parties take their turns to be photographed by the weeping willow or the heather garden. The bride is central to all photographs, whether of wedding party, extended families, or newlyweds. The personnel not being photographed—and any passersby: it's hard not to stop and watch—stand behind the photographer, creating an audience. Maids fluff the bride's veil, powder her nose, arrange her train around her feet. She turns this way and that, drops her chin, raises her flowers an inch at the photographer's request. It is a heady experience for a woman. One of the brides quoted in Lewis's thesis told him, "Finally, I got center stage in something." Finally. Having "center stage," being the focus of all eyes is so highly prized in today's culture that many of us, relegated to the background, feel diminished until we get our turn in the spotlight. And once in the spotlight, some hate to leave. One California couple, Christie Jeans and Brian Davis, profiled in the spring 2002 edition of *Elegant Bride,* chose to marry in Venice. Their photographer helped them find a church that would perform the rite for two non-Italians. After an early afternoon ceremony, "Christie and Brian stole away with their photographer to record the day against the dazzling staging of Venice." They roamed the city in their wedding finery, posing in gondolas and piazzas. Finally the sun went down and the newlyweds joined their guests for a dinner "which, luckily, in Venice, starts around nine o'clock," noted the bride. What is more real here—the wedding or the pictures? Promising to share a life with another person, or being photographed in the costume of someone who has just made that promise, in front of an exotic background?

Christie and Brian's pictures are great, though. Part of the mission of a wedding photographer is to record an ideal event, and in this case the man did his job. For the majority of brides and grooms with a less ambitious vision, an important reason to hire a professional photographer is that he or she can retouch. Smudge on the dress? Blemish on the chin? Whoosh: the pro makes them vanish. What's more, the progression of standard wedding pictures—the procession, the vows, the receiving line, the first dance—depicts a stately, predictable, and correct event. Video, which has the advantage of being fresh and lively, often introduces an element of risk, and mars the perfect facade of the ideal wedding memory. A still photograph will capture the bride's poignant dance with her father, but the video will record that Dad can't dance. The photographers Lewis interviewed in Minnesota pointed out that the shots they sold the most prints of were the formal portraits and family groups, the pictures that could be posed, framed, and lit to flatter. The photographs that depict what really *happened*—the action photographs, as it were—are less popular.

Photography is such a basic element of the wedding ritual that we take it for granted. If you've been married, you have wedding pictures. If you have wedding pictures, they'll fall into certain categories: the formal portraits, the pictures that tell the story of the wedding, and the candids. It's standard procedure to agree on a list of shots with the professional photographer, who is likely to know, better than the bride and groom, what images they will want of their wedding. Part of what's recorded is the assemblage of people, since weddings unite large family groups. But, as Lewis points out, some of what's being captured is *stuff*. The regalia of a wedding is expensive and fleeting; this is where the Cinderella myth really applies. The dress is worn once, the flowers fade, the cake is eaten, the coach turns back into a pumpkin. But they are all recorded meticulously on film. Formal portraits of the bride often depict her from the back, looking over her shoulder, so that her gown's bustle and the tiny fabric-covered buttons running down her spine can be captured forever. Many wedding albums feature a shot of the cake before it's cut, often with the bride's bouquet placed next to it. The photographs attest that all of these beautiful creations existed before the clock struck twelve and everyone went back to being normal workaday people.

CHAPTER 11

This Is Not Real Life

Wedding photographs memorialize the greatest spending spree most couples will ever know. If it weren't for the pictures, poof! There's twenty thousand dollars gone up in smoke, for what really amounts to a big party. That, at least, is the average spent on a wedding today, give or take a few thousand dollars. The size of the "wedding industry" as a whole is reported to be anything from $22 billion to $70 billion in annual revenue. This includes money spent on honeymoon travel as well as purchase of a home and all the attendant costs of furnishing it, which seems like a pretty broad way of defining wedding costs. Still, even without factoring the price of a flat-screen TV and wall-to-wall carpet into the accounting, weddings are a formidable expense. Part of the reason for this is demographic. Brides and grooms both work now, and the median ages at first marriage in 2000 were 26.8 for men, 25.1 for women. (In 1970, those medians were 22.5 for men, 21.7 for women.) In contrast to the situation thirty years ago, couples often pay for their weddings themselves or share the cost with their parents. More of them (though still a small fraction) are using wedding consultants, who may tend to mount more elaborate wedding productions. And the size of today's wedding is large: in 1997 *Bride's* estimated the average at 250 guests. Mobile as we are in America now, bride and groom may well come from different parts of the country. Having been to different universities, perhaps, and held one or two jobs, both may have large networks of friends with little overlap. That makes for a long invitation list.

Sometimes cultural values drive up costs, too. *The New York Times* ran a story in 1995 about a waiter in a Brooklyn restaurant who had saved thirty-five thousand dollars for his eldest daughter's wedding, which took place at a catering hall in Bensonhurst. Relatives from Italy flew over for the event, which celebrated family and hospitality in the most lavish way. Possibly these were the desires motivating Catherine Zeta-Jones and Michael Douglas in the planning for their November 2000 wedding. The bride called it "a simple, down-home affair" and told a reporter, "I don't think of it as a Hollywood wedding. I think of it as a family wedding. . . . There's something very homespun about it." The "family" elements no doubt included the presence of the bride and groom's three-month-old son, as well as the more usual parents of bride and groom and children from previous marriages. What was "homespun" about a 350-guest event at the Plaza Hotel that involved personnel like a lighting designer and a "wedding producer" is harder to discern, unless the bride was referring to the forty-voice Welsh choir that announced her arrival.

Only the Douglases (and their wedding producer) know for sure what this fiesta cost them, though they did earn some money back by selling exclusive photography rights to the British celebrity magazine *OK!* for $1.4 million. The average bride and groom don't have that option, though they may be spending a mere $900 for their wedding cake, or $1,000 for the gown, or $3,000 for the engagement ring. The numbers add up fast. The bride's and attendants' bouquets come in around $500. A four-piece band for four hours averages about $800. Photography is around $1,000 and the food alone for the reception (forget any rental fee for the space, forget liquor) amounts to an average of $7,500. These numbers come from the 1997 edition of Diane Warner's *How to Have a Big Wedding on a Small Budget.* Previous editions had sold more than 100,000 copies and her direct competitors, Denise and Alan Fields, have sold more than 300,000 copies of *Bridal Bargains.* Brides and grooms obviously have a keen interest in cost containment.

That's one way to cope with the high cost of a wedding: plan carefully and save money where you can. Another, less prudent way is going into debt. In July 2002, *New York* magazine ran a profile of a "money counselor" that included an interview with a young woman named A. J. Pierce. Though she already owed nearly $35,000 to various creditors, she was planning a $35,000 wedding to take place in three months. Confronted by the reality that she would return from her honeymoon to bills for another $22,000, she could only protest, "I just want to be a beautiful bride. . . ."

And who can blame her? Everyone wants to be a beautiful bride and to have the full bridal experience. They don't all need the Welsh choir, but they crave the strapless satin gown and the three-tier cake and the champagne. A few intrepid couples have even ventured, logically enough as they see it, into finding corporate sponsors. In a September 2000 *New York Times* article, Julia Chaplin reported on Tom Anderson and Sabrina Root, who persuaded twenty-four local businesses to donate goods and services, from the "castle" venue for the reception to the stretch limousine. In return, the groom credited each vendor by name before the first toast. The Andersons managed to save themselves some thirty thousand dollars and get on Oprah's afternoon TV show (prolonging their nuptial celebrity), but they do not appear to have sparked a trend. It's hard enough to line up suppliers for a wedding without trying to find ones who will provide their goods for free. Another novel approach came from a group of Orthodox Jewish rabbis in New York State. In response to the inflated expenditures on weddings in their community, the rabbis proposed guidelines for modest wedding celebrations. Orthodox Jews have large families (six to eight children are not uncommon) and they marry young, so parents have to pay for lots of weddings, and invitation lists mount easily to four hundred guests. The limitations suggested by the rabbis were very concrete: one musician rather than several, decorations costing no more than one thousand eight hundred dollars and a ban on open bars, dessert tables, and meat-carving stations.

However admirable these restraints are, however sensible the authors who tout rental wedding gowns and borrowed cars instead of limousines, they are fighting an uphill battle. The wedding industry may not account for $70 billion in annual revenue but it certainly produces millions of vivid and ambitious dreams. Simplifying, paring down, or eliminating expensive elements of a wedding is very difficult to do. Part of what makes it hard is the newness of the situation. Nobody, not even Elizabeth Taylor, gets married often enough to find it an ordinary experience. Each wedding must be unique. If you're marrying for the third time you don't want your wedding to replicate your first nuptial celebration. And unless we belong to the tiny handful of people who routinely entertain hundreds at formal parties, most of us feel at sea in the world of freelance waiters and rented ballroom chairs. We may not be desperate enough to sign on with a wedding planner but we're certainly going to buy a book or a magazine or two.

The problem is that seeking help and advice from anywhere within the wedding industry leads in one direction only: toward *more*. Rare indeed is the consultant, rare is the magazine article that will suggest that a lovely reception would be a quiet lunch for the newlyweds' immediate families. Magazines do not feature articles about homegrown bouquets or potluck receptions. These options would not make the advertisers happy. The advertisers (and they are legion: *Bride's* averages 700 ad pages per issue and has reached as high as 1,150) want to push the expenditure on weddings ever higher.

They have been very successful in the last twenty years. Angela Thompson, in a Ph.D. thesis, tracks a steadily rising curve in the cost of the average wedding. In constant numbers, the tab ran between $4,000 and $5,000 in 1983. By 1991 it had climbed to over $13,000. Ten years later it was up to $20,000—an increase of 400 percent in twenty years.

There are various reasons for the inflation in costs and elaboration of weddings that began in the 1980s. In some respects, a big splashy wedding fulfills an emotional need. Many couples today live together before marrying, so the wedding does not mark a pronounced change in their day-to-day life. When our wedding practices formed, in the nineteenth century, the wedding day made a bridge between two sets of radically different circumstances, as a young girl went from being a child to being the sexually active chief executive of a household. Today, the identity shift is not nearly so clean-cut—and not nearly so positive. A newlywed woman in the nineteenth century earned a new level of respect as she joined the honorable ranks of matrons. Now, every woman who marries in the twenty-first century has to figure out for herself what it is to be a wife, and she won't get a lot of cues from the culture around her. The job description for "wife" in 1875 was clear-cut and included perquisites like deference and freedom from supervision. Nowadays it's a lateral move at best, and one that involves unfamiliar but weirdly unspecified responsibilities. Many brides and grooms cohabit before marrying; they're almost certainly sexually active; they frequently return to the same jobs after the honeymoon. Thus, the once-in-a-lifetime flourish of a big wedding may serve to help couples mark the change between two nearly indistinguishable phases of life.

That flourish may also, at an unspoken level, be a hedge against disaster. No couple agrees to marry today without wary acknowledgment of The Numbers, that 40 percent to 50 percent failure rate. Angela Thompson, in her Ph.D. thesis, quotes Jeffrey Stockard, the president of the Association of Wedding Planners, as saying, "There's a thing called a demonstration. The bigger the demonstration, the more the commitment. So the bigger the wedding, the more the kids subconsciously are saying their wedding will work." Pamela Paul, in *The Starter Marriage,* phrases things just a little differently: "In our consumer society, it's almost as if we think that by spending money on our weddings, we'll be able to buy ourselves happy marriages."

Or at least relief from anxiety: anxiety about marrying and anxiety about mounting an elaborate, expensive social production to mark the marriage. Buying things to alleviate tension is a modern American coping mechanism. Primitive societies saw the rite of passage into marriage as a transition fraught with danger, and enacted rituals to protect brides and grooms. In our consumer society, maybe it's the magic of the dollar that we're invoking to protect each young couple. Spending money to keep up with the Joneses is also a favored American pastime, and both of these factors come into play when weddings are being planned. Did your best friend have a trumpeter playing in the church? A raw bar at the reception? Cuban cigars for the ushers? Say yes to all of the above. Even without refinements like wedding cake decor to match the lace on the wedding gown, the basic elements of the wedding have been ramped up in the last twenty years. A seated dinner at the reception is now the norm, rather than passed hors d'oeuvres or a buffet. Wedding favors are usually provided, as well as little welcome gifts for out-of-town guests. Since no bride and groom today feel the need to rush off to consummate their relationship, wedding receptions tend to last longer, often involving dancing, and there may be a brunch the next day as well, attended by the bride and groom. In today's mobile society, families and guests often travel long distances for a wedding, so there is distinct pressure to make the event worth their while. It's not at all uncommon for a wedding to stretch out over an entire weekend's worth of dinners and brunches and activities like hiking or spa visits or rounds of golf. Only the "going-away outfit," a demure little suit worn with a corsage, seems to have been dropped from the list of wedding necessities.

And then there is the astonishing array of goods and services eagerly made available to free-spending fiancés. Some involve outlandish refinement of traditional elements: you can pay up to forty dollars per serving for wedding cake (decorated with blown-sugar balls) or forty dollars per invitation (on paper threaded with gold leaf) before calligraphy and postage. It is always possible for the rich and famous to push the boundaries; if Melissa Rivers wants the Plaza Hotel to look like St. Petersburg in a snowstorm, thirty thousand roses and hydrangeas wired to a forest of twenty-foot birch trees, all bathed in a cool blue light, can make her wish come true. (And then mother of the bride Joan can wear a gown trimmed with sable, to carry out the theme.) But the hoi polloi can spend ridiculously, too. If you look at wedding pictures from the 1960s you see the guests sitting on humble folding metal chairs, but today, rental chairs come with their own little shrouds in white tulle or brocade tastefully colored to match the table linens—for an extra five dollars to ten dollars per chair. "Save the Date" cards are being urged on couples as part of the stationery they need to order, as are menu cards to ensure that guests know what they're eating. A catalog called "Exclusively Weddings" presents nearly five hundred items, from a tulle-and-bead-trimmed baseball cap ("Feel Like a Bride for More Than a Day") to a monogrammed silver-plate cover for the wedding video. It offers a set of three matching photo albums to accommodate the pictures from wedding parties, rehearsal dinner, and the wedding itself. Then there's a range of lace-trimmed linen handkerchiefs that can be embroidered with sentiments like "For your tears of joy" or "Thank you for raising your son to be the man of my dreams." The catalog even sells "designer rice" for guests to throw as the bride and groom leave the church. It has long been a custom to toss rice over the new couple, a practice that alludes to fertility. In recent years, though, rice has gone out of favor since birds reputedly get sick after eating the dry kernels. Birdseed replaced rice for a while, but now there is "environmentally correct rice which has been specially developed to dissolve in water and crush underfoot. Its heart-shaped grains add a romantic touch." You'd need a hard heart to opt for millet and sunflower seeds when good old rice has been so strenuously engineered for nuptial purposes.

If even the rice thrown at the bride and groom is heart-shaped for a "romantic touch," clearly no item is too small to overlook. What's more, if a couple goes to the trouble of supplying their guests with designer rice, they must believe that such efforts will be noticed. Which means that no minute element of the planning can escape scrutiny; everything, from the brand of champagne served to the color of the cherry tomatoes in the salad, must be *selected*. Yellow cherry tomatoes are trendy and up-to-date, the red ones something you might find on an airline dinner tray. Every detail is deemed to have meaning, and every choice reflects on the bride and groom.

This theme runs through all American lifestyle advertising, from car commercials to print ads for diamond jewelry. An individual's choice of watch, of beer, of sneaker is supposed to communicate his character to the casual observer. And if you are what you buy, it's never more true than on your wedding day. Guests are supposed to be able to interpret consumer choices (gold lamé tablecloths, Cornish game hens, a klezmer band) as facets of the couple's personality. Pamela Paul, in *The Starter Marriage,* cites a couple whose reception included a cigar bar, a martini lounge, and a massive ice sculpture. The bride said that she wanted guests to be struck by these features and to think, "Wow, *that's* Jennifer and Tom."

This attitude puts tremendous pressure on the people

planning a wedding. If the purchase of designer rice demonstrates that you care about the welfare of the birds that might pick it off the sidewalk, does the purchase of Uncle Ben's identify you as a sparrow-hater? And if you choose to have your reception at the same restaurant as your best friend, does that mean you're copying her? One of the difficulties in planning a wedding today is that, since the average wedding is quite large, people attend a lot of them. Let's face it, the basics *are* pretty similar, so the details do tend to get freighted with meaning. *The New York Times* ran an article in 2001 describing innovative substitutes for place cards. One couple, whose reception was held on Ellis Island, created passport-shaped cards to reflect the theme of entry into the United States. Each table at the reception was identified by country, and one page in the passport told the guest which country to head to for dinner. The center spread gave the couple's family trees, and the last page, the dinner menu. Another bride and her mother created two hundred music boxes to serve as place cards, each one programmed to play a different song that they had selected for each guest. The bride who opted for butterfly-shaped cookies (iced with the guest's name and table number) planted in boxes of wheat grass said, "I wanted people to say, 'How beautiful, how different.' It was a real first impression and gave you the feeling that everything was going to be special."

Sometimes this craving for differentiation leads couples back to their ethnic backgrounds. The celebration of a wedding has always been an occasion for families to refresh their sense of cultural origin. The validity, stability and even the future of a community are affirmed by a marriage, and often celebrated in the wedding. Music, food, dances, or costumes from the homeland have frequently marked exiles' weddings. But the story of the white wedding in America has, for the most part, been a story of assimilation and standardization. The upwardly mobile have reached for the white dress, the trays of champagne glasses, and the receiving line. Harlem photographer James Van der Zee immortalized many African American weddings during his career as a commercial photographer. Sometimes dozens of attendants crowd the frame, with the distinctions between flower girl and junior bridesmaid and bridesmaid clearly delineated by style of hat and flowers. The elaboration of the wedding party reflects the exuberance of a hard-pressed community reaching a measure of stability and prosperity—but the wedding vernacular, however exaggerated, is still that of the conventional nineteenth-century bridal. Katherine Jellison's research on the weddings in one Nebraska family demonstrated the shift from a celebration formed by German immigrant habits to conformity with the commercial bridal standard. Sophie Bischoff married from the farm, but nearly sixty years later, her great-niece Ann Hardy married in a manner indistinguishable from any other girl who wed in 1985. Because she was an urban working woman, rather than a young farm bride, she had the money and sophistication to want and to pay for "all the elements of a modern commercialized wedding: hothouse flowers, engraved invitations, a catered reception, a honeymoon cruise." There was no German flavor at all in her planning.

That trend is reversing, though. The WASP ascendancy is fragmented and the entire concept of assimilation as the American dream has come under question. Should the country be a melting pot, with its elements assuming a common form? Or a mosaic, with each contributing its unique sparkle to the whole? The "mosaic" notion is gaining strength. In the bridal world, new attention is being paid to the practices of different cultural groups, from the elaborate three-day gatherings of Gypsy weddings to the multicourse banquets of the Chinese celebration. While fifty years ago only the most recent immigrants wed in the style of their ancestors, now couples are eagerly adopting practices that their parents may have disdained as "too ethnic." A Mexican American bride may feel conspicuous doing the "dollar dance" at her reception, when guests pin currency to her gown while dancing with her—but she may equally feel a sweet solidarity with the older women in her family who did the same thing. Weddings look both backward and forward, so the incorporation of old-fashioned ceremonial practices is perfectly fitting.

Which is not to say that some couples aren't reaching a little hard for any way to differentiate their weddings from what they see as the run of the mill. If the groom elects to wear a kilt even though his family left Scotland 350 years ago, he isn't really mining some vein of cultural loyalty. He's enacting a fantasy. But then, so are every other bride and groom, to one extent or another. In Nancy Savoca's film *True Love,* the young couple discusses the menu at the catering hall and establishes their color scheme. The caterer suggests that the mashed potatoes be tinted blue. Michael objects on the grounds that there is no blue food in real life. But, demurs the caterer, "This is not real life. This is your day, and you should feel that anything is possible, sort of a fantasy day." Not only is this the bride's opportunity to be treated like Julia Roberts, the cynosure of every flash attachment—it's the opportunity for the bride and groom together to live out the exotic scenario of their choice. In 1997 tough-guy actor Sylvester Stallone married his consort of nine years (and the mother of his daughter), Jennifer Flavin. Stallone did all the planning, instructing the bride only to bring her Armani wedding gown to Europe with her. The couple was wed in a civil ceremony at the Dorchester Hotel in London, then drove in a 1929 Rolls Royce to Blenheim Palace in Woodstock, the home of the Duke of Marlborough. There the marriage was blessed in the Churchill family chapel, with a full choir present. Scots Guards then escorted the wedding party and their handful of guests (and the photo crew from *InStyle* magazine) to a formal dinner in Blenheim's Saloon. Stallone told a reporter from *InStyle* that "To be invited by the aristocracy of Britain to use their extraordinary palace was too tempting. I thought it would be nice to get married in a historical place." In case readers inferred that the Duke had offered his house to Stallone on the basis of their warm friendship, the article clarified that "Permission to use the great house . . . was obtained through wedding guest and Planet Hollywood CEO Robert Earl."

It may take the bankroll of a Stallone to act out a British aristocratic fantasy (as Madonna also did at her Scottish castle wedding to Guy Ritchie), but grandiosity is not the only option. The July 2002 issue of *Modern Bride* reported on the wedding of two Nickelodeon employees, Abby Miller and Mike Pecoriello. The couple chose to be united at the Stepping Stones Children's Museum in Norwalk, Connecticut. Glitter, bubbles, a photo booth, cupcake decorating, and rock candy centerpieces carried out the childlike theme. Civil War reenactors have been married on the battlefield. Brides and grooms are united on skis, under water, in the passenger compartments of hot-air balloons. Nearly two thousand couples have exchanged their vows amid the spectacular stalagmites and stalactites of the Bridal Cave near Lake of the Ozarks, Missouri, according to a story in the June 23, 2002, *St. Louis Post-Dispatch*. In case the cave lacked appeal, an accompanying article described the antics of the Reverend Frank Borst, a minister who will perform ceremonies in the guise of Groucho Marx or Charlie Chaplin.

If fantasy has a brand name in America, though, that's probably Disney, and the Mouse has gotten onto the wedding bandwagon. Both Disneyland, in California, and Walt Disney World, in Florida, have developed very substantial wedding businesses. Though the two facilities are run separately, they offer similar services. Of course wedding and reception will take place in one of Disney's attractive venues, and of course all of the standard elements of a wedding—the food, the flowers, the music—provided by Disney will rival what could be had anywhere else. Only Disney, though, can bring Mickey to the party. For a fee, the cartoon characters (Mickey and Minnie, Pluto and Goofy, even Cinderella's wicked stepsisters) can appear at a reception in a variety of different outfits. In fact, Disney can make a lot of different dreams come true. Promotional materials from Walt Disney World offer weddings with a movie-star theme in which "The bride arrives in a star motorcade down Hollywood Boulevard for an official handprint ceremony at the Chinese Theater. . . ." Naturally, Cinderella's glass coach can be pressed into service for the bride's arrival at the ceremony. Even an "Aladdin" theme is possible, though tantalizingly, the press release offers no further details. In a dizzying example of life imitating commerce, couples planning their celebrations visit Franck's studio, inspired by the character of wedding planner Franck in the 1991 remake of *Father of the Bride*.

Weddings are acknowledged nowadays to be a kind of fantasy—and who does fantasy better than Walt Disney? Cathleen and Michael Clyde married at Disneyland and arrived at their reception in Cinderella's coach.

Statistically, not many brides and grooms avail themselves of Disney's rather pricey options: according to a *Los Angeles Times* story from October 10, 2002, the cost of a wedding and reception package at Disneyland starts at forty thousand dollars, with cartoon characters and fireworks extra. Only about two hundred couples a year marry at Walt Disney

World in Florida. Many of them, though, are visitors from far away, so their celebrations fall into the new category of "destination weddings." This is an especially twenty-first-century phenomenon. A bride and groom—often daunted by the cost and logistics of planning the standard elaborate stateside wedding—elect to marry in an exotic location to which neither of them has geographic ties. Their immediate families and a handful of friends travel to the chosen destination, where the wedding is celebrated in some picturesque spot, then the guests vanish and the newlyweds stay put for the honeymoon. This is now such big business for some beach resorts in the Caribbean and Mexico that their travel ads feature special wedding packages in which they promise not only to provide all the legal documentation but also the bride's bouquet, wedding announcements, and the cake. *Modern Bride* estimated in 2001 that as many as 11 percent of weddings are now planned this way, and a little subindustry has sprung up to handle it. If you don't want to buy, say, the Sandals resort's package, you can hire a local planner to pull together the event. Long-distance planners are also available, as are books, and a lot of the research can be done on the Web. In fact, the entire phenomenon depends heavily on the instantaneous exchange of information across long distances. Comparing images of different beachside wedding pavilions in the Virgin Islands online is no different from comparing the views of country inns much closer to home.

At first glance the "destination wedding" doesn't seem too different from that time-honored option, the trip to Las Vegas. But a celebration in the Virgin Islands with two dozen relatives still involves months of planning and coordination. And though the gambling capital is cleaning up its image to attract a more staid, settled visitor, the hallmark of the Vegas wedding is still speed. Got an impulse to wed the one you're with? You can be hitched within a few hours of reaching town. (It'll take longer if you want to rent a wedding dress for an hour, of course.) The Clark County Marriage License Bureau, conveniently located next to the Golden Nugget casino on the Strip, is open twenty-four hours on the weekends and until midnight during the week. No blood test is necessary. If one of the three dozen chapels in town is busy, you can just drive a few yards to find one without a line. In any event, the ceremony only takes about fifteen minutes, less time than you'd spend to renew your driver's license.

The Vegas wedding has its roots in the early history of Nevada, which in the nineteenth century was one of the states with the loosest divorce laws. Residency requirements were short, grounds on which divorces were granted, quite generous. In fact divorce became a tidy little sector of the tourist industry beginning as early as the 1910s. In 1931 the Nevada legislature passed a bill reducing the required residency to six weeks and ensuring that divorce cases were tried privately (no gawkers or reporters allowed). Divorce was quite a healthy industry during the 1930s and '40s, to the extent that in 1946 Nevada granted 148.9 divorces per thousand residents.

One of the attractive features of the Nevada laws concerned the waiting period between divorce and remarriage—there was none. It was thus possible for a man to be severed from his wife on Thursday and remarried to a new woman on Friday. This haste may seem pointless to us, but for most of the last century divorce was still potentially scandalous. The wish to swap partners implied ardent sexual desire that could not be legitimately satisfied outside the bonds of matrimony.

The only way to keep it respectable was to marry as soon as possible. Las Vegas is also conveniently located for Hollywood's perpetual marital shuffles, which in turn gives it a kind of raffish luster for the rest of us. Elvis Presley and Priscilla Beaulieu, Frank Sinatra and Mia Farrow, Cindy Crawford and Richard Gere—there's glamour for you!

The luster of the city, raffish or not, cannot be denied. Young-Hoon Kim, in his Ph.D. thesis, points out that Las Vegas is supremely *festive*. With its flashing lights and extravagant architecture and round-the-clock gambling, the city looks nothing like most people's real life. Marrying here, in fact, could be the ultimate fantasy, unconnected to humdrum daily existence. Repeat your vows to Elvis? This can be done: there are justices of the peace who double as Elvis impersonators. Tie the knot on a roller coaster? The "New York, New York" casino can accommodate you. Want a beachside wedding without that pricey airfare? See if Mandalay Bay will loan you their beach with the artificial waves. (Las Vegas may be landlocked but geography should be no barrier to imagination.) Become a bride at 3 A.M.? Shoot craps in your wedding gown? The locals have seen it all before. Thousands of couples find this appealing: in 2001, Clark County issued 123,143 marriage licenses. That figure is double what it was in 1985.

However, except for those many thousands of couples who participated in a Vegas wedding, few have actually witnessed one because there the guest list is usually short. A handful of family members may be invited along or the wedding chapel may have to enlist employees to witness the vows. Marrying in Las Vegas is apparently not a matter of seeking community approval for a match. If anything, it's about privacy. Kim interviewed one woman whose ex-husband, of

In Las Vegas, you can be serenaded by an Elvis impersonator—and married by one. It may be unconventional, but this bride's emotion is certainly genuine.

whom she was very fond, chose to be remarried there. She was disappointed by his choice, feeling that it shut out his friends and family. "I think his wedding should have been for the other—you know, the people who love him . . . I just felt like I was being left out. I wasn't allowed to stand there with them and show, Yes, this is a good thing. I support you." In effect, this particular wedding fantasy eliminates one of the traditionally essential aspects of marrying. Weddings used to be public so that everyone in the community knew that a man and a woman had joined their lives intentionally and willingly. Everyone present saw the same thing: the exchange of vows, the groom's putting on the ring, the officiant blessing the couple. It was a public event because the newlyweds' status in the community had changed and everyone needed to know it.

That is no longer true. Marriage doesn't change much anymore, except, perhaps, a couple's expectations of each other. A bride and groom no longer need to be seen to be believed. Their friends and families may wish to express their support of a marriage—for years couples have submitted to larger weddings than they really want in order to please parents or relatives. Choosing to marry in Las Vegas ignores the wider social implication of marriage, reducing it to its impact on the couple alone. "This is between us," a Vegas wedding says. "It's not about the rest of you."

Of course, many of the pairs who marry in Las Vegas are not first-time brides and grooms. Clark County doesn't track this statistic, but Kim interviewed 103 couples. In this tiny sample, at least one partner in 54 percent of the couples had been married before. Traditionally, couples on a second or third trip up the aisle care less about full-scale ritual, so the stripped-down nature of a Vegas wedding may be especially appealing. For most of the period since 1850, the fuss and ceremonial of the white wedding has been reserved for the previously unmarried. When Gloria Morgan married the divorcé Reggie Vanderbilt in 1923, for instance, it was in a quiet ceremony before fifty people. Gloria, though entitled to virginal white, wore a silver-gray silk faille dress (which she wore again to her daughter Gloria Vanderbilt's wedding in 1941, sending a very peculiar signal about who was the center of attention). Throughout the 1950s and '60s the etiquette experts and bridal magazines held the line on second weddings: no white dress, no veil, one attendant at most, and keep the celebrating down to a dull roar. By the 1970s, that rhetoric was softening. In 1976, *Bride's* conceded that a second-time bride could wear white, though the very traditional organza and alençon lace might look inappropriate. There was still some shock value attached to the visibly pregnant bride, which was exploited in the 1979 film version of *Hair.* Beverly D'Angelo, in a drug-induced dream sequence, is a beautiful bride in white who reveals her advanced pregnancy to her groom only at the end of the ceremony.

In those days, that disclosure still had some impact. No more—an article in *The New York Times* in June 2002 described the growing wedding business of high-end maternity designer Liz Lange. At the upper end of the socioeconomic scale, women tend to marry late. A spate of new information about declining fertility after age thirty-five may have contributed to the sense that proven fertility in a bride is something to show off and celebrate. Certainly children at a wedding are increasingly visible. When Madonna married Guy Ritchie, their son, Rocco, made his appearance in a kilt like his father, and almost half of the celebrity couples whose weddings are covered in *People* or *InStyle* feature either the couple's children or offspring from a previous relationship. What's startling about the weddings, though, is that the bride often dresses as if she were a twenty-three-year-old virgin. Actress Andie MacDowell, forty-three, married Rhett Hartzog in 2001 wearing a white Vera Wang ball gown. Fifty-year-old talk-show host Joan Lunden married in a white gown with a crystal headpiece and an elbow-length veil, her three daughters, aged twenty, seventeen, and thirteen, serving as her bridesmaids. Traditionally royalty maintains the customs of the past with more rigor than the rest of us, but in August 2001 Crown Prince Haakon of Norway took as his wife Mette-Marit Hoiby, who'd had a son in a relationship with another man. The bride—it was, after all, her first wedding— walked up the aisle in a long-sleeved white dress with a modest tiara and a tulle veil. She wore, in other words, the traditional regalia of a virgin, though son Marius appeared with her and her new husband on the balcony of Oslo's Royal Palace after the wedding.

In other words, the white dress and veil is now just a costume. It doesn't symbolize virginity, as for a while it was thought to do. The veil could not possibly represent a kind of haberdashery hymen, removed at the hands of the groom. The traditionally discreet coverage of a bride's fleshly charms has evaporated into strapless, skintight sheaths. Even the covey of bridesmaids, once virgins themselves, are often replaced by matrons, sometimes pregnant to boot. In a new trend, attendants cross the gender barrier. Angie Harmon, at her wedding to football player Jason Sehorn, had "bridesmen" and women have been selected as ushers. (They wear black, to blend in with the tuxedo-clad men.) In fact, very little of the symbolism of the wedding has maintained its significance, and as the significance fades, alterations in the practices become ever more common.

So is it *all* a fantasy? It's pretty clear that a wedding is not "real life," but does its traditional form have any meaning at all? When the set of rituals most of us use took their shape in the middle of the nineteenth century, they weren't terribly far removed from the rituals of festive social life. The religious ceremonial had its own form, of course, but the reception following was basically a formal version of an "at home" or open house. The food would be more festive, the decorations of the house more elaborate, everyone's clothes the very best in the closet, but only the presence of a cake and a toast to the newlyweds would really set the event apart.

Traditions must be flexible to survive, though. Over the years, this fairly simple celebration has accumulated all kinds of complications that have somehow become mandatory. A bride now expects bridal showers and a rehearsal dinner and brunches before or after the wedding. Menus now include not merely cake and something to drink a toast with, but multi-course meals and champagne, while an hour or so of congratulations to the bride and groom has stretched into four or more hours of photography, a receiving line, dancing, a meal, toasts, the cutting of the cake, the throwing of the bouquet, the throwing of the garter, and a ceremonial departure—all announced by the man leading the band. Wedding gifts have gone from optional tokens presented by the couple's family to obligatory checks. Or high-powered kitchen appliances selected on the Web that may be exchanged, virtually, for the technically advanced knives the bride decided she'd rather have. Or even for a share of the mortgage (yes, it is now pos-

It's not about virginity any more. Model Kristin McMenamy's pregnancy is
emphasized by the chiffon gown created for her by Chanel designer
Karl Lagerfeld (seated, in dark glasses).

sible to register to have your housing loan paid off by your
wedding guests).

And yet it's not all meaningless. Yes, weddings cost a lu-
dicrous amount of money today and yes, much of that cost is
prompted by the impulses of our consumer-oriented society.
Yes, many brides and grooms are acting out a fantasy and yes,
the wedding industry milks them for all it's worth. Still, if you
scrape away the grandiosity and consumer overkill, the basic

elements of today's formal wedding are fundamentally similar to those of 150 years ago. This complex and mutable tradition has real staying power. Americans wouldn't marry the way they do unless this process satisfied some need.

We crave ritual. The informality and practicality of daily life in the twenty-first century deny us that experience of ritual time which nothing is allowed to interrupt. And because the conventions of the nineteenth-century marriage do not completely satisfy today's needs, new rituals keep cropping up. Getting engaged has become one of them. It no longer means getting over that awkward moment when one of you does or does not actually say, "How about if we get married?" Somehow, a couple arrives at *that* decision, then the groom must come up with a way to formally present his intended with her ring. There may be a level of secrecy involved: some couples know that they will "get engaged" on a specific date, while some men go to elaborate lengths to secrete a ring in a glass of champagne or a sheaf of roses to surprise their fiancées. It's as if the mere intention to marry, in spite of the odds against marriage succeeding, is so remarkable that it must be emphasized in a formal undertaking. Then there's the unity candle. In the last twenty years, many brides and grooms have chosen, at the end of their ceremonies, to light a candle on the altar before which they've made their vows. Bride and groom each take up a slender taper and together they put those flames to the wick of a slightly larger candle. The two individual flames produce a third one, which stands for the couple, united. It's a visual elaboration of what has just occurred verbally, and it's becoming extremely popular.

In addition to ritual, we need community and connection. Say what you will about the rigors of wedding planning—the process nevertheless unites disparate people with a common interest. One of the avowed functions of prewedding parties like engagement parties and showers is to introduce the various elements of the bride's and groom's social networks. Sometimes when you read wedding announcements, it's not even possible to discern where the bride and groom met. They're from different states, went to different colleges, work in different industries. Assembling the people the couple cares about from far-flung locations is one of the most important functions of today's elaborate weddings. The bachelor party has begun to grow from just one wild evening before the wedding to an entire weekend, often in an exotic setting. There may be scheduled activities, like gambling or skiing or fishing, and there is probably a fair amount of behavior not fit for mixed company, but the result is a group of ushers who share not only their affection for the groom but also the social bond formed by time spent in each other's company.

Some of the wedding-based activity on the Web is clearly driven by this need for connection. Many of the wedding sites like theknot.com maintain message boards where brides in the planning stages can post questions and answers to questions like "Can my bridesmaids wear black?" and "Has anyone tried serving fish at the reception?" Brides often use wedding-based screen names like JuneBride23 or WeddingBelle. Some sites also permit couples to post wedding-themed Web pages that offer details about their celebrations. This allows the couple's friends to log on to get news of the wedding plans like the choice of a band or the location for a barbecue, or logistical details like times or directions. They even have "guest book" features that permit visitors to the site to virtually sign their names with brief messages. As little as thirty years ago, the bride's friends would have been more involved in helping with wedding preparations, by addressing invitations (now often done by a professional calligrapher) or boxing morsels of cake for the guests (the baker now takes care of it). Logging onto your friend's wedding Web page is not quite the same as picking up her Aunt Tillie at the train station to bring her to the rehearsal dinner, but it's a kind of connection nonetheless.

And people want to participate. If a friend of yours is getting married, you want to share in his or her pleasure and you want to express your support. Maybe part of the elaboration of today's weddings comes as a response to the increasingly heavy role of commerce. Embroidering a tablecloth for a young bride took a lot of time and made clear how much you cared about her, how much you hoped for her future happiness. Decorating the church altar with flowers from your own garden did the same thing. Now those tasks are assumed by the pros. It has become harder and harder for the people who love a bride and groom to get their hands onto something personal that conveys their affection and their estimation of how important marriage is. Simply trotting down to Williams-Sonoma or Target and buying the biggest stock pot on the shelves doesn't satisfy that need. Some of the multiplication of auxiliary events may have its source here: no, you can't bake a ham for the reception, no, they really don't want a china vase that was your grandmother's, but you *could* give a wine shower.

The average engagement now lasts over a year. Part of the reason it's so protracted is that planning such an elaborate event takes a lot of time. It's hard to book many venues for the prime times (Friday night, Saturday afternoon or night), especially during wedding high seasons of June and Sepember. Popular sites are reserved at least a year in advance, so if a bride has her heart set on The Old Mill Inn overlooking the waterfall, she's going to have to get in line. But the corollary is that everyone has a longer time to build connections to each other, and to the bride and groom as a couple.

Ultimately, even though few weddings today mark much of a practical change in a couple's life, they do stand for something. The extended engagement and intricate planning of a wedding allow a couple's friends and family a chance to participate and time to adjust to a couple's change in status. For it is a change. And the fact that society no longer dictates the form of that change makes it, in some respects, harder to discern. Most marriages are based on an expectation of sexual fidelity, and most, despite the odds, on an expectation of permanence. People really mean it when they say "until death do us part." Beyond that, though, the culture doesn't go. Society will not indicate, explicitly or implicitly, that one partner or another should earn more money, spend more time taking care of the children, or change the oil in the car. It's no longer broadly clear whether it's better to be married or single or divorced or married but living in different cities for complicated personal reasons. You don't need to be married to have children, and you don't need children to be married. All you need is another person that you want to spend your life with.

And maybe this is the crux of the matter. Most brides and grooms know, by now, what it's like to live alone. They can do it. They can support themselves and do the taxes and put the cat out at night. Some people like it better that way. But some people don't. Some people find another human that they'd rather be with, for richer, for poorer, in sickness and in health, snoring or grouchy or growing out a bad haircut. Or on parole. Or undergoing chemo. Or winning the lottery. Society at large no longer cares much, so this may be the ultimate expression of self-determination. This country has always supported the individual's attempt to make the most of him- or herself, and maybe in the end, getting married falls into that category. It certainly falls under the description of "the pursuit of happiness."

No wonder we celebrate. And if the celebration is grandiose and commercial, exuberant and inclusive and larger than necessary, isn't that the American way?

Selected Sources

For further information, readers may find the following sources helpful.

INTRODUCTION

Marilyn Yalom's *A History of the Wife* (HarperCollins 2001) is very good on the early history of European marriage. John Gillis's *For Better, For Worse: British Marriages, 1600 to the Present* was published by Oxford University Press in 1985. Van Gennep's thinking on ritual has been widely incorporated into many anthropology studies. Edward Westermarck's 1930 *A Short History of Marriage* (Macmillan) provided some of the earliest cross-cultural research on marriage. Eric Hobsbawm writes about tradition in the introduction to *The Invention of Tradition* (Cambridge University Press 1983). Early American marriages are covered in *And The Bride Wore . . .*, an especially well-researched history of mostly English weddings written by Ann Monsarrat (Dodd, Mead 1973).

CHAPTER 1

P. T. Barnum refers to Tom Thumb's wedding with considerable pride in his autobiography. He wrote many versions, but I used

Struggles and Triumphs, Or Forty Years' Recollections, published in 1871 by the American News Company. *P. T. Barnum: America's Greatest Showman,* by Philip W. Kunhardt Jr., Philip W. Kunhardt III, and Peter W. Kunhardt (Knopf 1995) provided some context, as did *Barnum Presents: General Tom Thumb* (Macmillan 1954) by Alice Curtis Desmond.

Mollie Dorsey's journals were edited by Donald F. Danker and published as *Mollie: The Journal of Mollie Dorsey Sanford in Nebraska and the Colorado Territories, 1857–1866* by the University of Nebraska Press in 1959. Charlotte Perkins Gilman's *Women and Economics* (1899) was published by Small, Maynard & Co. Harvey Green's *The Light of the Home* (Pantheon 1983) and Ellen Rothman's *Hands and Hearts: A History of Courtship in America* (Harvard 1987) paint a vivid portrait of the Victorian American wife. Adele Sloane's journals were published in 1983 by Doubleday as *Maverick in Mauve,* with additional commentary from Louis Auchincloss. I quote from Constance Cary Harrison's *The Well-Bred Girl in Society* (Doubleday 1898) and from an 1872 edition of the Book of Common Prayer. I used Charles Scribner's Sons' 1968 edition of *The Age of Innocence,* and Fords, Howard & Hulbert's 1887 edition of Henry Ward Beecher's *Norwood, or Village Life in New England.* Eleanor Cohen Seixas's diary is published in Penelope Franklin's *Private Pages: Diaries of American Women, 1830s–1970s* (Ballantine 1986). The quotation from Jane Carlyle on pages 21–22 comes from *And the Bride Wore . . .* Louisa May Alcott's *Little Women* has been available in many editions since its 1868 publication; I used a Signet Classic paperback from 1983. Jessie Wilson's wedding is described in Wilbur Cross and Ann Novotny's *White House Weddings* (David McKay 1967). Harper Brothers published Mary Elizabeth Sherwood's *Manners and Social Usages* in 1897.

CHAPTER 2

The account of Queen Victoria's wedding comes from *And the Bride Wore* . . . Linda Otto Lipsett's *To Love and to Cherish: Brides Remembered* was published by The Quilt Digest Press in 1989. Catherine Zimmerman's *The Bride's Book,* an invaluable source for anyone interested in wedding dresses, appeared from Arbor House in 1985. Information on chemical dyes is in Francois Delamare and Bernard Guineau's *Colors: The Story of Dyes and Pigments* (Abrams 2000). My copy of Laura Ingalls Wilder's *These Happy Golden Years* is from Scholastic, 1971. Vicki Jo Howard's Ph.D. thesis for the University of Texas at Austin (2000), entitled *American Weddings: Gender, Consumption, and the Business of Brides,* is the source for the Rochester bride's notebook of wedding costs. The trousseau information comes from *To Love and To Cherish.* My own *Victorian Treasures: An Album and Historical Guide for Collectors* (Abrams 1993) provided the background on decorative arts objects that were often given as wedding presents, while Henry James's novel *The Golden Bowl,* which touches on the subject, was published by Charles Scribner & Co. in 1904. Thorstein Veblen's *The Theory of the Leisure Class* was published in 1899 by Macmillan & Co. Consuelo Vanderbilt Balsan's memoir *The Glitter and the Gold* appeared from Harper & Brothers in 1952. Lee Furman Inc. published Grace Lumpkin's *The Wedding* in 1939. The weddings of Nellie Grant and Frances Folsom are covered in *White House Weddings.* Historical information about wedding cakes comes from Simon Charsley's *Wedding Cakes and Social History* (Routledge 1992).

CHAPTER 3

Macmillan & Co. published *Learning How to Behave: A Historical Study of American Etiquette Books* by Arthur Schlesinger in 1946. John H. Young's *Our Deportment: Or, The Manners, Conduct, and Dress of the Most Refined Society* appeared from F. B. Dickerson in

1879. Dixon Wecter's *The Saga of American Society* (Charles Scribner's Sons 1937) is an excellent social history of America's upper
crust. The information on American heiresses' marriages comes
from *To Marry an English Lord* (Workman Publishing 1989), which
I wrote with Gail MacColl. *And the Bride Wore . . .* provided the information about George V's wedding to Princess May of Teck. The
development of the popular press is covered in three sources: Lois
Banner's *American Beauty* (Knopf 1983), Simon Michael Bessie's
Jazz Journalism: The Story of the Tabloid Newspapers (Russell & Russell 1969), and John Tebbel and Mary Ellen Zuckerman's *The Magazine in America, 1741–1990* (Oxford University Press 1991). *White
House Weddings* is the source for the details of Nellie Grant's and
Alice Roosevelt's weddings and the press coverage they attracted.

CHAPTER 4

The turbulent period of the 1920s and its effect on America's young
people is the subject of Paula Fass's *The Damned and the Beautiful:
American Youth in the 1920's* (Oxford University Press 1977). Phyllis Blanchard and Carlyn Manasses's *New Girls for Old* was published in 1930 by Macaulay. Further background comes from
Robert and Helen Lynd's *Middletown in Transition: A Study in Cultural Conflicts* (Harcourt Brace 1937) and from Ellen Rothman's
Hands and Hearts. Zelda and Scott Fitzgerald's story is told in
Nancy Milford's *Zelda* (Avon 1970). Elaine Tyler May's *Great Expectations: Marriage and Divorce in Post-Victorian America* appeared
in 1981 from the University of Chicago Press.

Jean Worth is quoted in Vicki Jo Howard's Ph.D. thesis.
Mrs. John Alexander King's *Weddings: Modes, Manners & Customs*
was published by the Butterick company in 1927, while T. E.
Lindquist published Mary E. Lewis's 1947 *The Marriage of Diamonds and Dolls.* Jeanette MacDonald's wedding dress and other
bridal fashions are described in Catherine Zimmerman's *The Bride's
Book.* Once again, *White House Weddings* provided details of Jessie

Selected Sources

Wilson's wedding. *The World's Most Unforgettable Weddings: Love, Lust, Money and Madness* (Citadel Press 2001) by Deborah McCoy includes an account of Harry Truman's wedding. Katherine Jellison's research on the Bischoff family appeared in "Getting Married in the Heartland: The Commercialization of Weddings in the Rural Midwest." The article was published in the fall 1995 issue of *Forum,* Ohio State University's magazine. John Modell's *Into One's Own: From Youth to Adulthood in the United States, 1920–1975* was published by the University of California Press in 1989. Dance history, including Vernon and Irene Castle's influence on it, comes from an essay in *Dance: A Very Social History* (Rizzoli 1986) by Dan McDonagh. Barbara Norfleet's enchanting *Wedding* (Fireside 1979) contains information on early wedding photography. Charles Wesley Lewis's Ph.D. thesis for the University of Minnesota (1994) is entitled *Working the Ritual: Wedding Photographs as Social Process.* It looks at wedding photography in considerable detail.

CHAPTER 5

Simon Michael Bessie's *Jazz Journalism* covers the invention of tabloid newspapers. Mary Nichols's delicious *Champagne Cholly: The Life and Times of Maury Paul* was published in 1947 by E. P. Dutton & Co. It may be catalogued in some libraries under her pseudonym, "Eve Brown." Robert T. Elson's *Time Inc., 1923–1941* (Atheneum 1968) is the source for the founding of *Life.* Sandy Schreier's *Hollywood Gets Married,* published in 2002 by Clarkson Potter, is full of glorious photographs of weddings on-screen and off. The Banky-LaRocque wedding is described in Bernard Rosenberg and Harry Silverstein's *The Real Tinsel* (Macmillan 1970). Elizabeth Kendall's *The Runaway Bride: Hollywood Romantic Comedy of the 1930's* was published by Alfred A. Knopf in 1990. "Dorothy Dix" was the pseudonym of Elizabeth M. Gilmer. *Dorothy Dix— Her Book* appeared in 1926 from Funk & Wagnalls. Paula Fass's *The Damned and the Beautiful* discusses the dawning of the youth culture and consumer society. Marisa Keller and Mike Mashon's *TV Weddings* was published in 1999 by TV Books.

CHAPTER 6

Glenna Matthews's *"Just a Housewife": The Rise and Fall of Domesticity in America* (Oxford University Press 1987) and Nancy Cott's *Public Vows: A History of Marriage and the Nation* (Harvard University Press 2000) describe marital politics in postwar America, while Barbara Ehrenreich's *The Hearts of Men: American Dreams and the Flight from Commitment* (Anchor Press 1983) looks at the masculine view of the domestic idyll. Betty Friedan's influential *The Feminine Mystique* was published by Norton in 1963. *Father of the Bride,* by Edward Streeter (with illustrations by Gluyas Williams), came out in 1948 from Simon & Schuster. *TV Weddings* is the source for weddings on television. The discussion of Barbie's nuptial options owes a great deal to *Barbie Fashion Vol. I, 1959–1967* by Sarah Sink Eames (Collector Books 2002).

CHAPTER 7

Judith Balaban Quine's *The Bridesmaids: Grace Kelly, Princess of Monaco and Six Intimate Friends* (Weidenfeld and Nicolson 1989) provides a detailed account of Princess Grace's romance and wedding. Geoffrey C. Munn's *Tiaras: A History of Splendour* (Antique Collectors' Club 2001) is the definitive work on the subject. Frank Deford's *There She Is: The Life and Times of Miss America* (Viking Press 1971) provides an irreverent history of that cultural institution. Lois Banner's *American Beauty* contributes a thoughtful analysis. Kitty Hanson's critical *For Richer, For Poorer* was published by Abelard-Schulman in 1967, while Marjorie Binford Woods's *Your Wedding: How to Plan and Enjoy It* was a 1942 Bobbs-Merrill publication. Cecil Beaton's diary is quoted by Ann Monsarrat in *And the Bride Wore . . .*

Selected Sources

CHAPTER 8

Naomi Wolf's essay "Brideland" appears in *To Be Real,* a collection of essays edited by Rebecca Walker (Anchor 1995). For the discussion of the manufacturing process, I am deeply indebted to John Burbidge, longtime designer for Priscilla of Boston, and Jill Northrop, manager of Dressed to the Nines in Morristown, New Jersey. Vicki Jo Howard's Ph.D. thesis includes information on rental wedding gowns in New York after World War II. Marcia Seligson's *The Eternal Bliss Machine: America's Way of Wedding* (William Morrow & Company 1973) is a detailed portrait of the bridal scene in the early seventies. She dwells with some relish on the excesses.

CHAPTER 9

William Chafe's *The Paradox of Change* (Oxford University Press 1991), Nancy Cott's *Public Vows,* Barbara Ehrenreich's *The Hearts of Men,* and Marilyn Yalom's *A History of the Wife* provide much of the background material for this chapter. Tiny Tim's wedding is covered thoroughly in Marisa Keller and Mike Mashon's *TV Weddings.*

CHAPTER 10

Arlie Hochschild's *The Second Shift* (Avon Books 1997) discusses the family/work conundrum. Statistics on marriage are available at *www.cdc.gov/nchs/fastats.* Pamela Paul's *The Starter Marriage* was published by Villard in 2002. *Diary of a Mad Bride* by Laura Wolf was published by Delta Trade Paperbacks in 2001. Lois Smith Brady's columns for *The New York Times* have been collected into a volume called *Vows: Weddings of the Nineties from The New York Times* (William Morrow & Company 1997). Martha Stewart's 1987 *Weddings,* from Clarkson Potter, can be said to have launched an empire. Amy Spindler's *New York Times* article on weddings ran on

August 30, 1998, and was called "Critic's Notebook: The Wedding Dress That Ate Hollywood."

CHAPTER 11

The cap on wedding spending proposed by a group of Orthodox rabbis was covered by Francine Parnes in *The New York Times* on May 25, 2002. The article was called "Religion Journal: A Big Wedding with a Smaller Bill." Diane Warner's *How to Have a Big Wedding on a Small Budget* (third edition) was published by Betterway Books in 1997, while the third edition of Denise and Alan Fields's *Bridal Bargains* from Windsor Peak Press came out in 2002. Angela Thompson's Ph.D. thesis for Brandeis University (1998) was titled *Unveiled: The Emotion Work of Wedding Coordinators in the American Wedding Industry.* Copious information on Disney weddings is available at *www.disney.go.com* and *www.disneyland.go.com. The Road to Reno: A History of Divorce in the United States* by Nelson Blake (Macmillan 1962) looks wryly at Las Vegas's role in the Nevada divorce industry. Current statistics can be found at *www.co. clark.nv.us/clerk.* Young-Hoon Kim's Ph.D. thesis, *The Commodification of a Ritual Process: An Ethnography of the Wedding Industry in Las Vegas,* was for the University of Southern California, 1996.

Acknowledgments

Because I worked on this book for so long and talked to so many people about it, the end result involves a great deal of effort besides my own. (The mistakes, of course, are wholly mine.) Above all I have to thank my agent, Lynn Seligman, who never stopped urging me to turn this project from folders full of clippings into an actual book—and whose encouragement never flagged.

I am also indebted to my editor, Caroline White. Without her enthusiasm, sense of humor, eye for detail, and categoric knowledge of popular culture, *All Dressed in White* would be a lesser creation.

Laurel Cardone provided impeccable research. Ellen Horan found the glorious photographs. The staffs at the New York Public Library and the New York Society Library steered me to sources I never would have found on my own. Lisa Marie Rovito, Elizabeth Kendall, and Katherine Jellison provided expertise and direction. John Burbidge and Cile Bellefleur-Burbidge regaled me with wedding industry lore and hospitality, while Jill Northrop generously gave me an insider's view of the workings of a bridal boutique, Dressed to the Nines, in Morristown, New Jersey.

And then there were my friends and relatives who shared pictures, stories, books, and wisdom: Peggy Hamlin, F. Paul Driscoll, Charlie Pastre, Cathleen Clyde, Celeste McCauley, Wendy Hilboldt, Hikari Hathaway, Emily Mikulewicz. I am also grateful to the women

Acknowledgments

I accompanied to the altar as a bridesmaid: Jill Woolworth, Peyton Petty, Lisa Callahan, Claire Miner, Meg Whitman, Nancy Casserley, and Diane Jensen.

Of course none of this would have been any fun without Rick Hamlin, who twenty years ago was the world's most understanding groom.

Dedication page: André Snow, collection of the author; p. 10 Tom Thumb: Culver Pictures; p. 25 1860s wedding: Hulton Archive/ Getty Images; p. 34 Queen Victoria: Topham/The Image Works; p. 37 Worth gown: Copyright © Museum of the City of New York; p. 42 Bride in black: Bettmann/Corbis; p. 50 Grace McDonald: author; p. 56 Wedding in potted palms: The Granger Collection; p. 62 Tall cake: Hulton Archive/Getty Images; p. 71 Jennie Jerome: Culver Pictures; p. 74 Consuelo Marlborough: Culver Pictures; p. 80 Queen Mary wedding: Popperfoto/ Retrofile.com; p. 86 Nellie Grant: Culver Pictures; p. 102 Carol Gardner: author; p. 109 Jessie Wilson: Corbis; p. 120 Van der Zee Studio: James Van der Zee/ Library of Congress, Prints and Photographs Division, LC-USZ62-112472; p. 133 Vilma Banky: Bettman/ Corbis; p. 135 It Happened One Night: Culver Pictures; p. 150 Wartime cake cutting: Eliot Elisofon/Time Life Pictures/Getty Images; p. 159 Moon Gardner: author; p. 164 Barbie: Topham/The Image Works; p. 170 Princess Grace: Thomas D. McAvoy/Time Life Pictures/Getty Images; p. 175 Priscilla Presley: Bettman/Corbis; p. 180 Miss America: Hulton Archive/Getty Images; p. 187 Many bridesmaids: author; p. 201 Father of the Bride: Culver Pictures; p. 203 Peggy Hamlin: Mrs. Thornton Hamlin; p. 215 1950s wedding: author; p. 223 Sharon Tate: Hulton-Deutsch Collection/Corbis; p. 227 Luci Johnson: Bill Eppridge/Time Life Pictures/Getty Images; p. 230 Tiny Tim: Bettman/Corbis; p. 241 Hippies: Alan Carey/The Image Works; p. 246 Lorna Luft: Hulton-Deutsch Collection/Corbis; p. 251 Diana: Topham/The Image Works; p. 260 True Love: The Everett Collection; p. 264 1990s dress: Sean Cayton/The Image Works; p. 268 Adam Sandler: Nick Gossen/Courtesy of Adam Sandler.com/Getty Images; p. 279 Bridal party: Monika Graff/The Image Works; p. 297 Disney: Cathleen Clyde; p. 301 Vegas: John Storey/Time Life Pictures/Getty Images; p. 306 Pregnant bride: Eric Robert/Corbis Sygma